Professor Rusk
invites your comments
and remarks concerning
The Other End of the World.

Please contact
Professor Rusk at
219 Cherokee Trail
Seymour, Tennessee 37865

the other end of the world

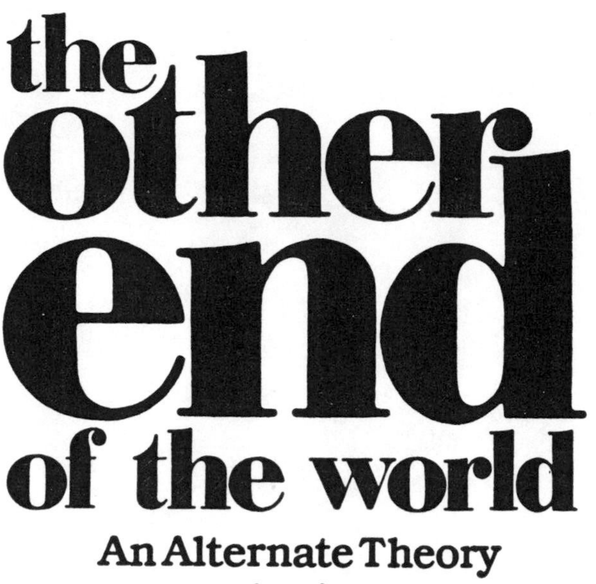

An Alternate Theory
Linking
Prophecy and History

by Roger Rusk

Plantation House, Inc.
Knoxville, Tennessee

All quotations from the Bible are from the
King James Version except as noted

0-945378-00-9

P.O. Box 51428 Knoxville, Tennessee 37909

ACKNOWLEDGMENTS

Many people have made this book possible. My wife, whose chief contribution has been her patience, love, and confidence, has been my mainstay and helpmate. My son, Bob, has donated secretarial time of his office staff. This includes the endless hours of repetitious typing of Maryellen Kasten and Donna DeLozier, the latter having entered the entire work, after frequent changes, on a word processor. Special thanks are extended to Doe Barbee who painstakingly produced the calligraphic clock face. Finally, gratitude and thanks are given to Paul Cowell, publisher and friend, for his stimulating discussions concerning the possibilities of this work.

The Author

Prologue

The Other End of the World is written for thoughtful Christians who have more than a superficial interest in prophetic scriptures. The hope is that the reader will take the time to personally evaluate the scriptural references, examine the appendixes, and prayerfully approach this unique presentation of prophetic scriptures.

Roger Rusk has spent sixty years in an aggressive pursuit of truth. As a college professor in the natural sciences and a Bible teacher, he has devoted his life to an examination and reevaluation of information passively accepted by those with less interest in life. Many of the chapters of this book were originally given as lectures. Much of this material and all the style is an adaption from oral presentation. Rusk's methods are inductive, not explicit. His desire for the hearer-reader to be in the thought process is essential to an understanding of this book. A clear understanding of this book will necessitate the reader's involvement with scriptures quoted but need to be read in context. Much is implied by the list of material in the bibliographies.

Although the views expressed in this book will seem new to modern readers of prophetic literature, the truth is that these views closely parallel those of the reformation fathers. Since the turn of the century most books on Bible prophecy have exploited current events and imposed future details on the reader that have simply not been Biblically based. In an effort to be interesting many books have erred to the side of sensational. Roger Rusk believes that our efforts to be predictive about specifics often produce a loss of credibility ten years later.

The reader will find the great themes of prophecy and an overview almost always lacking in modern presentation. The goal of the author is to give us comfort in the midst of unfolding current events because of an awareness of God's hand in it all.

It will be tempting to categorize Rusk's views and place him in some box of misunderstanding. Do not reject the material presented just because you disagree. Only disagree if an alternate view can be more clearly understood and substantiated.

Because some of these were independent papers given over a period of years there will be some lack of continuity and some repetition. The repetitions are sometimes deliberate in that a single passage fits into more than one context of thought. No effort has been made to popularize this material by providing easy answers or personal conclusion. Rusk's goal is to cause the reader to personally evaluate the weight of the material presented and arrive at a conclusion as a result of thought and prayer.

Paul Cowell

CONTENTS

PART I
FOREGROUND:
AN INTRODUCTION

Chapter 1
What in the World is Going On?

What are you going to do tomorrow? What are your plans for next week-end? Where are you going? Are you certain that your intentions will be realized? Isn't it wonderful how we can toy with the future as if we owned it? Yet, for each of us, there is no guarantee that there will be a tomorrow.

In additon to our concern for our personal lives, there is a concern for what is happening in our community, our nation, and the world. Some of us are very concerned about what may happen tomorrow, next week, or next year. There is a book which addresses future things. We call it the Bible. About thirty-five percent of the Bible is prophetic literature. There is also prolific secular literature today which concerns the future. Man has a deep-rooted, innate interest in what is going to happen to him.

Men are also turning to other guides. There has been a widespread revival of interest in astrology. We are encouraged to look at our horoscopes to see what may happen in our lives, to see what we should do. There is also an increasing interest in the occult, in psychic phenomena of various sorts, and in science fiction which attempts to portray future life in a world of space travel, encounters with beings from other worlds, and multi-dimensional existence. All these indicate man's interest in his own future. We are faced with the prospect of eventual nuclear annihilation.

Millions are currently experiencing starvation. New diseases stalk the earth. The nations of the earth are so heavily in debt that a world-wide financial disaster is assured. Incentives for increased productivity are not very effective in our culture. Can mankind continue to live as we have for centuries past?

Where are we going? Where are we now? Is there any way of being sure of any answers? A poll conducted a few years ago by U.S. News and World Report shows that the people of America are deeply concerned about their public life. They are convinced that something is wrong, but they do not know what it is. They are mystified by the activities of men in high places. They wonder if truth in government is lost forever.

We are plagued with a surplus of confusion and a scarcity of leadership. We have amassed mountains of knowledge, but generated only molehills of wisdom. Where do we go for understanding?

When you leave a public meeting that lasts an hour, you will be more than a million miles away from where you were when you came in. That is how fast the earth is traveling through space; more than a million miles an hour. Now Christians believe that this space ship — Planet Earth — came with a book of instructions called the Bible. This book tells us how to keep the ship operating, how to maintain order among the crew members and passengers, how to communicate with the Captain, and how to insure safe arrival at our destination. All these instructions and more are in this book.

Francis Schaeffer's book called *He Is There and He Is Not Silent* develops the idea that not only God Is, but He can do whatever pleases Himself. Not only CAN He communicate with His creation, He DID. Not only CAN He act in history, He DOES. And God continues to act in human history, dealing with men and nations. Then what on earth is God doing?

God isn't doing anything He did not tell us about. The prophet Amos wrote, "Surely the Lord will do nothing, but He revealeth his secret to His servants the prophets." He has told us what He is going to do. Through the prophet Isaiah, God makes it plain that He is the author of history. In verse after verse in Isaiah chapters 40 to 48, He shows that HE is bringing about whatever comes to pass. Our God is in truth the Sovereign Lord of history.

History can be rationalized according to at least three theories. One viewpoint is that history is open ended; it just goes on and on in an evolutionary manner, made up of human experience, but having no purpose. Goodness and human wisdom will lead us to some dreamed of Utopia, or our evil and folly will lead us to destruction. Either is possible and nature affords no preference. Another view is that history is cyclical; it just keeps repeating itself. Civilizations flourish and die. Nations come and go, and mankind never learns. Still another view is that history is climactic; we are living toward some great climax. There is a purpose, a designed goal, a destination. This view involves human responsibility. It involves an accounting for man's behavior. We read about such things as a judgment, a harvest, and a day when God triumphs. This is the Biblical view, the Christian view.

Since God has told us the story agead of time, which is a prophecy, we can follow His revelation by looking at history. An adequate interpretation of history and prophecy should include several considerations. We should study the selection of a people from out of the world to be God's servant. This is a continuing story we can trace throughout the Bible and in real history. We should include a study of the rise and fall of empires, which we find outlined for us in the second chapter and the seventh chapter of the book of Daniel, and in portions of the book of Revelation. An adequate interpretaion to history should take into consideration world powers, such as the Papacy, which exercised political domination over the nations of Europe for thirteen centuries; and Islam, which held sway over the Holy Land for thirteen centuries. It should take into consideration the mightiest nation this earth has ever known, the United States of America, as well as its modern enemies. It should take into consideration great movements, such as the spread of the early church, the Reformation, and the modern phase of world missions. Is it not significant that in about two hundred years the Gospel has been taken all over the world, and now about one half of the population of the world has shut its doors to Christian missions? And what of the great apostasy at the end of the age preceding the Second Coming of Christ?

An adequate interpretation of history should consider such subjects as the Church and the Kingdom of God, Israel and the Jews, and as Grattan Guiness said 100 years ago, if you have not yet learned the difference between Israel and the Jews, you are yet in your prophetic infancy. It should take into consideration the world system that goes under the name of Babylon in the Bible; Political Babylon, Ecclesiastical Babylon, and Economic Babylon, as described in the Old Testament and in the book of Revelation. It should take into consideration the continuing work of Satan, and the greater work of the Holy Spirit.

There are four general theories of the relationship between history and prophecy.

1. Prophecy is symbolic Literature. The prophetic scriptures teach us only spiritual truth, and although they use the phraseology of history for giving us that spiritual truth, these scriptures have nothing to do with actual history.
2. There is a Preterest theory, which states that the history about which the Scriptures speak happened back in the days of the Roman Emperors when the Christian were severly persecuted. It is all finished now, and we are not to look for anything else as a historical fulfillment of the prophecies except the developing world under the influence of the Church.
3. The Futurist theory of prophecy claims that the main events described by the prophets have not yet begun. They are postponed until the time of the Second Coming of Christ.
4. The Historicist view states that all of history is included in the messages of the prophets. There are no gaps, and the intervening centuries since Christ was here are all very much included in the prophetic messages.

Currently, there is a very popular view of history and prophecy in circulation among Christian people. In its present form, this general view is little more than a hundred years old. There are hundreds and even thousands of books written about it, and it is virtually the only study of prophecy which is available in Christian bookstores. It presents a future history of events on the earth not involving Christians. It appeals to our spiritual vanity in that it sets forth the proposition that we will be removed out of the world before these prophetic events begin to happen. It presents us with an escape from persecution and reality. It denies the relevance of current world history as well as most of what happened in the 1900 years since the first century. It forgets the teachings of the giants of our faith in former generations, especially during the time of the Reformation. It consists of a system of inferences of questionable Biblical support. By calling for the removal of the Church before the world undergoes the greatest crisis of the ages, no reasonable test of the scheme is available to us in any meaningful way, such as the one we find in the 18th chapter of Deuteronomy. This is the Futurist view of prophecy.

There is another view, an older view, the Historicist view, which was freely taught until the latter years of the nineteenth century. It is the Protestant view. It was recognized and developed by the men who opened the Bible after the Dark Ages and gave the Bible to all the people. This view is based on the teaching of Luther, Calvin, Huss, Wycliff, Knox, Latimer, Cranmer, Ridley, Hooker, Newton, and a host of others; many of whom were burned at the stake or beheaded in the 16th and 17th centuries. These men freely gave their lives for their beliefs rather than recant when they were accused of heresy. Their faith was tested in the literal fires of tribulation. The general system of prophetic interpretation which included the current history of their day was formulated by these men several centuries ago. Others today should account for their own loyalties to their favorite scholars, but this was their loyalty. This view might be called "The Other End of the World", because it is a story that church people do not hear about very often today. We have forgotten our Reformation heritage when it comes to teaching Bible Prophecy.

You will find this story first of all in the Bible; all of it, not just a few selected passages. The Bible presents us with a series of covenants, or contracts. Some of them were freely given by God to man without any conditions. Some of them were entered into by mutual agreement between God and man, with conditions guaranteeing blessings or penalties. As in all contracts there is a great amount of fine print. We need to read carefully in order to see just what it is the Lord is presenting to us in the

Bible, not only in the Gospel of Jesus Christ, but also in the prophetic passages dealing with history.

Older commentaries and church histories exhibit this view. You will find it when you study the lives of the martyrs of the church. You will find it in the writings of Wycliff, and yet the new *Wycliff Bible Commentary* takes a view different from that of Wycliff. You will find it in the older printings of Halley's Bible Handbook, but the new printing omits it or alters it. You will find it in some of the historical notes in the old *Scofield Reference Bible,* but those have largely been eliminated, or edited in such a fashion as to be hardly recognizable in the New Scofield Bible. You will find it by careful study; in the Bible, in the libraries, and in the literature that has long standing.

The Gospel is so simple a child can understand it, yet the prophetic scriptures are so complex that a satisfactory understanding does not come from superficial reading. It comes only by careful reading and thoughtful study. Scripture presents three purposes of prophecy. Soothsaying and annual predictions are not the purpose of the prophetic scriptures.

1. The first purpose is to show that God is the author of history. This is set forth plainly in Isaiah.
2. Another purpose of prophecy is to give enough evidence to condemn disbelievers by the Word when the historical events do occur.
3. Still another purpose is to give comfort and understanding to believers as history unfolds. As it happens, you will understand, not before.

Understand what? We are commanded to WATCH. What does watch mean? It means to be aware of what is going on about us. There is an interesting passage in the latter part of the 12th chapter of Ezekiel. It is summed up in the last two verses, which read, "Son of man, behold, they of the house of Israel say, The vision that he seeth is for many days to come, and he prophesieth of the times that are far off. Therefore say unto them, Thus saith the Lord God; There shall none of my words be prolonged anymore, but the word which I have spoken shall be done, saith the Lord God." In other words, the time has come for God's promises to be fulfilled. The day is NOW.

This is the most exciting generation since the time of Christ. More than 15,000 people in the United States are at least one hundred years old. They have lived more than one half of the life of this nation. Isn't that amazing? Some of us have lived more than a third! This has been the most exciting third, and the excitement builds. Yes, this is truly the most exciting generation on earth since Christ was here.

Will civilization as we know it survive? This has now become a legitimate question among thoughtful people. Let us read something from the Gospel of John, in the 12th chapter. "And there were certain Greeks among them that came to worship at the feast: They came to Philip, and desired him, saying, Sir, we would see Jesus. Philip told Andrew, and Andrew and Philip told Jesus. And Jesus answered them, saying, The hour is come that the Son of man should be glorified. Verily, verily, I say unto you, Except a corn of wheat fall into the ground and die, it abideth alone; but if it die, it bringeth forth much fruit." What kind of an answer was that? Here were these Greeks who asked to see Jesus. Soon there would be Italians, Germans, Frenchmen, and others. Do you realize that in His incarnation God limited Himself? Jesus could be in only one place at one time? But if He died and resumed His eternal nature, without the limitations of this frame of flesh, He could be everywhere at once. Then He could see these Greeks, and the Italians, Germans, Americans; everywhere.

In this situation, Jesus was speaking of His own death. But isn't this true for each of us, that in order to be born again, we must first die? Paul says, "I die daily". We die unto self and live more and more unto Him. In the spiritual order of things, death precedes life.

Are we to achieve a great society of peace and righteousness throughout the world by man's efforts alone? If we could, who would get the credit? There are many of the prophets that speak of the day that is fast arriving. The world as we know it cannot continue, even on a physical basis. Must this civilization die, in order to be born again as the Kingdom of God? Think about that for a little while. Today, we see raging the most vicious spiritual warfare this world has ever known. It seems that this is Satan's last attempt to take over the active control of the nations of the world, in order to thwart the return of Christ. It would be easy if it were not for certain people; you, and you, and you, who are the Christians in the United States. Of course there are Christians in many lands, in many places, but the headquarters for the Christian enterprise on this earth is now in America. We are being attacked as perhaps no other people have ever been attacked in recent history; in our churches, in our family life, in our government, in our morals, in our faith, and in the very foundations of our society. There is one certainty about Satan attacking us; we can counterattack! And our weapons are spiritual weapons, if we would but use them.

There is increasing tension and competition among nations for the dwindling natural resources of the earth, as we move toward a period of real shortages of energy and materials. Is there enough human wisdom for our problems and perplexities? The issues of society are fast becoming the issues of a total society, a world society; they are fast becoming issues of the Kingdom of God on earth. The Club of Rome, in presenting its report, *The Limits to Growth,* offers a solution. Let the scientists find the level at which human life can be sustained on earth, and let the governments get together, and provide us with a beneficent dictatorship to enforce all the rules and regulations devised by the scientists for continuing life. The Bible has much to say about such an arrangement. It is the Lord Jesus Christ who is going to rule this planet earth, according to his laws. The King is coming! How long will it be? How soon? When? When we BEG Him to come. When we cry out for help in our troubles. When human effort and human wisdom are exhausted. When we have endured sufficient chastisement.

There is an increasing separation of God's people from the world around them, with increasing difficulties that accompany such separation. In this gathering storm our faith and patience will be tested. Just who do we think we are, that we should escape any tribulation? Christians in other lands have endured much suffering, even death, in this century; then why should we be spared? "Whom the Lord loveth, He chasteneth." Other generations of Christians have gone through the fire; why not us? What are our false gods today? Are they not gods of the good life, gods of affluence, gods of our possessions? Do we think too highly of these things? Then in our chastisement, will not God touch us right in the middle of our materiality?

One of the Ten Commandments says, "Thou shalt not take the name of the Lord thy God in vain, for the Lord will not hold him guiltless that taketh his name in vain." That word "take" means to take up, to bear aloft as on a banner, to lift up as a standard, to wear as a label. We have been called a Christian nation throughout the world. We have borne the name of Christ; but in vain? We may be in for a bit of a spanking, and we may be already half way to the woodshed. When it comes, despise not thou the chastening of the Lord. We have a sure rendevous with the Lord Jesus Christ.

We are going to have a great prayer meeting one of these days; a great prayer meeting. "If my people, which are called by my name, shall humble themselves, and pray, and seek my face, and turn from their wicked ways, then will I hear from heaven, and will forgive their sins, and will heal their land." When we meet that requirement, God will surely deal graciously with us.

Bibliography

1. Beegle, Dewey M. *Prophecy and Prediction.* Ann Arbor. Pryor Pettengill Publisher.
2. Lindsey, Hal. *The Late Great Planet Earth.* Grand Rapids. Zondervan Publishing House. 1971.
3. Sargent, H. N. *The Marvels of Bible Prophecy.* London. The Covenant Publishing Company LTD. 1938.
4. Shaffer, Francis A. *The God Who Is There.* Downers Grove, Illinois. Intervarsity Press. 1968.
5. Toffler, Alvin. *Future Shock.* New York. Bantam Books. 1970.
6. Toffler, Alvin. *The Third Wave.* New York. Bantam Books. 1980.
7. Wilkerson, David. *The Vision.* Old Tappan, New Jersey. Fleming H. Revell Company. 1974.

PART II
BACKGROUND:
OLD TESTAMENT BASICS

Chapter 2

The Charter of the Kingdom

God touches human history occasionally with great events. After the creation, the first such significant event was the sin of Adam and Eve and their expulsion from Eden. As men multiplied, they became corrupt, so God destroyed all but one family and human history began anew after the flood. Again, men multiplied and became corrupt and vain, building a tower in Babel to reach to heaven. God judged them, scattered them, and divided them by languages.

Men still would not obey and glorify God. In the first chapter of Romans, Paul tells us what happened. "Because that, when they knew God, they glorified him not as God, neither were thankful; but became vain in their imaginations, and their foolish hearts were darkened. Professing themselves to be wise, they became fools, and changed the glory of the uncorruptible God unto an image made like to corruptible man, and to birds, and four-footed beasts, and creeping things. Wherefore God also gave them up to uncleanness through the lusts of their own hearts, to dishonor their own bodies between themselves."

At that time, God initiated a program of reclamation, a program of bringing men who would trust him into an everlasting fellowhip with himself. An older catechism teaches us that "Man's chief end is to glorify God and enjoy him forever". God could have accomplished this purpose in any way he chose. He chose to attain this end by a program operating through history, that he might "bring many sons to glory". God could have ended human history at any time he chose. Since he did not, then he must have had some purpose in continuing it.

God's purpose in history is manifest again with the call of Abram, whose name he later changed to Abraham. We do not know how populous the world was in those days, but there were many tribes of people, small kingdoms of people, living all over the Fertile Crescent. This would include the countries surrounding the Persian Gulf, up the Euphrates Valley towards the mountains of the Caucasus and sweeping down through Syria toward the eastern shores of the Mediterranean all the way into Egypt. Out of all that mixture of people, God chose just one man; Abram. With the call of Abram, God was reducing the number of those who would be involved as his servants in carrying out his whole plan of salvation.

The declared purpose of God is conveyed to Abram as a set of intentions or promises, usually introduced by the words "I will". Nowhere will you find an "if". There are no contingencies and no conditions. God did not say, "Abram, IF you do so and so, then I will do such and such". God simply announced his purpose to Abram in a succession of completely unconditional promises. All these together we consider as God's covenant to Abram. Notice that it is a covenant to Abram, not with Abram.

The Scriptures contain many covenants or contracts, and like any contract, there is a great amount of fine print in them. Few people read all the fine print in these covenants and therefore miss some important points. It is in the fine print, that is, the detailed clauses, that we find the real intent of the covenant. At times the examination of these highly important small points will show that the whole program hinges on them.

We find the first mention of the promises to Abram in the twelfth chapter of Genesis. "Now the Lord said unto Abram, get thee out of thy country, and from thy kindred, and from thy father's house, unto a land that I will show thee: And I will make of thee a great nation, and I will bless thee, and make thy name great; and thou shalt be a blessing: And I will bless them that bless thee, and curse him that curseth thee: And in thee shall all the families of the earth be blessed".

In response, Abram left Ur of the Chaldees and moved up the Euphrates River to Haran into what is now Syria. When his father Terah died, he moved southwest with his nephew Lot into the land of Canaan, to a place called Sichem, or Shechem. Here, God appeared to him again and repeated his promise of the land.

After a short interlude in Egypt, Abram spent the rest of his life along the highland ridge running north and south between the Mediterranean Sea and the Jordan Valley. This high ground controlled the trade routes of the region, as well as providing a pasture land for flocks and herds.

In Genesis 13, look at verses 14 to 18. "And the Lord said unto Abram, after that Lot was separated from him, lift up thine eyes and look from the place where thou art northward, and southward, and eastward, and westward: For all the land which thou seest, to thee will I give it, and to thy seed forever. And I will make thy seed as the dust of the earth: so that if a man can number the dust of the earth, then shall thy seed also be numbered. Arise and walk through the land in the length of it and in the breadth of it; for I will give it unto thee. Then Abram removed his tent, and came and dwelt in the plain of Mamre, which is in Hebron and built there an altar unto the Lord." What do we look for? Small tribes somewhere? If this thing comes to pass, we should look for many people.

In Genesis chapter 15 we read that the Lord appeared to Abram and Abram complained. In paraphrase, "You promised me a great many seed and you haven't even given me one child." In chapter 15, verse 4, "And behold the word of the Lord came unto Abram in a vision saying, This shall not be thine heir (that is, Ishmael); he that shall come forth out of thine own bowels shall be thine heir. And he brought him forth abroad, and said, Look now toward heaven, and tell the stars, if thou be able to number them: so shall thy seed be. And he believed in the Lord: and he counted it to him for righteousness." In the next verse, Abram raises a question. "And he said unto him, I am the Lord that brought thee out of Ur of the Chaldees, to give thee this land to inherit it. And Abram said, Lord God, whereby shall I know that I shall inherit it?" He asked for a sign. So the Lord said, "All right, Abram, get some sacrificial animals, a ram, a goat, a heifer and two birds. Divide them into two parts and lay the pieces along two lines. Of the birds, put one on one side and one on the other." What was all this about? This was the most serious, sacred, oath-taking ceremony we find anywhere in secular or sacred history in that part of the world. It was a symbolic way of passing through death, "The sun was going down and a deep sleep fell on Abram and a horror of a great darkness fell on him, and the Lord said, Know of a surety that thy seed shall be a stranger in a land that is not theirs, and serve them that shall afflict them four hundred years. And also that nation, whom they shall serve, will I judge: and afterward shall they come out with great substance. And thou shalt go to thy fathers in peace; thou shalt be buried in a good old age. But in the fourth generation they shall come hither again, for the inquity of the Amorites is not yet full." (The two chief constituants of the Canaanites were the Amorites and the Hittities.)

"And it came to pass, that when the sun went down, the Lord asked Abram to get up and walk between those pieces." No! The account does not say that. "And it came to pass that when the sun went down, and it was dark, behold a smoking furnace, and a burning lamp that passed between those pieces." The Lord God himself, not Abram, walked between those pieces signifying, "Abram, I am going to keep my word if I have to die". And he did! On the cross. This shows the unilateral feature of the covenant. Abram was not asked to do a thing. God himself promised, and pledged his very life as a guarantee.

We know that Sarah was disappointed that she did not have a child. She gave Abram Hagar, her Egyptian handmaid, as a concubine, and of that union came Ishmael. Hagar's son, Ishmael, inherited some of these general promises given to Abram, such as the multiplicity of seed. Ishmael is the father of the Arabs. The Arabs are a Hebrew people; they are a Semitic people; they are descended from Abram. Please remember who the Arabs are when considering problems of the Mideast.

In chapter 17 Abram was ninety-nine years old. "The Lord appeared to Abram and said, I am the Almighty God; walk before me and be thou perfect. I will make my covenant between me and thee, and will multiply thee exceedingly." And Abram fell on his face: and God talked with him, saying, As for me, behold my covenant is with thee and thou shalt be a father of many nations. Neither shall thy name anymore be called Abram, but thy name shall be Abraham, for a father of many nations have I made thee." Abram means exalted father. Abraham means a father of a multitude. We call him Abraham from now on. "I will make thee exceedingly fruitful, and I will make nations of thee, and kings shall come of thee." Nations. There is one word in the Old Testament for "nations". It is Goyim. It is translated nations, heathen, people, gentiles; all one and the same Hebrew word. "I will make gentiles of thee and kings shall come of thee." There were not anything but gentiles in his day. Not too appropriate, is it? "I will establish my covenant with thee and thy seed after thee in their generations for an everlasting covenant, to be a God unto thee and to thy seed after thee. I will give unto thee and thy seed after thee the land wherein thou art a stranger, all the land of Canaan, for an everlasting possession. And I will be their God." God then introduced the rite of circumcision as a sign of this covenant.

In chapter 18, verses 18 and 19, in view of the impending doom of Sodom and Gomorrah, God appeared again to Abraham. "And the Lord said, shall I hide from Abraham that thing which I do? Seeing that Abraham shall surely become a great and mighty nation, and all the nations of the earth shall be blessed in him? for I know him, that he will command his children and his household after him and they shall keep the way of the Lord, to do justice and judgment: that the Lord may bring upon Abraham that which he hath spoken of him." In chapter 17, verse 18, Abraham was hopeful about his son Ishmael, but Sarah was going to have a child. In Genesis 21:12 we read, "And God said unto Abraham let it not be grievious in thy sight because of the lad, and because of thy bondwoman; in all that Sarah hath said unto thee, hearken unto her voice; for in Isaac shall thy seed be called." Besides these two, Abraham had other children, but these he sent back into the east countries, away from Ishmael and Isaac. He also had six sons by his second wife Keturah, whom he married after the death of Sarah. "But in Isaac shall thy seed be called." Of all the descendants of Abraham, only those coming through Isaac will be the principal part of this mainstream of covenant relationship. In 22:15-19, "And the angel of the Lord came unto Abraham out of heaven the second time. And said, By myself have I sworn, saith the Lord, for because thou hast done this thing, and hast not withheld thy son, thine only son, that in blessing I will bless thee, and in multiplying I will multiply thy seed as the stars of the heaven, and as the sand which is upon the sea shore: and thy seed shall possess the gate of his enemies: And in thy seed (singular) shall all the nations of the earth be blessed; because thou hast obeyed my voice." In thy one seed shall all the nations or gentiles of the earth be blessed because thou hast obeyed my voice. Paul quotes this in Galatians. The New Testament presents to us the one seed which is Christ.

When Isaac became a young man he went back to the east country and found Rebekah for a wife under unusual circumstances. To Isaac and Rebekah were born two sons: Esau and Jacob. Here is another covenant detail. Before the children were born, so that it would not be dependent on anything they would ever do, God made a choice (see Romans 9:10-12). The story is in Genesis 25. "The elder shall serve the younger." You know what happened. Esau was born first, all red like a hairy garment, so they called his name Esau, which means hairy. After that his brother came out and his hand took hold on Esau's heel and his name was called Jacob, since the name Jacob means heel.

Esau was the first born, and had the birthright, which was the right to inherit the father's worldly goods. Esau sold his birthright for a bowl of soup. The birthright was his to sell, so in exhaustion he sold it to Jacob. Imagine Jacob teasing Esau with a bowl of good stew until Esau sold him his birthright. The birthright is the right of inheritance of all the material possessions that the father owned. Someone may think that there was also a connotation of spiritual leadership in the family associated with the birthright. There was no inherent spiritual blessing involved. This was largely a material blessing, the birthright in the natural, legal sense.

In addition to the birthright there was indeed a special spiritual blessing that passed from generation to generation. This was transmitted by a kind of last will and testament spoken orally. Rebekah knew that Jacob was to have preeminence and she connived with Jacob concerning a plan to get this blessing from Isaac. Rebekah helped Jacob dress up with goat skin so he would feel hairy to the touch, because Isaac was going blind. Jacob went in to Isaac and deceived him into thinking he was Esau. Consequently Jacob received the blessing from Isaac that Isaac intended to give to Esau. But once spoken it was binding. This was an irrevocable legal act. Jacob not only bought the birthright from Esau but received the blessing from Isaac, their father. Therefore, Jacob was now in line for those covenant blessings which would be his, down through his life and beyond. The story is in Genesis chapter 27.

In the first five verses of Genesis 26, the Lord appeared to Isaac and promised some of these same blessings he had given to Abraham. Verse 5 is very significant. "Because that Abraham obeyed my voice, and kept my charge, my commandments, my statutes, and my laws." This was 430 years before Mt. Sinai. What kind of laws did they have then? The law was from the beginning. Else why find fault with Cain for slaying Abel? There is a special way in which the law fits in with the covenant at Sinai which we will present in a later chapter.

Jacob went back to the east country to his Uncle Laban and worked 22 years for his wives and his flocks and herds. He had 12 sons. Joseph was sold as a slave by his brethen into Egypt and later rose to power there; becoming vice-pharaoh of Egypt. In Genesis 48, Joseph had a visit with Jacob his father. Joseph could not come back into that shepherd family. Joseph had become the vice-pharaoh of Egypt. Jacob did not expect Joseph to take off his regalia of authority and quit his office of administering the economic affairs of Egypt just to become the young boy in a family of shepherds that had come out of Canaan. In paraphrase, Jacob said, "Now you have these two boys, Ephraim and Manasseh. I am adopting them. Since I cannot take you back into the family, they are going to be mine just like Reuben and Simeon and Levi and my other sons. If you have any other children they are yours, but these two are mine." So Jacob adopted Ephraim and Manasseh, therefore making 13 sons for Jacob. This adoption was purely a unilateral affair on the part of Jacob and the boys did not even have to be present. But then Joseph brought the two boys to Jacob. Jacob said, "Who are these?" Jacob's eyesight was failing, like his father Isaac. "These are my two boys, Ephraim and Manasseh." "Well, bring them over here." Jacob, called by his name Israel on this occasion, and speaking under inspiration, crossed his hands, put his right hand on the younger boy's head and his left hand on the older boy's head and pronounced a special blessing upon them. We find it in chapter 48, verse 15. Joseph objects,"You put your right hand on the younger boy's head." "I know what I'm doing." "And so he set Ephraim before Manasseh", (Ephraim being the younger son.) This passage presents the adoption of the two boys, the blessing of the two boys, with regard to the multitude of seed, and other blessings.

The next chapter contains Jacob's last will and testament, spoken orally, in which he said something about each of his sons. In chapter 49 of Genesis, two sons are predominant. Judah is likened to a lion. Here is the beginning of the association of the symbol of the lion and Judah. Also to Judah is given the scepter, the right to rule, the kingship. A number of these sons are symbolized by animals which were later used as signs in the camp of Israel. We have studied the story of Jacob and Esau in Sunday School lessons repeatedly. Discerning students realize the difference between the birthright, which Esau sold to Jacob, and the Blessing, which Jacob obtained from his father Isaac by deceit. What happened to the Birthright and the Blessing in the next generation? Look very carefully at Jacob's prophecy concerning Joseph in Genesis 49:26. It reads, "The blessings of thy father have prevailed above the blessings of my progenitors unto the utmost bound of the everlasting hills: they shall be on the head of Joseph and on the crown of the head of him that was separate from his brethen."

Here, in Genesis 49:22-26, Jacob transfered the blessing to Joseph with a most unusual statement. In verse 26, who is "thy father"? Is it not Jacob, who is speaking? Who are "my progenitors"? Are they not Jacob's father Isaac and grandfather Abraham? Then the passage can be read, "The blessings which I, your father, Jacob now pronounce upon you, Joseph, shall greatly exceed the blessings which I received from my father Isaac and my grandfather, Abraham." What a blessing! If there is any place in all of the Scripture where a particular family of people were designated as a special recipient of God's special blessing, it is here in verse 26.

Not only did Jacob confer upon Joseph these special blessings, but the Birthright also was given to Joseph after Reuben disqualified himself. Joseph was the oldest son of Jacob's beloved wife Rachel. Just as the circumstances of life brought both the Birthright and the Blessing to Jacob, so, likewise, did Joseph receive them both also.

Here in the closing passages of the book of Genesis, Jacob prophesied concerning his sons, about 400 years before the Old Testament (Mt. Sinai) and over a thousand years before there ever was a Jew. Let it be emphatically stated that none of the descendants of Joseph are ever called Jews in the Bible.

A few hundred years after Jacob's death, the people fell into slavery and God sent Moses to lead them out of Egypt in the Exodus. When they arrived at Mt. Sinai, something very strange happened. The ceremony at Mt. Sinai was a wonderful wedding ceremony. In it there is a courtship, a proposal, an acceptance, a period of getting ready, and a presiding minister. The Lord spoke his vows, the people of Israel spoke spoke their vows. The people became very nervous with some bridal jitters during the ceremony. They even ran away for awhile. There was music, a wedding feast; the whole ceremony is complete. It was a wonderful ceremony when God married Israel at Mt. Sinai. This is a covenant, a contract; but a highly conditional one. God said, if, if, if, right on down the line. And the people accepted those conditions.

First of all the law is given and written for them as part of the marriage contract. With no other people did God ever enter into contract on the basis of that law like He did with Israel on that day. And that law is more than the Ten Commandments. After hearing the Ten Commandments, the people ran away. That is all they heard. But in Exodus 21, 22, 23 there are more laws and judgments. All are a part of the contract.

Later, the Lord added something, knowing that the people of Israel could not keep the contract. He added a whole set of laws called ordinances in which there would be a symbolic atonement and forgiveness of sin. He set up a priesthood within the tribe of Levi, from among all the descendents of Aaron, the brother of Moses. Aaron and his sons were to be the priests to administer the ordinances whereby the people should be mindful of their sin, and in ceremony the people would seek to atone for their sin. Without understanding how God would do it, these ceremonies looked forward to the time when God would make full provision for their sins and forgive them. The whole arrangement is highly symbolic. This is treated in detail in the Book of Hebrews which you should read concerning the priesthood. The ordinances were the part of the law which Jesus nailed to the cross, as mentioned in Ephesians 2:15. That is the law which Jesus completed. He did away with the whole system of animal sacrifices and the Levitical priesthood. Jesus took care of sacrifice for sin by his death on the cross as our high priest.

Your attention is now called to Deuteronomy 33, where Moses blessed the tribes very much as Jacob had blessed his sons. Here, Levi received a large portion because of the priesthood. To Levi was entrusted the administration of the ordinances given at Mt. Sinai. Notice particularly verse 7, which sounds as if Judah is going to be in a little trouble at sometime. In verse 12, we read, "And of Benjamin he said, the beloved of the Lord shall dwell in safety by him." Is Jesus the beloved of the Lord? Were the Galileans Benjaminites?

Beginning with Deut. 33:13, there is a long passage dealing with Joseph. The blessings of Israel to Joseph are repeated and augmented. The people of Joseph are to become wealthy and militarily strong. Joseph is likened to a bullock and a unicorn. This word unicorn is properly a wild ox, and is so translated in some versions. These are special blessings to Joseph, including the birthright.

In summary, the Lord God of Heaven and Earth, declared a covenant relationship with one man, Abraham, and his progeny through whom he initiated a program of reclamation for his disobedient and sinful creatures. This program includes the selection and multiplication of a family of people to be his servants in this program. Not only was there a people, but a land, laws to govern life, priests, and kings. What is this combination of king, laws, land and people, but a kingdom? In God's proposal to Israel, in Exodus 19:6; God said, "And ye shall be unto me a kingdom of priests, and a holy nation." Yes, the promises to the fathers, to Abraham, Isaac, Jacob, and Jacob's sons were nothing less than the charter for God's kingdom on earth, the kingdom into which all men of faith would come. The life, teachings, work of redemption, and coming reign as king of Jesus Christ are inherent within these promises which comprise the framework and purpose of God in human history.

Chapter 3

Her Tent and My Tent

We have considered the wonderful promises that God made to Abraham and what happened to them. Abraham had several descendants at that ancient time and God had promised many, many descendants later on. We saw that the various wonderful promises given to Abraham were divided by Jacob among his twelve sons. Actually there were thirteen sons, because he adopted the sons of Joseph in the place of Joseph. Joseph could not come back into the little family; he was Vice-Pharaoh of Egypt, a foreigner. We have examined Moses' blessings of the tribes. There are two chief divisions here: the throne and the kingdom, the scepter and the birthright, if you please. Now we want to explore the paths along which these two divisions of promise flowed throughout the Old Testament. Moses included a number of promises set aside for the tribe of Levi. Moses was a Levite, and at Mt. Sinai, when God made the law a written part of the contract with the people of Israel, he added a system of ordinances administered through the Levites having to do with sin and the atonement for sin. These are the laws that the New Testament tells us were nailed to the cross; they were finished with the work of Christ on the cross. Christ did not do away with "thou shalt not murder"; he did not do away with these ten commandments at all. We must understand, when Paul is referring to the law, which law he is talking about.

During the period of the judges, the tribes were struggling more or less single-handedly against their Canaanitish neighbors. Nothing of covenant importance happened nationally until the time of Samuel, who is called the last of the judges and the first of the prophets. Samuel did not write a book of prophecy, but the historical record shows that he spoke prophetically of many things. During the days of Samuel, the people clamored for a king. They wanted to be like their neighbors who had visible rulers. Samuel warned them it would cost them much more if they did that. The people wanted a king anyway, and Saul was crowned. David endured much under the reign of Saul. After the death of Saul, David was chosen king over the tribe of Judah only. David took the hill of Zion, the city of the Jebusites, which later became Jerusalem. Jerusalem was really in the tribal territory assigned to the tribe of Benjamin. It was always counted as part of the tribe of Judah because David took it. The men of Judah crowned David king, not in Jerusalem, but in Hebron. David reigned as king over the tribe of Judah only for seven years.

Through all the bickering between the sons of Saul and the people of Israel of the various tribes, the people of Israel finally got together and decided that they would like to have David rule over them as well. David was crowned king of all of Israel for another 33 years, making a total reign of 40 years.

David established a strong kingdom over all the territory that we can imagine the language of the Old Testament would give to Abraham. It extended from the Sinai desert all the way to the Euphrates River, and from the Gulf of Aquaba south of the Dead Sea all the way north to Mt. Hermon. He was on friendly terms with the Phoenicians and with the kings of Tyre and Sidon. Everything was in good order.

Having attained a great kingdom and established peace, David wanted to build the Lord a house of worship. The Lord sent Nathan the prophet to David. Beginning with II Samuel 7:8, we read the message. In verse 11, Nathan said, "Also the Lord telleth thee that he will make thee a house", and in verse 13, "He (David's son) will build a house for my name, and I will establish the throne of his kingdom forever." This is God's covenant to David in which God established a perpetual throne. This initiated the fulfillment of the promise that God made to Abraham, "kings shall be of thee." This also was in line with the promise to Judah that the "scepter shall not depart from Judah till Shiloh come, and unto him (that is, Shiloh) shall the gathering of the people be". Here was an earthly king with a heavenly charter. David's throne would endure forever, as long as the sun shines and the moon shines, as long as the stars shine, as long as the earth remains, David's throne will be there. God promised David a perpetual throne.

David died, and Solomon became king. Solomon continued the great wealth and influence of the kingdom of Israel. However, Solomon disqualified himself. He married strange wives, and went after their gods. Although he had prayed for wisdom and the Lord gave him wisdom, Solomon was very unwise regarding strange women, hundreds of them. He brought in all their idols and began to worship them. In I Kings 11:11, God promised to tear the kingdom away from Solomon.

At this point we are introduced in I Kings 11 to a strange man, Jeroboam. He was not of the tribe of Judah; he was of the tribe of Ephraim. In I Kings 11:28, Jeroboam is identified as belonging to "The house of Joseph", not the tribe of Joseph. The tribe of Joseph is used in one place where it means "Manasseh". In another place, where the tribe of Joseph is used in the Bible, it means, "namely, Ephraim". In other words, the tribes of Ephraim and Manesseh became the progeny of Joseph. But, in I Kings 11 this is not the Tribe of Joseph, it is the House of Joseph.

If we go back into the book of Samuel we find that David had trouble with his son Absalom. Absalom rebelled and wanted to become king, but David would not touch him. In fact, rather than punish his son Absalom with military forces, although Absalom was running around with his own soldiers, David left the country. He went across the Jordan River to the East. As he was going away from Jerusalem one of the followers of Absalom named Shemei cursed David. David did not reply, and went on across the Jordan.

Shemei was of the tribe of Benjamin. After the news of Absalom's tragic death, David began his journey back to Jerusalem. As the king returned he came to Jordan, and the men of Judah came to Gilgal to meet the king and conduct him over the Jordan. Shemei, the son of Geru, a Benjamite, hastened and came down with the men of Judah to meet king David. This is the same man, the very fellow, that cursed David when he left. There were a thousand men of Benjamin with him. Shemei fell down before the king when he was come over Jordan, and said unto the king, "Let not my lord impute iniquity unto me, neither do thou remember that which thy servant did perversely the day that my lord the king went out of Jerusalem that the king should take it to his heart. For thy servant doth know that I have sinned. Therefore, behold I am come the first this day of all the House of Joseph to go down to meet my lord the king." So here was a Benjamite claiming to be in the House of Joseph.

What is the difference between the tribe of Joseph and the House of Joseph? Ephraim became so dominant among the other tribes, being the birthright tribe, that the 11 tribes were known as "Ephraim" or the House of Joseph. They became the "dominion" over which the tribe of Judah ruled in the days of David and Solomon. The people of all the 11 tribes were called "Israel", "the House of Joseph" in contradistinction to Judah. Throughout the Old Testament, in all the numberings of the soldiers, the men of Judah were always considered separate and apart from the rest of Israel. We are getting into the proposition that the people of God, the descendants of Abraham, the children of Jacob, were considered to be two people. In Psalm 114:1-2, we find, "When Israel went out of Egypt, the house of Jacob from a people of a strange language, Judah was his sanctuary and Israel his dominion." There was a difference between Judah and Israel. Judah was the locale of the throne, the sanctuary and the theocracy, administered by the Levites who were the lawgivers. Judah was in the center of the government, of the whole theocracy of Israel. We have already read from I Chronicles that the birthright was Joseph's, and the genealogy pertained to Judah, that is, the genealogy of the king. The birthright belonged to Joseph; the scepter belonged to Judah.

Look further at I Kings chapter 11. Jeroboam went out of Jerusalem, into the countryside, and Ahijah the Shilonite, a prophet, found him. Jeroboam was clad in a new garment and the two of them were alone in the field. Ahijah caught the new garment that was on Jeroboam and tore it into 12 pieces. He then said to

Jeroboam, "Take thee 10 pieces. For thus saith the Lord, the God of Israel, behold I will rend the kingdom out of the hand of Solomon and give 10 tribes to thee. But he (Solomon) shall have one tribe for my servant David's sake and for Jerusalem's sake, the city I have chosen out of all the tribes of Israel." How many pieces does that make? Eleven. Where is the other one? There were 12 pieces. The twelfth piece represented Judah, the tribe of the king, and that was not a part of the kingdom, the "dominion" over which the king with Judah ruled. The king and the tribe of Judah are identified here. The kingdom consisted of the 11 tribes; not 12, not 13, but 11. And so the prophet told Jeroboam that God was going to give him 10 of these 11 tribes and that Solomon (or his son) was going to keep one "for David my servant's sake", because the Lord had promised David that he should never want a man to rule over the house of Israel. Not Judah, but Israel. There had to be somebody from Israel there in contradistinction to Judah for the Lord to keep his promise to David.

When Soloman died, Rehoboam, his son, inherited the throne. In I Kings 12:6, Rehoboam asked the old men, who had served his father, for advice, and they counseled moderation. Rehoboam forsook the counsel of the old men, and consulted with the young men who had grown up with him. They advised more drastic measures and increased taxes. Rehoboam then announced, in verse 11, "And now whereas my father did lade you with a heavy yoke, I will add to your yoke: my father hath chastised you with whips, but I will chastise you with scorpions." No wonder the people of Israel complained.

There are several places in the Bible where the term "all Israel" means Israel in contradistinction to Judah. It does not include Judah, because there is also "all Judah" which means Judah excluding Israel. It is a peculiar expression, but do not think that "all" means everybody. It means "all the people of Israel" and "all the people of Judah". In verse 16 "All Israel" means these 11 tribes. They rebelled. "What portion have we in David?" We are the birthright people. We do not belong to that scepter bunch. "Neither have we inheritance in the son of Jesse."

Who is the son of Jesse? David. These people had no inheritance in the scepter; they had inheritance in the birthright of Joseph. "To your tents, O Israel." What does that mean? A call to arms, a war cry. "Now see to thine own house David." So Israel departed unto their tents. "But as for the children of Israel which dwelt in the cities of Judah, Rehoboam reigned over them. They started fighting over this affair! Hold on. Look at verse 20. They made Jeroboam king over all Israel, not including Judah, but all Israel.

Jerusalem was originally in the tribal territory of the tribe of Benjamin, but because David took it, Judah claimed it. Benjamin occupied a strip of land just north of Judah. They were next door neighbors. In the middle of verse 21, we read, "all the house of Judah with the tribe of Benjamin". In other words, Israel rebelled and ran away with the kingdom. Rehoboam was the king over Judah alone. But here was Benjamin, a piece of the kingdom, that came with Judah. Who divided the people? God did! "This thing is from me." What God hath put asunder let no man join together! God brought about this division for a purpose to be worked out in history. The birthright people were to have a different history and a different destiny than the scepter people. That is the theme we are going to be following.

From then on there were two kingdoms. The kingdom of Israel in the north whose capital city finally became Samaria. The kingdom of Judah in the south with the capital city of Jerusalem. Only kings from the line of David ever ruled in Judah. In Israel it was first one king then another, first from one family, then another.

Now there is a further division of tribes when this split came about. Jeroboam became disturbed. In I Kings 12:27, Jeroboam said, "if this people go up to do sacrifice in the house of the Lord in Jerusalem, then shall the heart of this people turn again unto their lord, even unto Rehoboam king of Judah, and they shall kill me, and go again to Rehoboam king of Judah." What did he do? He built two golden calves, and he said, "Behold your gods, O Israel." The calves were the symbol of whom? Joseph, Ephraim; they made calves which were idols to themselves. The Levites were sprinkled in cities throughout all the tribes, since they did not have any tribal territory. The Levites did not want to minister to the worship of two golden calves, which became a great sin. Then Jeroboam made a house of high places, and made priests of the lowest of people which were not of the sons of Levi, and maneuvered the Levites out of a job. As a consequence, Levites moved from all their cities throughout all the tribes of Israel to Judah. A new group of people came into being, which included the king, the tribe of Judah, the tribe of Benjamin, and the tribe of Levi. This new grouping became known thereafter as the kingdom of Judah. The Levites had no tribal inheritance in the land, no farms. The Levites were still a part of the theocracy, the civil servants, but only one family of them administered the ecclesiastical system of the land, namely, the priests of the family of Aaron, who were just a small portion of the tribe of Levi. The Levites taught the people the law; the Levites were the school teachers. The Levites were the tax collectors; they were the ones who collected the tithe, and they gave a tenth of the tithe to the priests. The Levites moved into the kingdom of Judah. From then on it was Judah, Benjamin, and Levi. This kingdom of Judah lasted for several hundred years.

Judah had good kings and bad kings but in Israel they were all bad kings. Jeroboam, the first king of Israel, is repeatedly called, "Jeroboam, the son of Nebat, who made Israel to sin," by worshipping the golden calves. They worshipped the golden calf, and they worshipped Baal, and they worshipped all kinds of idols. But they had no official worship for the Lord God anymore. Occasionally there would be an individual here and there who was faithful.

In the 17th chapter of II Kings we find that the empire of Assyria was spreading out and making contact with Egypt. The Kingdom of Israel was in the way. This Assyrian campaign against Egypt lasted many years. By this time the people of Israel had lost their power. They were fragmented. They did not have strong armies and they did not have a good economy. Shalmanezer, the king of Assyria, besieged Samaria for three years. The city fell, and Hoshea, the king of Israel, was taken captive. This brought to an end the kingdom of Israel in Old Testament times. The kingdom of Judah in the south continued for another 130 years.

The Assyrian invasion of Israel began about 745 B.C. and Samaria fell about 721 B.C. This invasion is recorded on the cuneiform inscriptions of the Assyrians. These people on the coast that were in the way of their invasion of Egypt were called the house of Omri, who was one of the Kings of Israel. They were also called Bit-sak by the Assyrians, which is the same as the Hebrew Beth Sac, which simply means the "house of Isaac". It is carved in stone in the museums today, stones which have been dug out of the ruins of the Assyrian empire. This kind of thing is not in the history books, but in books of the archeology of Assyria.

We find a summary in II Kings 17 of all the sins of the people of Israel. And the Lord kept on testifying against them through his servants the prophets, but they would not listen. Notice in verse 16 of chapter 17 . . . "and worshiped all the host of heaven, And served Baal." What does that mean? The constellations; astrology. They caused their sons and daughters to pass through the fire to Molech, which is part of Baal worship. That would be burning them up, would it not? They did not have abortion in those days; they just waited and pitched unwanted babies into the fire, as part of their religious worship. They "used divinations and enchantments and sold themselves to do evil in the sight of the Lord and provoked him to anger, therefore the Lord was very angry with Israel and removed them out of His sight. There was none left but the tribe of Judah only." This is a reference to the southern kingdom of Judah. Neither did Judah keep the commandments. Look at verse 21. "For . . . unto this day." When is that? The day this was written or edited, which was some time later. Days of the Chronicles?

What happened next? "The King of Assyria brought men from Babylon, from Cutha, and from Ava, and from Hamath, and from Sepharvaim and placed them in the cities of Samaria instead of the children of Israel and they possessed Samaria and dwelt in the cities there." There were some of the people of Israel, the country folk, the hillbillies, the small farmers, who did not get collected and shipped off to Assyria; the invaders did not take every single man. So these Cuthians and others that were brought in, foreigners who were from beyond the Euphrates, were settled in the land, and in due course of time they intermarried with the poor of Israel that had remained in the land. What did this mixture become? The Samaritans. In the days of Jesus, the Jews had no dealings with the Samaritans. When men went back and forth from Judea to Galilee, they had to travel along a route east of Jordan. About double the walking time.

The Assyrians did not stop with taking people of the 10 tribes. One of the Assyrian inscriptions has a story of lining up 200,150 men of Judah, and marching them to Assyria with the people of Israel. Another item tells us that one of the kings of Assyria besieged all the fenced cities of Judah and took them. Later, Jeremiah tells us the name of the three that were not taken. They were Jerusalem, Lachish, and Azekah. The Assyrian inscription says they took 46 fenced cities. In other words, by adding to the Biblical account which is accurate, some of the details furnished by the Assyrians, the whole story fits together.

Now let us look for the demise of the kingdom of Judah. We will find that in the last chapter of II Kings. By then we have another empire which has risen to take the place of Assyria, namely, Babylon. We enter a period of time called the Babylonian captivity of Judah. Not Israel; Israel was not there. The Babylonian captivity of Judah. This invasion extended from 604 B.C. down to 586 B.C. Nebuchadnezzer took the field of battle in 606 B.C. as head of the armies of his father Nabopolasser. His father died. Nebuchadnezzer had to go back to Babylon to assume the office of the King of Babylon. It was not until two years later that he returned to the field of battle, headed toward Egypt, and found Judah in his way. There were three principal captures of Jerusalem; one was in 604 B.C., one in about 598 B.C., and the final one in 586 B.C. Now the first was not much more than a capture of loot; not many people. The second one in

598 B.C. included the king, a young king named Jechoniah, or Coniah, or Jehoiachin. Here is one man that has three names in the Bible. The Babylonians set up Coniah's uncle as king in his place, a man by the name of Zedekiah. In II Kings 25 we begin to read about this. The King of Babylon would be Nebuchadnezzer. In verse 21, he smote the people of Jerusalem and slew them. "So Judah was carried away out of their land." There was a small group of the people of Judah left, which was not carried away. We read of it in verse 22. This group got into a little trouble and these people that were left killed Gedaliah, the appointed governor. They became afraid of the King of Babylon and fled to Egypt.

Where were the children of Israel during this time? We are not told in the Scripture. Archeologists tell us some things about. They settled in the cities of the Medes in the country between the Caspian Sea and the Black sea, northern Media, south of the Caucasus Mountains. Now there are some stories to the effect that when the Babylonians rose up and shook off the power of Assyria that many of these people of Israel said, "Let's get out of here". And they went through the narrow passages of the Euphrates River, and got into the country north of the Black Sea. That is another story we will get into a little bit later. We find that story in the books of the Apocrapha which we do not consider inspired scripture and it has a history whose reliability may be in question. But there is one thing not in question; the books of the Apocrypha represent Jewish thought at that time.

The people who went into Assyrian captivity were never called Jews. What does the word Jew mean? Little Judah. It is a diminutive. The difference is explained if you transfer the letters from the Hebrew directly into English. If you go by letters, you have Yehuda for Judah, and Yehudi for Little Judah, which is the word we translate "Jew". There cannot be a little Judah unless big Judah is gone. Yehudi means a remnant of Judah. After the Assyrians took Israel and parts of Judah away, that which was left of the house of Judah could be called little Judah or Jews. But it was not used generally until the time of the Babylonian captivity when Jeremiah used it several times. Some of the other prophets of that era used it. We are going to see that it was used officially for quite some period of time after the return from Babylon.

Look at Jeremiah, chapter three. Many of the prophets spoke concerning these two people, Israel and Judah. In the Appendix there is a list of scripture in Isaiah, Jeremiah, Ezekiel, Amos, Hosea and other prophets that speak of Israel and Judah. Micah begins with "The word of the Lord that came to Micah which he saw concerning Samaria and Jerusalem", Samaria being the capital city of Israel, Jerusalem being the capital city of Judah. Micah saw things concerning these two kingdoms. Jeremiah lived at the time of the Babylonian invasion. He saw the judgment that God was pronouncing on Judah and advised them to bow their heads and accept it. They did not like that and inflicted all kinds of hardships upon him, that we learn about when we read the personal history of Jeremiah.

In Jeremiah chapter 3 beginning with verse 6, Jeremiah accuses the people of Israel with spiritual harlotry. Harlotry or adultery in the words of the prophet means spiritual unfaithfulness. God had married all of the people of Israel at Mt. Sinai. When the people worshipped other gods, they committed spiritual adultery. This had happened a hundred years before the time of Jeremiah, but it is Jeremiah who announced that a just God had given the nation of Israel a divorce. Israel, but not Judah. Nowhere in the Bible does it ever say that God divorced Judah. This lesson in Jeremiah 3 is a lesson to Judah about Israel. The object lesson is plain since Jeremiah speaks of the people "to the north". Israel was located north of Judah, and when Israel was carried into Assyria, they were sent even farther north.

The invitation to return is spoken by Jeremiah to the people of Israel while the kingdom of Judah was still in the land. What kind of return is promised? A representative one, because these people of northern Israel carried with them the covenant promise of a multitude of children. Therefore, the return would be "one of a city and two of a family", not a mass return. Also, the House of Israel and the House of Judah would be together when this return occurs, according to Jeremiah 3:18.

In Jeremiah 31:31 we read, "Behold, the days come, saith the Lord, that I will make a new covenant with the house of Israel, and with the house of Judah." If there is to be a new covenant, it will be new with respect to a covenant which is old. What is the old covenant? The covenant of marriage of Mt. Siani which the people broke by committing spiritual adultery, when "I was a husband unto them". The old covenant was made in terms of the commandments, statutes, and judgements, with the addition of all the ordinances regarding disobedience and atonement for sin. The ordinances were to be administered by the priests and Levites. The day would come, when there would be a new covenant, not like Sinai, administered by a new priesthood, not in the line of Aaron. This story is the subject of the book of Hebrews.

The book of Genesis comes before the book of Exodus. The covenant which God made to Abraham precedes the covenant which God made with the people at Mt. Sinai. The promises precede the Law. The covenant at Mt. Sinai is within the framework of the promises made to Abraham. The new covenant also will be within the provisions of the promises made to Abraham. See Luke 1:54,55 and Luke 1:72,73.

The adulterous behavior of the people of Israel under the name of Jerusalem is described in the indictment we find in Ezekiel Chapter 16. Some of this language is rather extreme and raw, so the chances are that this chapter has not been studied in Sunday School classes. In the end, however, God promises a future restoration of his people to a covenant relationship.

In retrospect, the people of Israel are regarded as two separate and distinct people in Ezekiel chapter 23 where their sinful character is again related. Here, the language is very indelicate, and this chapter is rarely discussed openly. Read it yourself. It is a parable of two sisters, Aholah, and Aholibah, which are names for Samaria, the capital of the House of Israel, and Jerusalem, the capital of the House of Judah. The temple in Jerusalem replaced the tabernacle, a tent which covered the ark of the covenant in the wilderness. This was the place God had chosen to manifest his presence to the people of Israel. The place of God's presence was in the holy of holies in the temple. Therefore, Jerusalem is referred to as Aholibah, which means "my tent is in her". The people to the north, however, had broken away from the worship of the God of Israel from the days of Jeroboam and established calf worship and idol worship. God was not present among them. Therefore, Samaria is Aholah, or "her tent". God had brought about the division of the people into two kingdoms, but the God of Abraham had no place in the worship of the northern tribes. God cut them loose and divorced them. The two peoples were called "my tent" and "her tent". There were two people, two daughters of one mother, two sisters, two wives, two sheepfolds and two adulterous women. This duality is recognizable all the way through the prophets and Old Testament history.

Chapter 4
Figs and Figs

As nations fall and others rise in the course of history, careful observers might possibly notice that one particular change in political power is of more importance than others. Such was possibly the case when Daniel the prophet and prince of Israel experienced the turnover of sovereignty from Belshazzar the Babylonian to Darius the Mede. Although Daniel had interpreted the handwriting on the wall to Belshazzar, there was still the question in Daniel's mind concerning the significance of the momentous events to the people of Israel. So in the very first year of Darius, Daniel sought a better understanding of the meaning of that day and found it in the writings of Jeremiah the prophet, who had sent a letter to the captives of Judah in Babylon, among whom was Daniel himself.

A copy of this letter is in the 29th chapter of the book of Jeremiah. However, it is addressed to a particular portion of the people whom Nebuchadnezzar had carried into Babylon, and the entire captivity is portrayed in figure in the 24th chapter of Jeremiah. In order to better understand the message of the ninth chapter of Daniel, it will be advantageous if we first become familiar with the contents of these two chapters in Jeremiah.

In the 24th chapter of Jeremiah the prophet had a vision in which God showed Jeremiah two baskets of figs; one of good figs, one of bad figs. This vision occurred after the time that Jeconiah the king with his princes and ten thousand of the people of Judah had been taken to Babylon. Read Jeremiah 24:1, 29:16-19, and II Kings 24:8-17. This vision occurred during the reign of Zedekiah, the last king of Judah, and the very last in the line of David to reign in the Old Testament.

In the vision, the good figs are a symbol of the people who had already gone into captivity (verse 5), and the bad figs are a symbol for the people who were still remaining in the land of Judah (verse

8). The bad figs are yet to be carried into captivity, and this was to be a longlasting captivity among "all the kingdoms of the earth for their hurt", just as some of the people of Judah and most of the people of Israel had been taken captive by the Assyrians more than a hundred years previously. The House of Judah had been reduced to Jerusalem and its environs, and only two other fenced cities. Compare Jeremiah 29:17 with II Kings 17:5-23. Since that earlier captivity, this remnant of the people of the Southern Kingdom of Judah had been known as Jews, a name which means simply "little Judah". The vast majority of the people of Israel and Judah had been driven from the land before the name Jew was applied to this remnant. Does the Bible ever use the word Jew to mean all the people of Israel? According to Jeremiah 3:11, Ezekiel 16:46-52, and Ezekiel 23:31, this remnant of Jews was more deserving of punishment than all of Israel before them.

The good figs are to go into exile in Babylon for a limited time of only seventy years. They are to be brought back to the land of Judah for their good and for the good purpose of God. They are not to be misled by the false prophets among them who claim they are to return in a very short time. They are told to settle down and live normally in Babylon, for it will be a long time, 70 years, before any of them or their children would return to Jerusalem and Judah. Upon their return, these good figs are to enjoy the blessings of God in a renewed spiritual fellowship with him. Is there any other promise of any other group who are to go into captivity and return at that time? If so, where is the Scripture? Daniel refers to this group alone as the basis for his consideration in Daniel 9:2.

All this history is inherent in the messages of Jeremiah which Daniel read. When Darius conquered Babylon, we can imagine that Daniel asked himself, "Is this the time when the promise of a return will be fulfilled"? Daniel seeks his answer from God. Daniel understood by books the time. Is it necessary to be a Daniel, especially chosen and prepared by God, before anyone today may understand by books (the prophets, including Daniel) the significance of our own times, or may any devout Christian understand by searching the Scriptures? If not the latter, then why were they written? This may bring up the problem of placing confidence in various prophetic teachers who have all the outward marks of devotion and sincerity, but whose predictions just do not fit subsequent history.

The prayer of Daniel is a wonderful prayer and serves as a model for the intercession of a ruler for his people. This is not a prayer of personal penitence. Daniel is not personally responsible for all the past sins of his people. Yet Daniel identifies himself with the sinful people, because he is racially and nationally their pre-eminent representative before nations and before God. This is primarily an intercessory prayer, although Daniel was not a priest. This was most appropiate, for Daniel was probably of the royal line of David as one of the princes mentioned in II Kings.

The admission of sin is complete. It can only fully be understood if we read Leviticus 26 and Deuteronomy 28 in connection with Daniel 9:5-15. In these passages we see that disobedience to the commandments of God and disregard for all teachings and warnings of the prophets are responsible for the punishment of the people. Daniel names the transgressors as the men of Judah, the inhabitants of Jerusalem, and all Israel. Daniel confesses the sin of all the people of Israel, regardless of their present circumstances wherever they are. Judah and Jerusalem were the special subjects of Jeremiah, but all Israel were already entered into the time of their punishment before the time of Jeremiah. Here, Daniel is looking backward, and sees all Israel had been driven from the land over a hundred years before the Babylonian exile began. All Israel is included in the prayer of confession, because Daniel is at the last end of the transgression as predicted by Moses.

As pointed out, the eminence of Daniel in the courts of Babylon and Medo-Persia was such as to make him the foremost representative of Israel. In this sense he could pray for "my people". But all Israel was never captive to Babylon, and in no other passage is there any indication that Daniel ever prayed in behalf of all of Israel.

Now we come to Daniel's prayer of petition in verses 16-19. It is a very remarkable prayer, for in it Daniel seems to sense the limits of what he can pray for according to God's purpose as Daniel understands it. The secret of the meaning of God's answer lies within this prayer of petition.

First, let us consider what Daniel did not pray for. He did not pray for a restoration of all the people of Israel who had sinned. He did not pray for all the land of Israel which had been cursed, nor for the removal of the curses on the people which had been pronounced by Moses so long ago. He did not pray for God to restore the throne of David by setting up a new king. He did not pray for the return of the people of Israel from their Assyrian captivity. He did not pray for the reunion of the House of Israel and the House of Judah as foretold by other prophets.

Then what was included in Daniel's prayer of petition? He asked for only two things: the city of Jerusalem and the Sanctuary. Nothing more. He prayed for Jerusalem in verse 16, and for the Sanctuary in verse 17. There is no further request. The people of Israel and Judah had profaned the name of God. Daniel was bold enough to make these two requests because the city of Jerusalem was the place that God chose "to put his name there," as mentioned so often by Moses. Daniel prayed that God would uphold his own name by doing something about the city and the sanctuary that would bring honor to God's Holy Name. The answer to Daniel's prayer is not long in coming. It comes in the person of the angel Gabriel, whom Daniel "had seen in the vision at the beginning". What vision? There is no vision recorded in the 9th chapter of Daniel. Gabriel? Vision? Where is this combination found? In only one other place in Daniel: in the 8th chapter.

This vision in the 8th chapter of Daniel is a vision concerning the Sanctuary. It occurred in the third year of Belshazzar, the last king of Babylon, which would be followed immediately by the first year of Darius. The interval between the vision of the 8th chapter and Daniel's prayer in the 9th chapter was at most a matter of months. It could have been several weeks, but it is not impossible that it was a matter of only a few days.

In this vision of the Sanctuary, an evil person called a "little horn" is to rise up out of one of the remnants of the "goat" empire (the Greek) who is to desecrate the Temple. Some think this was fulfilled by Antiochus Epiphanes about 175 BC who sacrificed a pig on the altar in the temple at Jerusalem and killed many of the Jews. However, the language of Gabriel in the interpretation of the vision in verses 23-25 implies that the desolating personage will be manifest just prior to the coming of Christ in judgment. If taken literally, the 2300 days of verse 14 would last only about 6 years, and we know there was no cleansing of the Sanctuary in that period of history. If, however, we consider the time as 2300 years, a very accurate lunar-solar time cycle, we must consider that the vision pertained to something that would happen after a very long time.

The passage is difficult. Gabriel is commanded "make this man to understand the vision," but Gabriel's interpretation is not clear to Daniel. Gabriel did not complete his mission, for Daniel closes chapter 8 by stating that none understood it, which would include Daniel himself. Gabriel's mission is never completed unless it is completed in chapter 9. After Daniel became concerned with the status of the Sanctuary, Gabriel is sent again to give Daniel wisdom and understanding, and the implication is strong that Daniel did indeed understand. In Daniel 9:23, we read, "therefore understand the matter and consider the vision". We can expect, then, that Gabriel's message in chapter 9 will be both an answer to Daniel's prayer and a more complete revelation concerning the vision in chapter 8. One thing becomes certain. Both chapters concern the Sanctuary.

The content of God's answer to Daniel's prayer as conveyed by Gabriel is contained in 9:24-27. This is one of the most controversial passages in all of prophetic Scripture, since it has become one of the chief points of dispute between those of the futurist school of interpretation and the adherents to the historical interpretation which was followed by most of the Reformers. In working through this passage, the question should not be how does this fit into our preconceived notions, but rather what does it say and what does it establish?

The first statement to be examined concerns the time. "Seventy weeks are determined upon thy people and upon thy holy city." The wording is simply "seventy sevens". The word for seven, SHABUA, in ordinary weeks would be 490 literal days, approximately 1 year and 4 months. Nothing of significance to the Sanctuary happened in such a short interval of time in that era of history. All agree that the statement is symbolic and refers to a much longer period of time. Taking a year for a day, the time is 490 years. This would be seven times as long as the captivity period of seventy years endured by the Good Figs of Jeremiah 24 and 29. So a sevenfold period of time is announced for the restoration of the Sanctuary.

Following is a list of six purposes for the seventy weeks, six objectives to be accomplished in this time span. Each should now be examined in turn.

A. To Finish the Transgression

What transgression is unfinished? Did not the people go the limit in rebellion against God and in the pollution of the land? Did not Daniel just finish a great prayer of confession for all the transgressions of his people? But the one great and awful crime was not yet done—the bruising of the heel of the seed of the woman—the slaying of the Son of God, the anointed one, the Messiah. The greatest of all transgressions is to take place in this seventy week period, and not until this act is accomplished is the transgression of the people complete. The cup of iniquity must be completely filled.

"Is there anything more ghastly than the failure of the Hebrew people from the beginning to the end? They were always failing and they never failed more disastrously than when they wanted a king "like the nations." In that act, as God said to Samuel, they had rejected him from being king. It had gone on through the ages, and the last thing the Hebrew people did to prove their ultimate and appalling catastrophic folly and sin was to crucify the Son of God." This quotation is from Dr. G. Campbell Morgan,

Parables and Metaphors of Our Lord, page 316.

In Acts 2:33, Peter says, "Him, being delivered by the determinate counsel and foreknowledge of God, ye have taken, and by wicked hands have crucified and slain." Again, in Acts 3:14,15 Peter declares, "But ye denied the Holy One and the Just, and desired a murderer to be granted unto you; and killed the Prince of life, whom God has raised from the dead; whereof ye are witnesses." In Stephen's defense before the Sanhedrin, he gave a lengthy review of God's dealings with his people in the Old Testament, and ended his testimony in Acts 7:51, 52 by exclaiming, "Ye stiffnecked and uncircumcised in heart and ears, ye do always resist the Holy Ghost: as your fathers did, so do ye. Which of the prophets have not your fathers persecuted? And they have slain them which showed before of the coming of the Just One; of whom ye have been now the betrayers and murderers." In 1 Thessalonians 2:14, 15 Paul is plain-spoken and says, "--for ye also have suffered like things of your own countrymen, even as they have of the Jews: who both killed the Lord Jesus, and their own prophets, and have persecuted us; and they please not God, and are contrary to all men."

Thus we see that the "thy people" of Daniel included those who were responsible for the death of Christ. What else is there left to do in the way of transgression? This purpose was certainly fulfilled within the seventy weeks.

B. To Make an End of Sins

The verb, "to make an end of," is CHATHAM, which is used also to mean finish, complete, seal, seal up, perfect, accomplish. The principal use is seal or seal up. The same word is used in Job 14:17, "My transgression is sealed up in a bag." The meaning is not that men will no longer sin, but that sin will be taken care of. This does not say that all sin shall cease. This idea is borne out by the following Scriptures. Romans 10:4: "For Christ is the end of the law unto righteousness to everyone that believeth." II Corinthians 5:21: "Him who knew no sin he made to be sin on our behalf, that we might become the righteousness of God in him." Hebrews 9:26 "But now once at the end of the ages hath he been manifested to put away sin by the sacrifice of himself." 1 Peter 2:24: "Who his own self bare our sins in his body upon the tree, that we, having died unto sins might live unto righteousness." I Peter 3:18: "For Christ hath also once suffered for sins, the just for the unjust, that he might bring us to God, being put to death in the flesh, but quickened by the Spirit." This purpose was accomplished by Jesus the Messiah.

C. To Make Reconciliation for Iniquity

The word for "make reconciliation" is the Hebrew word used most often for "make atonement". The word "atonement" is used only once in the New Testament, in Romans 5:11, but the Greek word is the same one used for "reconciled" in the previous verse. Now read this and other verses.

Romans 5:10, 11: "For if, when we were enemies, we were reconciled to God by the death of his Son, much more, being reconciled, we shall be saved by his life. And not only so, but we also joy in God through our Lord Jesus Christ." In II Corinthians 5:18, 19: "And all things are of God, who hath reconciled us to himself by Jesus Christ, and hast given to us the ministry of reconciliation; to wit, that God was in Christ, reconciling the world unto himself, not imputing their trespasses unto them; and hath committed unto us the word of reconciliation." Hebrews 2:17: "Wherefore in all things it behooved him to be made like unto his brethren, that he might be a merciful and faithful high priest in things pertaining to God, to make reconciliation for the sins of the people."

Who else has made an effectual reconciliation for iniquity? Surely this is the distinctive work of Jesus the Messiah.

D. To Bring in Everlasting Righteousness

Another such promise is also in the Old Testament, for in Isaiah we find, "--but my righteousness shall be forever, and my salvation from generation to generation." Also in Isaiah 61:11 we read, "For as the earth bringeth forth her bud, and as the garden causeth the things that are sown in it to spring forth; so the Lord God will cause righteousness and praise to spring forth before all the nations." The following New Testament references indicate the fulfillment of this promise. Romans 3:21, 22: "But now the righteousness of God without the law is manifested, being witnessed by the law and the prophets; even the righteousness of God which is by faith of Jesus Christ unto all and upon all them that believe; for there is no difference." Romans 5:17, 19, 21: "For if by one man's offence death reigned by one; much more they which receive abundance of grace and of the gift of righteousness shall reign in life by one, Jesus Christ. For as by one man's disobedience many were made sinners, so by the obedience of one shall many be made righteous. That as sin hath reigned unto death, even so might grace reign through righteousness unto eternal life by Jesus Christ our Lord." Romans 10:3, 4: "For they being ignorant of God's righteousness, and going about to establish their own righteousness, have not submitted themselves to the righteousness of God. For Christ is the end of the law for righteousness to everyone who believeth." 1 Corinthians 1:30: "But of him are ye in Christ Jesus, who of God is made unto us wisdom, and righteousness, and sanctifiction, and redemption." Ephesians 4:24: "And that ye put on the new man, which after God is created in righteousness and true holiness." Philippians 3:9: "And be found in him, not having mine own righteousness, which is of the law, but that which is through the faith of Christ, the righteousness which is of God by faith." 2 Peter 2:24: "Who his own self bare our sins in his own body on the tree, that we, being dead to sins, should live unto righteousness."

Surely, Jesus the Christ, ushered in everlasting righteousness.

E. To Seal the Vision and Prophecy

This is somewhat obscure. Literally, it says, "And seal up the vision and prophet". What vision? What prophet? Or prophecy? Do we await the second coming of Christ for this "sealing up" or is that the time when all things shall be revealed? Surely this purpose is to be attained between the time of Daniel and the coming of Christ in glory at the end of the age.

Jesus was the Great Prophet of whom Moses and the prophets spoke. Jesus prophesied. Paul prophesied. So did Peter, James, and John. Since the apostles fell asleep, we do not consider any of the writings of Christian teachers as true prophecy in the sense of additional direct revelation of God to His people. Although much of the Revelation of Christ to John is in symbol, and contains things that are sealed, the intent is "revelation", for in Revelaion 22:10 we read "Seal not the sayings of the prophecy of this book; for the time is at hand."

Christ himself is sealed, for in John 6:27 we read "for Him hath God the Father sealed". So whether it be prophet or prophecy, Jesus the Messiah fulfilled this purpose also.

F. To Anoint the Most Holy

The expression is used in the Old Testament for holy things, holy places, and holy persons. Aaron and his sons were anointed to the office of the priesthood. The tabernacle was anointed by Moses in the wilderness. All the things in the tabernacle were anointed, which would have included the holy things in the Holy of Holies. David was anointed king. The same word for anointed which is used in Daniel 9:24 is also used in Isaiah 61:1. This is translated into the same Greek word in both the Septuagint translation of Isaiah 61:1 and in the quotation in Luke 4:18. When Jesus quoted Isaiah, he claimed that "This day is this scripture fulfilled in your ears". Jesus was anointed by water, by the Holy spirit, and by the voice of the Father when he was baptized by John.

The demon in the man in the synagogue at Capernaum exclaimed "I know thee who thou art; the holy one of God". Peter calls Christ the Holy One and Just in Acts 3:14. In Acts 4:27, Jesus is called "--thy holy child Jesus, whom thou hast anointed". In Peter's opening of the Gospel to the gentiles in Acts 10:38, he says, "How God anointed Jesus of Nazareth with the Holy Ghost and with power". In Hebrews 1:9 there is a quotation of Psalm 45:7, which says, "--therefore God, thy God, hath anointed thee with the oil of gladness above thy fellows". Certainly Jesus is the Most Holy Person ever to be anointed.

In Hebrews 9:11-14, we read, "But Christ being come a high priest of good things to come--by his own blood entered in once into the holy place, having obtained eternal redemption for us. For if the blood of bulls and goats, and the ashes of a heifer sprinkling the unclean, sanctifieth to the purifying of the flesh, how much more shall the blood of Christ, who through the eternal Spirit offered himself without spot to God, purge your conscience from dead works to serve the living God"? Further, in verses 24 and 28 we read, "For Christ is not entered into the holy places made with hands, which are the figures of the true; but into heaven itself, now to appear in the presence of God for us. --So Christ was once offered to bear the sins of many--".

It would be profitable to read the entire passage in Hebrews 9 and 10 at this point. Surely, by entering into the most Holy Place, into the very presence of God, through the veil of his own flesh and by the offering of his own blood, Jesus has made it possible for us with "Boldness to enter into the holiest by a new and living way".

In summary, it has been shown that each and every one of these purposes of the seventy weeks involves sin and the atonement for it. Each of these purposes was achieved by Christ at his first advent. Is there any one of them left unfinished or unfulfilled? They all have to do with the Sanctuary, in which Christ serves as our great high priest, and not with the Throne on which he will sit in judgment when he returns in power. These six objectives deal not with judgment, but with sacrifice.

Chapter 5
Who Is He?

We have examined the purposes of the Seventy Week period which God ordained for the people of Daniel and the Holy City Jerusalem. We are now ready to look at the fulfillment in history of those purposes.

In Daniel 9:25, we read, "know therefore and understand, that from the going forth of the commandment to restore and to build Jerusalem unto the Messiah the Prince shall be seven weeks, and threescore and two weeks: the streets shall be built again, and the wall, even in troublous times."

The intention is for Daniel to understand the message. Since Daniel wrote it down, can it also be said that it is intended to be understood by others as well? Is it not the purpose of the word of God to transmit understanding to God's people in other times than the particular time in which the message was first received? Verse 23 ends with "therefore understand the matter and consider the vision." What vision? There is no account of a vision in the ninth chapter of Daniel.

The ninth chapter of Daniel concerns the Sanctuary; so does the vision in the eighth chapter. Gabriel is the heavenly messenger in both chapters. Concerning the vision in the eighth chapter, Daniel said, "but none understood it". In the ninth chapter, Gabriel said, "Understand . . . and consider the vision," referring to the vision of the Sanctuary.

Continuing in the reading of the 25th verse, we see a division of time into 7 weeks and 62 weeks, a total of 69 weeks, extending "unto Messiah the Prince". This passage introduces the chronological problem of establishing some dates. There are two ways of approaching the problem. The first involves finding a beginning point and counting forward, and the other an ending date and counting backward. It will be gratifying if we can find two schemes which agree.

Before examining this problem, consider the possible relationship of the 70 weeks to the 2300 days of the sanctuary vision in chapter eight. If the 2300 days are literal days, either already fulfilled, or yet to come, how can the 70 weeks (490 years) be considered as measured off or cut off out of the 2300 days? Does not the "cutting off" imply that 490 years is a shorter span of time than the 2300 days? Since it is a concensus that the 70 weeks is symbolic of 490 years, does this not demand that the 2300 days must be a larger period such as 2300 actual years? Is not this relationship strongly implied by the common elements "sanctuary" and "Gabriel" in both chapters?

There is apparently little disagreement that the rebuilding program occupied 49 years or the first 7 weeks of the 70 weeks period. The only disagreement would be concerning the particular 49 years of history which correspond. We need to find a satisfactory over-all chronology.

When did the 70 weeks begin? Which commandment is the reference point? The commandment of Cyrus, or that of Artaxerxes, or some other? Nebuchadnezzar took Jehoiakim, king of Judah, captive in 604 B.C. In 598 B.C. Nebuchadnezzar took Jehoiachin, or Coniah, king of Judah, captive into Babylon. A number of people from Jerusalem who were leaders and of the nobility, probably including Daniel and his three friends were also taken to Babylon at this time. This group of people were symbolized by the "good figs" of Jeremiah 24:5 and 29:2. In 586 B.C., Nebuchadnezzar captured Zedekiah, the last king of Judah, and the remaining people in Jerusalem and destroyed the city. These were the "bad figs" of Jeremiah 24:8 and 29:16-19. Note again that the "good figs" are to return after 70 years of captivity, but the "bad figs" are to enter their long-term punishment at that time.

If the 490 year period began immediately following the first 70 year period after 598 B.C., then 490 years did not reach the Christian era. There must be some other way to consider it. Any of the captivity dates result in dates too early for the 70 weeks period. It should be noted that the Protestant commentators of the eighteenth and nineteenth centuries are almost unanimous in their agreement on 457 B.C. as the date of the commandment of Artaxerxes to build Jerusalem. This commandment is the only one quoted verbatum in the Bible, recorded in Ezra 7:11-26.

In all, there were four commandments. They are:

(1) The decree of Cyrus for the rebuilding of the House of God 536 B.C. Ezra 1:1-4.

(2) The decree of Darius for the resumption of the same work in 519 B.C. Ezra 6:1-12.

(3) The decree of Artaxerxes to Ezra (recorded in Chaldee) in 457 B.C. Ezra 7.

(4) The commission to Nehemiah from the same king in the 29th year about 444 B.C. (Nehemiah 2). The first two are too early for 490 years to reach Christian era.

Which Commandment? Consider the following points:

(1) Nehemiah's commission was verbal only. There was no written document.

(2) Work was already well under way. Nehamiah's commission was to augment or carry to completion this work. Nehemiah's work of building the city was done in 52 days.

(3) No new phase of work was committed to Nehemiah. The decree to Ezra included all previous commandments and more.

(4) Ezra believed his responsibility was to consumate the purpose of God. Ezra's prayer is of great significance. Read Ezra 9:5-17.

(5) Counting from the time of Nehemiah, 445 B.C. or 444 B.C., 490 years takes us to 40-50 A.D., too late for Messiah and unmarked by any significant historical event.

(6) Prideaux (Connexion, Vol. I., p. 332) says: In the 15th year of Darius Nothus, ended the first seven weeks of Daniel's prophecy. For then the restoration of the church and state of the Jews in Jerusalem and Judah was fully finished, in the last act of reformation which recorded in Neh. 13:23-31, just 49 years after it had been commenced by Ezra in the 7th year of Artaxerxes Longimanus. This was 408 B.C.

(7) Ezra himself considered the series of decrees as "the commandment". Ezra 6:14 "and they builded it, and finished it, according to the commandment of Cyrus, Darius, and Artaxerxes, kings of Persia." The 3 decrees were steps or stages of the "commandment", which was made complete in the recorded decree of Artaxerxes.

"And after threescore and two weeks shall Messiah be cut off, but not for himself" (Daniel 9:26). Notice that it says "after" and not "at the end of" the 69 weeks. To think that the cutting off of Messiah happened immediately as the 69 weeks are finished is not consistent with the general sense of the rest of the verse. The verse seems to look beyond the scope of the 70 weeks just enough to show the relation to the longer period of Israel's punishment already begun in Assyria and Babylon.

The word for "cut off" is KARATH: it means to be cut down or cut off. Its most frequent means to "make covenant", which is accompanied with the cutting of sacrificial animals. How appropriate, since the "cutting off" of Messiah established a new covenant with his people. He was cut off, not for himself, but for the sins of his people.

"The people of the prince that shall come" are obviously the Romans, who destroyed Jerusalem in 70 A.D. It was an event, like the cutting off of Messiah, which came sometime "after" the 69 weeks. The destruction of the "city and the sanctuary" is pronounced. Why apply this to some far distant invasion of the sanctuary when the primary and obvious fullfillment is so evident? When did the 69 weeks end? "Unto the anointed one the Prince." When did Jesus become the Messiah? If you say at Christ's birth, then the 70th week ended when He was 7 years old. What about Luke 2:11? What about Gabriel? If you say at his Baptism or beginning of his ministry, then you must admit that at least the first 3½ years of the 70th week elapsed before his death. If you say at his death, where is the scripture? And how do any such scriptures compare with the following:

(1) John 1:41 - Andrew said, "We have found the Messiah".

(2) Matt. 16:13-20 - The disciples knew him as Messiah.
(3) Luke 4:41 - Demons knew him as Messiah.
(4) John 4:25,26 - Jesus claimed to be Messiah.
(5) Mark 14:61,62 - He admitted to the high priest that he was Messiah. .

All these events happened before his death.

If you say that there is a gap or parenthesis in Prophetic time because the Jews are now under Gentile rule, then how can the 70th week ever take place under the rule of a persecuting anti-christ? The Israelis became an independent nation on May 16, 1948. Did the 70th week begin then? It should have ended in 1955! What are we waiting for? Or did it begin with the 6 day war in 1967? More than 7 years have gone by since then.

The second approach may be more simple and more satisfying. Just when did Jesus become the Messiah? When was the Messiah manifested? When did he assume the office and function of Messiah? When was the "annointed one" introduced on the stage? When he was anointed! Acts 4:27 - "Whom thou didst anoint" When? Acts 10:38 - "God anointed him with the Holy Spirit and with power." Luke 4:18 - "The Spirit of the Lord is upon me; He hath anointed me to preach..." Already done at Jesus' appearing in the synagogue. Jesus said, "This day is this scripture fulfilled." Luke 3:21,22, "Jesus also being baptized, and praying, the heaven was opened, and the Holy Spirit descended in a bodily form as a dove upon him, and a voice came out of heaven, "Thou art my beloved son; in thee I am well pleased." Jesus was thrice anointed at his baptism:

(1) By John with water;
(2) By the Holy Spirit;
(3) By the Father with words "This is my son" - a prince.

Is there any other event in the life of Jesus which could possibly be the anointing? If so, what scripture would support another annointing? Conclusion: Jesus was introduced as the anointed one - the Prince - at his baptism and opening of his ministry.

Now let us examine very carefully Daniel 9:27.

(1) And he shall confirm the covenant with many for one week;

(2) And in the midst of the week he shall cause the sacrifice and the oblation to cease;

(3) And for the overspreading of abominations he shall make it desolate, even until the consummation;

(4) And that determined shall be poured upon the desolate.

Who is "He"? Here is one of the greatest stumbling blocks in all prophetic scripture. The position we take with respect to this personage determines in the main the entire structure of a system of interpretation including many other prophetic scriptures. Futurists and historicists alike attach much significance to the proper identity of this "he" but arrive at quite different answers. Seldom does so much depend upon the proper exegesis of a single word. However, "he"is not there!

The word does not even appear in the original language of the text!

"He shall confirm" is one word. It is the 3rd person singular of the future tense of the verb "to confirm". It is usual in many languages for the personal pronoun to be included within the verb form.

Therefore it becomes necessary to search for the antecedent subject of the verb, "he shall confirm".

Read the passage again (verses 24-26). Verse 24 refers to the works of Messiah. Messiah is the primary person discussed in verse 25. Messiah is the primary subject of verse 26. Analyze verse 27 by any set of grammatical rules you wish and in any language you wish, English, Greek, or Hebrew. Parse it, diagram it. Who is He?

Messiah is He! He is Messiah!

Is there any way of making "the people of the prince that shall come" the subject of "he shall confirm"? How can the prince be the subject of anything but the verb "shall come" in a subordinate clause? "To confirm" means to make firm or strengthen something already in existence. The Hebrew word is translated "strengthen" elsewhere. It nowhere connotes the creation or bringing into existence of something new. Why no "karath", to cut a covenant? "The covenant" is which covenant?

Many current prophetic teachers claim that the "he" is a reference to some far distant antichrist that will appear on earth in the future. This interpretation calls for a gap or parenthesis of more than nineteen hundred years between the 69th week and the 70th week. Was there a gap between the 7 weeks and the 62 weeks? A long interval simply cannot be induced from the language here. The idea must be part of the presuppositional base applied to the passage. In other words, it must first be assumed and then the passage interpreted to fit the assumption. If the Romans are the people who destroyed Jerusalem in 70 A.D. how can they be the people of a prince who has not yet appeared after 1900 years?

How can Messiah be the subject of verse 27? Which covenant is to be confirmed? The Mosaic covenant is a highly conditional one; it cannot be confirmed, it can only be fulfilled by obedience. The Abrahamic covenant is unconditional. All of its provisions are by promise. It can be confirmed by restating the promise or executing these promises.

The announcement of Gabriel to Mary was considered as carrying out the promises to Abraham, for in Luke 1:54,55 Mary explains, "He hath helped his servant Israel, in remembrance of his mercy; as he spoke to our fathers, to Abraham and his seed forever".

When John the Baptist was born, the tongue of his father Zechariah was loosed and he prophesied concerning what the Lord God of Israel was doing. Among the words, we find, "to perform the mercy promised to our fathers, and to remember his holy covenants; the oath which he swore to our father Abraham." (Luke 1:72,72). Paul declares, in Romans 15:8, "Now I say that Jesus Christ was a minister of the circumcision for the truth of God, to confirm the promises made unto the fathers." In Galatians 3:16-19, we read, "Now to Abraham and his seed were the promises made. He said not, And to seeds, as of many; but as of one, And to thy seed, which is Christ. And this I say that the covenant, that was confirmed before of God in Christ, the Law, which was four hundred and thirty years after, cannot disannul, that it should make the promise of none effect. For if the inheritance be of the law, it is no more of promise: But God gave it to Abraham by promise. Wherefore then serveth the law? It was added because of transgressions, till the seed should come to whom the promise was made; and it was ordained by angels in the hand of a mediator."

The 70th week, therefore, began with the baptism of Jesus when the anointed one was anointed and ended on schedule 7 years later when the Sanhedrin officially rejected the Gospel, stoned Stephen, and drove the church from Jerusalem. During this week, the covenant which God made to Abraham, Isaac, and Jacob was confirmed by the ministry, works and death of Jesus Christ and by the Gospel preached by His disciples. Every major speech by the apostles to the leaders of the Jews proves this point. (Acts 2:14-40; Acts 3:12-16; Acts 4:8-12; Acts 5:29-32; Acts 7:1-60. Note that Paul did not offer the gospel in Acts 23, but did to the people in Acts 22).

The new covenant is not of such a nature that the bodily presence of Messiah is necessary before it can be confirmed. In Mark 16:20, we read, "And they went forth, and preached everywhere, the Lord working with them, and confirming the word with signs following." The "cutting off" of Messiah is an essential part of the "confirming", and the preaching of the efficacy of the "cutting off" was the message of confirmation to the people. In this connection, read also Hebrews 6:13-20; 9:11,12; 9:15-17.

Admittedly Daniel 9:27 is a difficult passage. However, let it be emphasized that it is not made any easier by trying to force it to say something it does not mean. There have been many variations in the translation of this verse in recent times, but none of these should alter what has been said about the identity of "he" as Messiah, particularly in view of the purposes of the 70 weeks as set forth in Daniel 9:24, all of which refer to the sanctuary and the work of the Messiah as the high priest of the sanctuary.

Continuing in Daniel 9:27, we read, "And for the overspreading of abominations, he shall make it desolate, even unto the consumation." The people of Israel were guilty of all manner of abominations. In Jeremiah 7:9-11, we read, "will ye steal, murder and commit adultery, and swear falsly, and burn incense unto Baal, and walk after other gods whom ye know not; and come and stand before me in this house, which is called by my name, and say, We are delivered to do all these abominations? Is this house, which is called by my name, become a den of robbers in your eyes? Behold, even I have seen it, saith the Lord." The word for "robbers" in the Septuagint, the Greek version of the Old Testament, is exactly the same one as used by Jesus when he says, in Matthew 21:13, "My house shall be called the house of prayer; but ye have made it a den of thieves". In Ezekiel 16:2, we read, "Son of man, cause Jerusalem to know her abominations." There follows a picture of Jerusalem showing the vile and base immorality into which the people of Jerusalem had sunk. No wonder Jesus should lament and exclaim "O Jerusalem, Jerusalem . . . Behold your house is left unto you desolate". Yes, Jesus pronounced desolation upon Jerusalem for the overspreading of the abominations of the people.

"And that determined shall be poured upon the desolate." Just what is determined? Jesus said, "There shall not be left here one stone upon another, that shall not be thrown down." He announced the utter destruction of Jerusalem which was accomplished in 70 A.D. by the Romans.

The long term punishment of the people of Israel is foretold in Leviticus 26. Most of the people had been banished from the land of promise many years before New Testament times. The few who returned from the exile in Babylon, the good figs, were given a temporary respite for the purpose of bringing forth Messiah, the seed of David from the tribe of Judah. This purpose being accomplished, there was no reason these people should not join their brethren already in their punishment among the nations. Therefore, the punishment determined by a righteous God was now in order, and Jesus pronounced it so by saying "Ye shall not see me henceforth, till ye shall say, Blessed is he that cometh in the name of the Lord."

In Daniel 9:27, we find "he shall confirm", "he shall cause the sacrifice to cease", and, "he shall make it desolate". Each one of these actions was accomplished or declared by Jesus the Messiah. The entire passage in Daniel 9 concerns the person and works of Jesus the Messiah. Surely "HE" is Messiah.

Chapter 6

Why Christ Died

Why did Christ die? There is a little verse in Mark that does not receive the attention it deserves. Immediately following the account of the triumphal entry of Jesus into Jerusalem, we read, in Mark 11:11, "And Jesus entered into Jerusalem, and into the temple: and when he had looked round about on all things, and now the eventide was come, he went out unto Bethany with the twelve." This sounds rather innocuous, doesn't it? But examine this closely. Jesus had taken his last journey from Galilee, declaring to his disciples that he was going down to Jerusalem to be killed. When he arrived in Jerusalem, he went into the temple, the sanctuary, and "looked round about on all things". He could see much of the city from the hill on which the temple stood. At the end of the day, he went out to Bethany, perhaps to the home of Mary and Martha and Lazarus.

The time had come for the greatest event of human history, the central event of human existence, the consummation of God's purpose with respect to the reclamation of sinful humanity. This was a real drama, not an acted drama. These were real participants, not just actors. Jesus himself was the author, the producer, the director, and the principal figure in this great drama. He was both the villain and the hero. He was the victim and the victor. He already knew the entire scenario. The whole drama concerned his own person and his work.

Now, at last, everybody was in town. Each would play his part. Each would say what he had to say; each would do what he had to do. Jesus himself would provide every cue. The high priest was provoked to take the action he did by what Jesus said. Pilate was like putty in the hands of Jesus; he had no escape.

Just why did Jesus die? There are several reasons. First of all, who killed Jesus? Oh, a squad of Roman soldiers executed him. Were they responsible for his death? No. They were merely carrying out the orders of Pilate. Concerning the Romans, Jesus said, "Father, forgive them; for they know not what they do." However, we can say that the Romans killed him. In a sense, the world killed him; the world of sinful flesh, the world system. The Jews killed him. It was a crowd of Jews in Jerusalem who cried out "Crucify him." It was the high priest of Judaism who pronounced the death sentence upon him for the crime of blasphemy. Because of our sins, you and I killed him. Finally, he killed himself. Every Gospel writer says that he cried with a loud voice and gave up the ghost. He willingly and willfully died for the sins of the world. Who killed Jesus? The question has many answers.

But why?

There are various reasons.

In Isaiah 51:4, we read, "Hearken unto me, my people, and give ear unto me, O my nation: for a law shall proceed from me, and I will make my judgment to rest for a light of the people. My righteousness is near; my salvation is gone forth, and mine arms shall judge the people; the isles shall wait upon me, and on mine arm shall they trust." Continuing in verse 9, we read, "Awake, awake, put on strength, O arm of the Lord; awake, as in the days of old." In Isaiah 52:10 we read,"The Lord hath made bare his holy arm in the eyes of all the nations; and all the ends of the earth shall see the salvation of our God."

"Who hath believed our report? And to whom is the arm of the Lord revealed?" What is this mighty arm of the Lord? The mighty arm of the Lord is Jesus on the cross. The suffering servant, who was led as a lamb to the slaughter. He who bore our iniquities, who was chastised for our sins. The entire 53rd chapter of Isaiah reveals that the mighty arm of the Lord is the mighty work of God in taking care of man's sin problem. The death of Jesus on the cross is the mighty arm of the Lord. There is a verse, Psalm 89:13, which says, "Thou hast a mighty arm: strong is thy hand, and high is thy right hand."

Included in the revelation of the angel of the Lord to Joseph in Matthew 1:18-23, we read, "And thou shalt call his name Jesus:

for he shall save his people from their sins." Jesus, Yeshua, Yehoshua, God is Salvation. In Luke 1, the angel repeats to Mary, "--and thou shall call his name Jesus." Simon, in Luke 2, says, "--for mine eyes have seen thy salvation." My eyes have seen your Jesus.

It is generally believed that the beginning of the Gospel in the Bible is in Genesis 3:15, where we read that God spoke to Satan and said, "I will put enmity between thee and the woman, between thy seed and her seed; it shall bruise thy head, and thou shalt bruise his heel." There is another early mention of the Gospel. In the 5th chapter of Genesis there is a genealogical list of names that makes boring reading. Few people ever read it twice. However, the list will bear close scrutiny. The meaning of the name SETH is given as APPOINTED in Genesis 4:25. What do these other names mean? We can find out by looking them up in Bible Dictionaries, Concordances, and other Bible helps. The following list was compiled as a result of such a search.

NAME	MEANING
Seth	Appointed
Enos	Mortal
Cainan	Sorrow
Mahalaleel	Blessed God
Jared	Come down
Enoch	Teacher or teaching
Methuselah	When he dies, it shall come, or his death will bring it
Lamech	Despairing
Noah	Comfort

Now put them all together. MORTALS ARE APPOINTED TO SORROW, BUT THE BLESSED GOD CAME DOWN TEACHING THAT HIS DEATH WILL BRING COMFORT TO THE DESPAIRING. The Everlasting Gospel is in these names! In these names, God promises to DIE in order to reclaim the human race. And he did.

Why did Christ die? To keep faith with Abraham.

Do you know the story of that awesome oath-taking ceremony when Abraham divided the sacrificial animal pieces into two rows? The story is in the fifteenth chapter of Genesis. God had just told Abraham that there would be an heir of his own through whom the promises of the many seed and the inheritance of the land would come. Then Abraham questioned God asking, "Whereby shall I know that I shall inherit it?" (vs. 8). Then God gave Abraham the instructions for the sacrificial ceremony. Such a ceremony is mentioned in Jeremiah 34.18. It was the most solemn of all oaths, because it symbolized death. The contracting parties pledged their very lives as surety for whatever agreement they entered into.

The sacrifical animals were divided and the parts arranged into two parallel rows. The parties to the agreement then walked up and down between the two rows of pieces signifying they would pass through death if necessary to fulfill the promises made. This was the ceremony for which Abraham prepared.

Then a strange thing happened. Abraham passed into a trance, or sleep, in great darkness. The Lord appeared to him and told him of the things to happen to his descendents after Abraham's life would end. In Genesis 15:17 we are told, "And it came to pass, that when the sun went down, and it was dark, behold a smoking furnace and a burning lamp that passed between those pieces." The Lord God Himself alone passed between those pieces. Abraham was not asked to walk through that ceremony at all. Only God made the oath. It was a completely unilateral promise. God was thus saying, Abraham, I will keep my promise even if I have to die. And he did. On the cross!

In Hebrews 6:13, we read, "For when God made promise to Abraham, because he could swear by no greater, he sware by himself." See also Acts 7:4-7.

When Jesus was in agony in the Garden of Gethsemane, he prayed, "O my father, if it be possible, let this cup pass from me; neverthless, not as I will, but as thou wilt". And again, "O my father, if this cup may not pass away from me, except I drink it, thy will be done."

What cup is Jesus talking about? Death? No, he left Galilee knowing that he was going to Jerusalem to die. Men die willingly. Men die happily. Men die victoriously. The martyrs who were put to death during the Inquisition in the sixteenth century glorified God as they died. They died praying. They died preaching. They died singing. They died quoting Scripture. They died triumphantly. Men are not afraid to die.

Then what was Jesus praying about in his agony in the garden? In Psalm 75:8, we read, "But in the hand of the Lord there is a cup, and the wine is red; it is full of mixture; and he poured out of the same: but the dregs thereof, all the wicked of the earth shall wring them out, and drink them."

Yes, in the hands of the Lord there is a cup. It is the wine cup of God's fury. In Jeremiah 25:15, we read, "Take the wine cup of this fury at my hand, and cause all the nations —to drink." In Isaiah 51:17 we read, "Awake, awake, stand up, O Jerusalem, which hast drunk at the hand of the Lord the cup of his fury; thou hast drunken the dregs of the cup of trembling, and wrung them out." In verse 22, "Behold, I have taken out of thine hand the cup of trembling, even the dregs of the cup of my fury; thou shalt no more drink of it again."

In Ezekiel 23:30-35, in reading of the two women, the two wives of the Lord, Aholah and Aholibah, Judah and Israel, we find the cup of astonishment and desolation. This is the cup of God's judgment for sin. This cup "containeth much". This cup contains the fury, the wrath, the indignation, and the judgment of God because of the sins of the people he has created. The cup of judgment is there because of God's holiness and righteousness. We all deserve that cup. Yet in his mercy, Jesus drank that cup for us. He drank it to the bitter dregs; my sins were in that cup, and your sins were in that cup. That is the cup Jesus prayed about: the awesome judgment of God for the sins of the world. "The soul that sinneth, it shall die," but, "The Lord has laid on him the iniquity of us all." Jesus bore our sins on the cross.

God married the people of Israel at Mt. Sinai. The account is given in Exodus in chapers 19-24. The ceremony is complete, beginning with God's proposal in 19:4-6, and ending with the pronouncement of the union by Moses, the officiating minister, in Exodus 24:8. There is an acceptance by the bride, the preparation of the bride, a special place for the ceremony, music, an altar, vows spoken by the husband, (commandments, statutes, and judgments). The bride responded with her vows, and the ceremony ended with a great wedding feast. This ceremony is known to us today as the Old Covenant, or the Old Testament.

God loved Israel with an everlasting love. In Jeremiah 31:3, we read, "Yea, I have loved thee with an everlasting love, therefore with loving-kindness have I drawn thee." Israel is called "Jeshurun" in the poetic language of Deuteronomy 32:15, 33:5, 26, and in Isaiah 44:2. The term means "my darling upright one". The Lord God became the husband to Israel at Mt. Sinai.

In course of time, Israel became an unfaithful wife. Israel consorted with other gods, other husbands, and became guilty of spiritual adultery. Israel fell into idol worship, Baal worship, and the worship of the queen of heaven. The general and widespread apostacy of the people became so great that God gave Israel a divorce. This applies specifically to the northern Kingdom of Israel in contradistinction to the southern Kingdom of Judah. In Jeremiah chapter 3, the prophet is addressing the people of Judah concerning their brethren to the north, who had been destroyed as a kingdom by the Assyrians more than 100 years before Jeremiah was speaking. In Jeremiah 3:8, we read, "And I saw, when for all the causes whereby backsliding Israel committed adultery I had put her away and given her a bill of divorce, yet her treacherous sister Judah feared not, but went and played the harlot also." A careful study of this chapter will show that Israel of the ten tribes was given a divorce. Although Judah became treacherous in her relationship to God, nowhere in scripture is it said that Judah was ever given a divorce. Do not the Jews, even today, claim to be bound by the Law?

There is a promise of better days to come. Beginning in Jeremiah 31:31, we read, "Behold, the days come, saith the Lord, that I will make a new covenant with the House of Israel and the House of Judah: not according to the covenant that I made with their fathers in the day that I took them by the hand to bring them out of the land of Egypt; which my covenant they brake, although I was a husband unto them, saith the Lord: but this shall be the covenant that I will make with the House of Israel; After those days, saith the Lord, I will put my law in their inward parts, and write it in their hearts; and will be their God, and they shall be my people."

Several questions arise. What is the significance of the term "House of Israel" used inclusively here? How is this restoration of an adulterous wife to be accomplished? How can a holy God enter into a new relationship with an unfaithful and adulterous wife? Perhaps the answer can be found in the Law itself as Paul explains in the first few verses of Romans 7. "The law hath dominion over a man as long as he liveth. For the woman that hath a husband is bound by the law to her husband as long as he liveth; but if the husband be dead, she is loosed from the law of her husband. So then, if, while her husband liveth, she be married to another man, she shall be called an adulteress: but if her husband be dead, she is free from that law; so that she is no adulteress, though she be married to another man."

According to this, the restoration of the unfaithful wife awaited the death of her husband. Therefore the husband of Israel died in order to set his adulterous wife free. Moreover, the efficacy of his death provided for the cleansing of his people, so that Hosea could exclaim, "And I will betroth thee unto me in righteousness, and in judgment, and in loving-kindness, and in mercies. I will even betroth thee unto me in faithfulness, and thou shalt know the Lord." Hosea 2:19, 20.

Now who is betrothed? A bride. In Isaiah 61:10, we read,
"I will greatly rejoice in the Lord, my soul shall be joyful in my God; for he hath clothed me with the garments of salvation, and he hath covered me with the robe of righteousness, as a bridegroom decketh himself with ornaments, and as a bride adorneth herself with her jewels." And in Isaiah 62:5, "For as a young man

marrieth a virgin, so shall thy sons marry thee: and as the bridegroom rejoiceth over the bride, so shall thy God rejoice over thee." The unfaithful wife becomes a righteous bride. A virgin? Israel is repeatedly called a virgin in the Old Testament. In Jeremiah 18:13, we read, "The virgin of Israel hath done a very horrible thing." And in Jeremiah 31:4, "Again I will build thee, and thou shalt again be adorned with thy tabrets, and shalt go forth in the dances of them that make merry." In Jeremiah 31:18-22, we read, concerning Ephraim, a prophetic name for the northern Kingdom of Israel, in verse 21, "—turn again, O virgin of Israel, turn again to these thy cities." (Judah is spoken of separately in succeeding verses).

Yes, the Husband-Redeemer of Israel died, and in this death, the unfaithful wife of the husband was transformed into a virtuous bride. What love! What a sacrifice!

Were God's promises to Abraham restricted to the descendants of Abraham alone? It says "all families of the earth" does it not, in Genesis 12? Is not this the same as "all nations" in Genesis 18:18? This is the very word translated "gentiles" throughout the Old Testament. God's choice of Abraham was the beginning of a program for the redemption of people of all nations (gentiles) throughout history. In Isaiah 49:6, we read, "It is a light thing that thou shouldest be my servant to raise up the tribes of Jacob, and to restore the preserved of Israel: I will also give thee for a light to the Gentiles, that thou mayest be my salvation unto the end of the earth." Thus the death of Christ was not only for the sake of Israel, but also for the Gentiles. In Romans 11:30-32, we read, "For as ye (Gentiles) in times past have not believed God, yet have now obtained mercy through their (Israel's) unbelief: even so have these also (Israel) now not believed, that through your (Gentile's) mercy, they (Israel) also may obtain mercy. For God hath concluded them all in unbelief, that he might have mercy upon all." Therefore, believing Gentiles are included in God's purpose in choosing Israel. So in Galatians 3:29, we read, "And if ye be Christ's, then are ye Abraham's seed, and heirs according to the promise." The death of Christ was to be efficacious for the Gentiles as well as for Israel.

When Jesus was before the Sanhedrin early that fateful morning in Jerusalem, the High Priest asked him, "Art thou the Christ, the Son of the Blessed"? And Jesus answered, "I AM I", using the very name of God as was used in Exodus 3:14, when Moses encountered God at the burning bush. The High Priest then said, "-What need we any further witnesses? Ye have heard the blasphemy: what think ye? And they all condemned him to be guilty of death." So Jesus was condemned to die for the crime of blasphemy, for claiming to be God. The Law is plain. Leviticus 24:16 reads, "And he that blasphemeth the name of the Lord, he shall surely be put to death." Jesus was either guilty as charged, or he spoke the truth. The Sanhedrin believed one way; we believe the other.

Who died on the Cross? The Blessed God, the God of Splendor of Genesis 5:12-17, who came down teaching that his death would bring comfort to the despairing. Who died on the Cross? The smoking furnace and the burning lamp who walked between the pieces of death pledging his life as a surety for the promises to Abraham. Who died on the Cross? The Husband-Redeemer of Israel, who loved his adulterous wife so much, that he desired to transform her into a chaste virgin whom he could marry again. Who died on the cross? The Born Child whose name is Wonderful Counselor. The Son Given, whose name is the Everlasting Father. Who died on the Cross? The Mighty God who bared his strong arm in the eyes of all nations, and all the ends of the earth have seen his Salvation. Who died on the Cross? The Coming Prince of Peace.

HALLELUJAH!!

Chapter 7
Unfinished Business

The time has come for us to consider some unfinished business. We have discussed several reasons for Christ's death on the cross. One proposition we considered was the death of the Husband-Redeemer to set free his adulterous wife, Israel, making of her a virtuous woman fitted for remarriage.

Are the promises to Israel in the Old Testament no longer valid? Were they all fulfilled by the close of the Old Testament record? Are they fulfilled in only a spiritual fashion since the days of Christ? Let us look in the scriptures to find some answers.

After the resurrection of Christ, and just before his ascension, the disciples were together talking with Jesus and asked him, "Lord, wilt thou at this time restore again the kingdom to Israel"? Acts 1:6. The disciples were puzzled. What do all these recent events mean? We recognize that you have died and now appear alive again. This is very important in the scheme of things. Does all this mean that all the things the prophets have declared concerning the restoration of Israel shall be accomplished at this time? The kingdom had been taken away from Israel for several hundred years. No king of the line of David had ruled in Jerusalem since Zedekiah, the last king of Judah, at the time of the Babylonian captivity. Such could have been their musing. Jesus did not reprimand them for asking the question. He did not say "No, that will never happen again." He said, it is not for you to know when. You have work to do first. Listen, "But you shall receive power after that the Holy Ghost is come upon you, and ye shall be witnesses unto me both in Jerusalem, and unto the uttermost part of the earth." Why did he not include Galilee? He was speaking to Galileans! He did not say that the kingdom will never be restored. There is something to be done first.

That brings up a problem in the general scheme we have been following. Let us consider now some statements that can be made by way of review, and it is along the line of this review that you should think of a question. This study was undertaken with the idea that not many readers would know the last chapter of the story. It is presumed that many of you as yet do not know it. Consider this review as the middle of a book, if you will. What propositions have posed certain problems or questions in your mind that we should resolve or answer before we get too far?

It may be wise, before we get into some New Testament studies, to consider a summary of all the propositions and ideas that we have been studying in the Old Testament. This summary is not complete, because it lacks the New Testament extensions of these ideas and the New Testament expositions. Let us see where we are before going ahead.

If there is any one scripture to be considered as the basis for this summary, it would be the first few verses in the twelfth chapter of Genesis, setting forth God's call to Abraham. This call to Abraham set him apart from all other men on the face of the earth.

Our first proposition is that God chose Abraham to be a recipient of God's blessing and to be a channel of God's blessing to others. This covenant of blessing was unconditional. There are several things we should consider. First of all, this was not some spiritualized, ephemeral, incorporeal proposition, but it involved a flesh and blood man, Abraham, who was to have flesh and blood children. This covenant is very much a part of this world. God set apart a man in this world to be a recipient of blessings and a channel of blessings. That means it is going to be very real, historically speaking, and that it is not some insubstantial, unhistorical proposition. It has to do with all subsequent history. The impact of this choice on the part of God is still being felt in the world. It is the secret of all earth history . . . all the history of mankind from that day until now and on into the future. God said, "I will do it." The promises were unilateral and unconditional.

Some may consider this as just folklore. Some may say that this is just what the people that came out of Old Testament times have said subjectively about themselves. Every tribe of men on the face of the earth has had some sort of belief that they are different from all other tribes, or nations, or peoples. Therefore, this is just the peculiar belief of a particular group of people. They think that they have been divinely appointed to do and be certain things.

Such an evaluation depends upon the beliefs concerning God's revelation to man in history. The best that we can say here is that the Bible says these things about Abraham. That brings into sharp focus our beliefs concerning the Bible. We have been exploring the meaning of the statement "God chose Abraham". What do we believe concerning the Bible? Is it folklore? Or is it really God's revelation to man?

We have two propositions before us that can be used as a test. One would be the coming of the person of Jesus Christ; the cross, the resurrection, the ascension, the whole set of events that are spoken of ahead of time by the prophets of the Old Testament. In Peter we have the challenge of the mockers who say, "Where is the promise of his coming, for since the fathers fell asleep, all things continue as they were from the beginning of the creation." Peter is saying that the time will come when all the Word of God will be discounted, and all relegated to ancient history and folklore and myth. The other would be that there comes another time in history when a testing will be made of the veracity of God's Word. That testing has to do with the gathering together of the people of God unto Christ when He comes the second time. We know that the New Testament teaches that there shall be a falling away — apostasy — a general feeling of disbelief in the things of which the Bible speaks.

The second proposition to consider is that the various blessings promised to Abraham were transmitted unconditionally to Isaac, Jacob, and severally to the sons of Jacob. This last means that some promises went to one son, and others went to another. There were many promises, and there were twelve, and eventually thirteen, sons of Jacob, counting the adoption of Ephraim and Manasseh in place of Joseph. That transfer of covenant blessings is a matter of Bible record as related in Genesis 48 and 49. As was said earlier, that happened several hundred years before the old covenant at Mt. Sinai and about 1000 years before there was a Jew. In Galatians 3:17, we read, "And this I say, that the covenant, that was confirmed before of God in Christ, the Law, which was four hundred and thirty years after, cannot disannul, that it should make the promise of none effect."

Particularly, the blessing pertaining to kingship and the one seed were transmitted to Judah. "The sceptre shall not depart from Judah." The blessing pertaining to material well being and the multiplicity of seed were transmitted to Joseph, under the heading of the birthright. We see Jacob blessing Joseph as part of his last will and testament, spoken orally before he died. These blessings of Joseph, or course, passed to Ephraim and Manasseh, the sons of Joseph.

Third, God chose the descendants of Jacob and constituted them into a nation at Mt. Sinai, to receive God's blessing, to be a blessing to other nations, and to obey God's commandments. In Deuteronomy 7:12,13, "And it shall come to pass because ye hearken unto these ordinances and keep and do them, that the Lord thy God will keep with thee the covenant of loving kindness which he sware unto thy fathers, and he will love thee, and bless thee, and multiply thee. He will also bless the fruit of thy body, the fruit of thy ground, thy grain and wine and oil and increase of thy cattle and the young of thy flock in the land which he sware unto thy fathers to give thee. Thou shalt be blest above all people." In Zechariah 8:13, "It shall come to pass that whereas ye were a curse among the nations, Oh house of Judah and house of Israel, so will I save you and ye shall be a blessing. Fear not , but let your hands be strong." In Exodus 19:5, "Now therefore if ye will obey my voice indeed and keep my covenant then ye shall be my own possession from among all people, for all the earth is mine." In addition to these references, there is a long list of particular blessings promised for the keeping of particular laws in Deutronomy 15.

This nation was constituted into a kingdom nation having a king, a priesthood, a people, a body of law, and a land. These are the ingredients of a nation which is a kingdom. In Exodus 19:6 this is expressly stated. "And ye shall be unto me a kingdom of priests and a holy nation." Peter, writing to Israel in the Dispersion, mentions this. In I Peter 2:9, "but ye are an elect race, a royal priesthood, a holy nation, a people for God's own possession, that ye may show forth the excellency of him who called you out of darkness into his marvelous light."

Obedience to God's commandments was made a condition of current blessing, with disobedience to be punished by eviction from the land of promise, with no abrogation of the unconditional covenant God made with Abraham. By current blessing, we mean the blessing for the time being by any one generation.

The fact that any one generation might disobey and be punished had nothing to do with the unconditional promises made to Abraham that his seed will receive the blessings. In Leviticus 26:3 "If ye walk in my statues and keep my commandments and do them, then will I give you rain." This is repeated in Deuteronomy, the 28th chapter. In verse 1, "and it shall come to pass that if ye will harken diligently to the voice of the Lord thy God to observe to do all his commandemtns which I command thee this day, the Lord thy God will set thee on high above all the nations of the earth, and all these blessings shall come upon thee."

In both these passages, the alternatives are set before the people very clearly. If you obey, these blessings will come, but if you disobey, then these chastisements and punishments will come.

In addition to the laws, statutes, and commandments, God instituted the law of ordinances symbolic of the atonement for sin and the maintenance of the relationship of righteousness between God and his people. These laws were administered by the Levitical priesthood, or rather the Aaronic priesthood. The whole system of sacrifices and offerings was for sin, for atonement; it was symbolic of what was yet to come, whereby the people would receive God's righteousness. The people did not earn it. They made offerings as vicarious atonement for sin; a substitutionary atonement was involved in all these sacrifices.

God chose David, in the line of Judah, as the king through whom God would establish his throne forever. This is a setting apart of a family within the family of Abraham, for we find that the promise was "the sceptre shall not depart from Judah until Shiloh come". It is through Judah that "kings shall reign". So this everlasting convenant is made to David by the Lord, as related in II Samuel 7, and the throne is set up forever.

The people of Israel were divided into two main groups according to the two main divisions of the covenant promises. On one hand, there is Judah, the sceptre, or throne, the house of David, as the family leading to the one seed; and the locale of the sanctuary. On the other hand, there is Joseph, who inherited the birthright, under the leadership of the tribes of Ephraim and Manasseh, characterized by the material blessings, the multiplicity of seed, the dominion over whom the King is to reign, the many seed promised to Abraham. So it is this natural division in the content of the promises to Abraham that forms the basis for the division among the people.

After Solomon, the entire people were divided into two kingdoms according to these main divisions. That is, the political cleavage came along the line of the natural division already existing, with the exception of Benjamin, who was loaned to Judah, for the sake of the promise that the house of David would reign over the house of Israel. Benjamin, Judah, and the Levites constituted the southern kingdom of Judah. Ephraim, Manasseh, and all the other tribes formed the northern kingdom of Israel. The capitals were Jerusalem and Samaria; the first kings, Rehoboam and Jeroboam. In Old Testament times, this division continued until each group of people was carried into captivity.

The people disobeyed God's commandments and were driven from the land as God had promised, as set forth in Leviticus 26 and Deuteronomy 28. Joseph-Israel, the northern people, were taken into captivity by Assyria, from which captivity they never returned. Judah-Israel, the southern people, were taken into captivity by Babylon, from which a remnant, the Jews, returned until 70 A.D. This was in keeping with Jeremiah's figure of the bad figs and the good figs, and the promise of the 70 years captivity. captivity.

God brought about a return of a certain remnant of Judah, Benjamin, and Levi, in order to further his purpose in the work of his son, Jesus Christ. We can read Jeremiah's letter to the captives in Babylon, and also the explanation of the limited return of this remnant in the ninth chapter of Daniel. Daniel read Jeremiah's letter and was led to understand what the angel was telling him about the return of a certain group of people to Jerusalem. This was not a re-establishment of the kingdom since no king of David ever ruled over this group of people. The purpose of this nation was to complete the work of the sanctuary, not the throne. This was a people placed back in Jerusalem for the purpose of bringing forth the Messiah. This work was accomplished by Christ at his first coming. The throne is the domain of his work when he comes again, the second time.

That the main body of the people, Joseph-Israel, did not return in Old Testament days is confirmed by three things: first, by Biblical history which is completely silent about such a return; second, modern Jewish scholarship as found in many references, shows very clearly, that the northern people never did come back or rejoin the people called Jews, and third, prophecy requires that they not come back, since the prophetic message concerns a far future reunion of the people under Christ. These people pass out of Old Testament history completely.

The promises of the Abrahamic covenant were repeated to the people by the prophets after they had been removed from the land. God's word to Abraham is still valid, even though the people were carried away into captivity. The people had been told they would be taken into captivity for disobedience, and therefore, this punishment was a part of, not a discontinuance of, the Abrahamic covenant. Therefore, the assurances of God's purpose in these promises to Abraham were repeated in written form, to the people after they had been carried away into captivity. In this connection, in Isaiah 11:11-16 we read, "it shall come to pass in that day that the Lord shall set his hand the second time to recover the remnant of his people that remain from Assyria, Egypt, . . . the islands of the sea, and shall set up an ensign for the nations, and shall assemble the outcasts of Israel, and gather together the dispersed of Judah from the four corners of the earth." This has yet to happen. Isaiah was writing at a time when northern Israel was being carried away captive by the Assyrians.

The future restoration of the people is to follow the return of the people to God in the latter days in far places. In the latter days, after the time of Christ, there is to be a spiritual return and this would happen while Israel is still away from the land in far away places. In Jeremiah 46:27, "But fear thou not, Oh Jacob my servant, and neither be dismayed, Oh Israel. For lo, I will save thee from afar and thy seed from the land of thy captivity, and Jacob shall return and shall be quiet and at ease, and none shall make him afraid."

The relationship of Israel to other people in this promised spiritual return is of such nature as to require fulfillment before the second coming of Christ. This is because they are to be an expanding, aggressive, warlike people, as we studied in a previous lesson. Also, there will be sin, which is not characteristic of the millennial reign of Christ. Therefore, there is to be a spiritual turning to the Lord, and the Old Testament prophecies are full of it.

The national restoration, under the Son of David, is yet sure, but associated with the reunion of Joseph and Judah, and the coming of Christ in judgment. We see this in the vision of the two sticks in Ezekiel 37, in Jeremiah 33:7,8, and a number of other scriptures which speak of the uniting of Judah and Israel, along with the coming of the Lord, under David their king.

How much further we can go, and how much more specific we can be in terms of Old Testament writings, may still be a question. This is a summary of the propositions we studied, the Old Testament "postulates", which form the basis of any New Testament study.

The question of time is a persistent one. In Genesis 49:1, Jacob begins his distribution of covenant blessings to his sons by saying,

"Gather yourselves together, that I may tell you that which shall befall you in the last days." These propositions and promises were for the distant future, not the immediate future.

Remember the story of Balaam who was hired by Balak to curse Israel? The angel of the Lord appeared to Balaam, and said, in Numbers 22:35, "Only the word that I shall speak unto thee, that thou shall speak." Balak was very angry because what he thought would be a curse turned out to be a blessing. Three times. Then Balaam said, in Numbers 24:14, "I will advertise thee what this people shall do to thy people in the latter days." Then follows the wonderful prophecy of the Star out of Jacob and the Scepter out of Israel who will have the final dominion. Now the Hebrew word for "latter" in this passage and the Hebrew word for "last" in Genesis 49:1 are one and the same. There are several other passages that use this same word which is translated either "last" or "latter".

Moses warned the children of Israel that they would be scattered among the nations for their disobedience. Then Moses said, in Deuteronomy 4:30, "When thou art in tribulation, and all those things are come upon thee, even in the latter days, if thou turn to the Lord thy God, and shall be obedient unto his voice; he will not forsake thee, neither destroy thee, nor forget the covenant of thy fathers which he swore unto thee." This was a prophecy spoken before the children of Israel ever set foot on the promised land.

Moses also warned the people just before he died. In Deuteronomy 31:29, he said, "For I know that after my death, ye will utterly corrupt yourselves, and turn aside from the way which I have commanded you; and evil shall befall you in the latter days; because you will do evil in the sight of the Lord, to provoke him to anger through the work of your hands."

In Isaiah 2:2 and Micah 4:1, in the last days, "the mountain of the Lord's house shall be established in the top of the mountains, and shall be exalted above the hills; and all nations shall flow unto it." In Jeremiah 23:20 and 30:24, the latter days are when the thoughts of the Lord will be executed. In Ezekiel 38:8, 16, the latter days are the time of Gog's attack. In Daniel 10:14, it is the time for the great battle between the king of the south and the king of the north. In Hosea 3:5, the latter days are the time for the people of Israel to "seek the Lord thy God, and David their king; and fear the Lord and his goodness." These are some of the Old Testament passages that speak of the last days or the latter days as a time yet to come.

Since the messages of the prophets contain references to the latter days and the last days as times still in the future, then all the more should we regard the prophetic statement of Jacob in Genesis 49:1 as referring to events not to be realized in Old Testament times.

As a first example, consider God's promise to Abraham concerning a multitude of seed. Was this accomplished in Old Testament times? It would seem so. In I Kings 3:8, Solomon said, "And thy servant is in the midst of thy people which thou hast chosen, a great people, that cannot be numbered nor counted for multitude." And in I Kings 4:20, we read, "Judah and Israel were many, as the sand which is by the sea in multitude, eating and drinking, and making merry."

However, God had foretold that the people would disobey his covenant, and be left few in number. In Leviticus 26:38,39, we read, "And ye shall perish among the heathen, and the land of your enemies shall eat you up. And they that are left of you shall pine away in their iniquity in your enemies' lands."

The judgment fell. In Hosea 9:11-16, we read, "as for Ephraim (the pre-eminent recipient of the blessing of the multiplicy of children), their glory shall fly away like a bird, from the birth, and from the womb, and from the conception. Though they bring up their children, yet will I bereave them, that there shall not be a man left . . . Ephraim shall bring forth his children to the murderer. Give them, O Lord, what wilt thou give? Give them a miscarrying womb and dry breasts . . . Ephraim is smitten, their root is dried up, they shall bear no fruit; yea, though they bring forth yet will I slay even the beloved fruit of their womb." Add to this Isaiah 48:18,19, which says "O that thou hadst hearkened to my commandment: then had thy peace been as a river, and thy righteousness as the waves of the sea; thy seed also had been as the sand, and the offspring of thy bowels as the gravel thereof."

Could a judgment be more explicit? Did God abrogate his unconditional promise to Abraham that his seed would be a great multitude? Not at all, for the promise is still for the future in the messages of the prophets. We read, in Hosea 1:10, "yet the number of the children of Israel shall be as the sand of the sea; which cannot be measured nor numbered; and it shall come to pass, that in the place where it was said unto them, ye are not my people, there it shall be said unto them, ye are the sons of the living God." Isaiah exclaims in 54:1-3 "Sing, O barren, thou that didst not bear, break forth into singing, and cry aloud, thou that didst not travail with child: for more are the children of the desolate than the children of the married wife, saith the Lord. Enlarge the place of thy tent, and let them stretch forth the curtains of thine habitations: spare not, lengthen thy cords, and strengthen thy stakes; for thou shalt break forth on the right hand and on the left; and thy seed shall inherit the Gentiles, and make the desolate cities to be inhabited." Thus we see that the ultimate fulfillment of the promise of many seed belongs to a time after the prophets spoke.

An examination of the other promises will reveal the same thing. When Jacob spoke his prophecies in Genesis 49, he declared that they pertained to the "last days". According to the prophets, the last days had not arrived in their times. When did the last days begin?

In the latter part of John 6, Jesus refers to the last day several times as the day of resurrection. He also refers to the last day as the time of judgment in John 12:48. Peter refers to Joel 2:28 as describing the events of the day of Pentecost which the disciples witnessed. Also in I Peter 1:20; we read of Christ, " but was manifest in these last times for you." In Hebrews 1:1,2 we read, "God who at sundry times and in diverse manners spoke in time past unto the fathers by the prophets, hath in these last days spoken unto us by his Son." In I John 2:18, we read, "Little children, it is the last time, and as ye have heard that anti-Christ shall come, even now are there many anti-Christs; whereby we know that it is the last time."

By these, we see that the writers of the New Testament considered that they were living in the last time or last days. They also expected the resurrection and judgement to be in the last time. Then are we not reasonable to say that the last days began with the first advent of Christ and will extend to the second advent when he comes to raise the righteous and judge the world? Then would not this interval between the two advents be the period of history in which the promises to Israel would be fulfilled? What are we waiting for? What is the remaining contingency? Has not Christ come as the Redeemer of his people Israel? When he comes again, will he not come as Judge but not as Saviour? Did not Mary say, In Luke 1:54, "He hath holpen his servant Israel, in remembrance of his mercy; as he spoke to our fathers, to Abraham and to his seed forever"?

How could the promises be fulfilled without the person and work of the one seed to which Paul refers in Galatians 3:16?

PART III

HIGH GROUND:

A THEORY OF HISTORY

Chapter 8
History and Prophecy

Note: This chapter differs in style and format from the others. It is an attempt to present more formally the philosophical basis and logical structure of the thesis developed in the book. In substance it is adapted from an article published in a professional journal some years ago and is offered here for whatever explanation it affords. It could be read again profitably after reading the remainder of the book. -- The Author.

After two world wars, a worldwide economic depression, the failure of two world peace organizations, and in the midst of world revolution, why has there been no new evangelical approach to a Christian interpretation of history? Is it because evangelicals are so involved and immediately concerned with the facts of revolt and apostasy that they cannot assimilate them into a general scheme? If so, how much more time is needed for them to develop a proper perspective? Is it because the only scholars interested in such matters are so blindly committed to interpretative schemes developed before the twentieth century that they are unwilling to adjust hypotheses and theories to new facts?

Any adequate and acceptable Christian interpretation of history must consider the following:

1. God has revealed to man a pattern and purpose of history.
2. There has been but one history.
3. Therefore, any interpretation must set forth the complete consonance of God's revelation with historical fact. This requires a continual reexamination of current theories, models, and perspectives. The history that has happened is in keeping with the revealed pattern and purpose.

God's plan of salvation is very simple—so simple a child can understand the basis for participation. However, God's historical pattern is very complex. It is so complex that men find it difficult to comprehend in just what we participate. This is particularly true of all which still lies ahead of us. The pattern as set forth in the scriptures is there for all to read, yet is so complex that no man has ever exhaustively set forth a statement of the historical proposition.

The fact of its revelation is claimed in Amos 3:7, "Surely the Lord God will do nothing, but he revealeth his secret unto his servants the prophets." The purpose of the revelation is threefold.

1. The revelation shows that God is the author of history. This is shown in Isaiah 41:20, "That they may see, and know, and consider, and understand together, that the hand of the Lord hath done this, and the Holy One of Israel hath created it." Again, in Isaiah 46:10,11, "Declaring the end from the beginning, and from ancient times the things that are not yet done, saying, My counsel shall stand, and I will do all my pleasure." This is suggested also in Isaiah 42:9, and Isaiah 44:7.
2. The revelation stands as a witness against unfaithful men as in Isaiah 46:8-10, "Remember this, and show yourselves men, bring it again to mind, O ye transgressors. Remember the former things of old: for I am God, and there is none else: I am God, and there is none like me." Also we read in Isaiah 48:3-5, "I have declared the former things from the beginning; and they went forth out of my mouth, and I showed them; I did them suddenly, and they came to pass. Because I knew that thou art obstinate and thy neck is an iron sinew; and thy brow brass; I have even from the beginning declared it to thee; before it came to pass, I showed it thee: lest thou shouldest say, Mine idol hath done them."
3. The revelation allows the faithful to understand and take comfort as history unfolds. Isaiah 52:6, "Therefore my people shall know my name: therefore they shall know in that day that I am he that doth speak: behold it is I." In Luke 24:25-27, "O fools, and slow of heart to believe all that the prophets have spoken: Ought not Christ to have suffered these things, and to enter into his glory? And beginning at Moses and all the prophets, he expounded unto them in all the scriptures the things concerning himself." In John 14:29,

"And now I have told you before it come to pass, that, when it come to pass, ye might believe." See also John 13:19 and John 16:4.

The one and only history is also sufficiently recorded for all to read. A thousand histories could be invented, but not one of these imagined histories would necessarily accord with the real history. There could have been many different histories; there has been only one. The particular written account of this history is highly determined by the pattern we adopt as presupposition grounds. However, since the pattern is from outside ourselves (revealed), we must admit the necessity of taking a very hard look at the facts that should be incorporated into our written accounts.

We believe that whatever history has happened is according to God's sovereign will and purpose, which is revealed to us in the Bible. If this history does not fit the pattern, we have not selected the pertinent historical facts and events, or we have misread the pattern, or we are mistaken in believing there is a revealed pattern. The preferred alternative for evangelical Christians is that we have misread the pattern. Our inadequacy in reading the pattern can be partially compensated by inducing the pattern from actual history. This is of secondary value and dangerous, since it is difficult to keep out natural, human, even merely logical presuppositional grounds. It is not at all easy to reduce the total pattern of history to logic. However, an attempt to do so may prove helpful to the extent it increases our faith and confidence in God. The pattern is truly "translogical", since its author is a transcedent God.

We believe the Bible teaches that history is neither open-ended nor cyclical, but climactic. In the Bible there is so much said of judgment, harvest, the fullness of time, the Day of the Lord, etc., that we cannot think otherwise. We are moving toward a great climax.

When shall the end be? When the issue of God's offer on earth becomes planetwide. When all peoples have heard. When "This gospel of the kingdom shall be preached in all the world for a witness unto all nations, then shall the end come." Communication and travel have made this possible in this century. The worldwide missionary enterprise has taken the gospel to governmental representatives of every soul on the face of the earth. The witness has been made to the nations. Nations and peoples have made their choice. Individuals here and there are still responding to the preaching of the gospel, but apostasy and revolt have set in.

We are now in a unique situation. The increase in world population is a problem to be assessed in terms of the capacity of the earth for people. For the first time in man's history the continued existence of life on earth is thought to be in the hands of man himself (nuclear warfare, etc.). Finally, man's venture into space raises questions regarding the ultimate habitat of man. These factors of witness, revolt, population, self-destruction, and space have brought mankind to issues concerning his final destiny, and this is just the situation the scriptures describe as that in which God resolves all history.

Let us now set forth a list of propositions which may be helpful aids in building a Christian interpretation of history. Some of these propositions may seem inappropriate and even discordant to those whose chief vocational concern has been the witness of the church. Some may be unreasonable to those who have restricted their study and teaching to the New Testament. More than a superficial reading of the entire Bible is imperative. There should be only one criterion: What does the Bible say?

1. God is Creator, man is creature; God is sovereign, man is subject. Our very creaturehood dictates that we are not masters of our own destiny. Almighty God is the Lord of History. We do not compose history; we comprise history. We are not God. We are too base, self-willed, ignorant, arrogant, inadequate, natural, earthy, and materialistic to provide for our own salvation. The world of man is separated from God who created it. Man not in full fellowship with God is said to be lost. The Biblical word for this condition is SIN. Yet if man is not a mere robot he must be endowed with choice.

2. God has provided a way to salvation, restitution, completeness, happiness, righteousness, triumph, glory, and eternal life. This way is found in history. God did not at a time ancient call for ultimate decision of all mankind and close the offer, but has allowed the offer of salvation to work out in time (history) that he may bring "many sons to glory". The central element of the offer is eternal life in the presence of God, which transcends all material existence. The offer is communicated to man by the death and resurrection of Jesus Christ. The essential response of man to the offer is acceptance of the free gift of eternal life by faith. The ultimate end of the offer is the reign of Christ in righteousness over the whole of creation. Thus history fulfills God's purpose. (I Corinthians 15)
3. In order that men be presented with the offer, of necessity there must be channels of communication through which the choice is presented. The channel itself was a matter of God's choosing, namely, Abraham and his descendents. We must admit as a matter of historical fact that God did not reveal Himself equally at that time to all divisions of mankind. This principal channel of blessings involves both a Person and a People: Christ and Israel, the one seed and the many seed of Abraham.
4. That the choice is real is attested by the following: there are men today who confess they do not believe in the God of Abraham, they are not related to God in Jesus Christ, and even some confess they are knowingly lost and without hope. On the other hand, there are men who confess they do believe in the God of Abraham, and are related to Him by faith in Jesus Christ. They are knowingly saved and are certain of eternal life. These facts of man's existence and his testimony are in keeping with the teaching of Scripture.
5. The church has been chiefly concerned with Christ, his Person, and work of redemption in providing the basis for the individual man's relationship to God. The church has been a fellowship of believers and a messenger of the offer to "whosoever

will." The church until recently has not been primarily concerned with the social issues of corporate society. Of late, the Marxists have offered a materialistic substitute salvation through authoritative corporate action which denies to the individual his personal sovereignty of choice. The church, through its social gospel, is becoming involved in some of these same issues.

6. The role of Israel, and subsequently the whole body of God's people in history, has not been too well understood. This part of the general scheme is not read or assimilted or incorporated into a general theory. The relationship of Israel to the church and the place of Israel in history as set forth in Old Testament Scriptures is especially unexamined. Any good interpretation of history requires a proper understanding of these matters, since, in addition to the person and work of Christ, history involves people. The following considerations show Israel's centrality to history:
   a. The specific promises to Israel near the end of Old Testament history which were not fulfilled in Old Testament times. This applies particularly to the main part of the people of Israel (The House of Joseph) who never became Jews. The many attempts to make of present day Jews the inheritors of promises never given to them only leads to confusion.
   b. The Old Testament promises that Israel is to be the agency of blessings brought to the Gentiles.
   c. The proposition consistently presented throughout the New Testament is that the Gentiles are added to (and not a replacement of), the corporate body of Israel. (Romans 11, Ephesians 2, Galatians 3, Revelation 21). The unconditional promises to Abraham have never been retracted, abrogated, or annulled.
7. The culmination of history is the ingathering of believers of all generations through resurrection into one people of God when Christ returns to reign over the earth. All our hopes for peace, health, and righteousness are centered in this one hope of His coming again. The details of the circumstances in

which He returns are not clearly understood since it is yet future. Beyond the glorious appearing of Christ, the details are even more obscure. However, we are confident that the tabernacle of God will be with men, and He shall dwell with them, and they shall be his people, and God himself shall be their God. (Hebrews 4, Revelation 21:3)

The great symphonic theme of the Bible is the story of Christ: His person, His work of redemption, His coming reign, and His final triumph. However, running throughout the entire symphony there is an alternate melody, a counterpoint, played with great pathos, now swelling, now dying, now lyrical with the joyous notes of a flute in harmony with the main theme. It is the song of God's people, without which the main theme would stand unadorned. This "song of the flute" is the song of a redeemed people. It is the melody of history. Isaiah 30:29 joyously proclaims, "You shall have a song as in the night when a holy feast is kept; and gladness of heart, as when one marches with a flute to come to the mountain of the Lord, to the Rock of Israel."

Chapter 9

All One Body We

So we sing the song. What do we mean by "one body"? Do we mean all believers of all variant shades of Christian faith, some sort of pan-denominational assembly of followers of Christ? Are we saying that the doctrinal and ecclesiastical differences which separate us into many worshipping groups are really not important when we meet at the foot of the cross? Do we include our grandparents and forebearers who are among the rightous dead? Dare we think of Old Testament stalwarts such as Noah, Abraham and David as members of the One Body? And here we stall.

In the resurrection will we find the City of God built up of many residential subdivisions? If so, there then will be one subdivision for the saints who lived from Adam to Noah, and another subdivision for those who lived from Noah to Abraham. Then sprinkled around the throne of the Holy City there will be other subdivisions for people in other ages, say from Moses to Jesus, or from Pentecost to the Rapture.

We are told in Hebrews 10:12-14, where we read, "But this man after he had offered one sacrifice for sins forever sat down on the right hand of God; from henceforth expecting till his enemies be made his footstool. For by one offering he hath perfected forever them that are sanctified." When is forever? Does it not include yesterday as well as tomorrow? It is certain that yesterday was the tomorrow to those who lived the day before yesterday. Is not God present at every instant of time as well as present at every point in space? God is every "when" at once as well as every "where" at once. Is there any past, present, and future with God? He is the Beginning and the End, the First and the Last. He is the Great I AM.

Suppose, in the resurrection, you recognize the patriarch Jacob, and walk up to him and ask, "Jacob, you old scoundrel, how did you get in here"? Would it not be reasonable to imagine he would look at you with those steely blue eyes, shake his white head, and answer "By the blood of the Lamb"! There is no other way, for anyone, regardless of the age in which one lives. The Old Testament saints believed that God would do something about their sins, and they looked forward to it in faith. We, today, believe that God did do something about our sins, and we look backward to it in faith. They did not understand it. Neither do we. It happened once, at the cross. Once forever. Christ did not appear to men in every generation and die as a sacrifice for their sins. "For then must he often have suffered since the foundation of the world: but now once in the end of the world hath he appeared to put away sin by the sacrifice of himself." (Hebrews 9:26). Once was enough. In olden times this expectation by faith was celebrated by blood sacrifices, for "without shedding of blood is no remission." The principal ceremony of the children of Israel was the Passover. The principal ceremony of Christians today is the Lord's Supper, which was instituted at a Passover feast. They looked forward to something just as we look backward to it. They believed as a matter of faith. So do we. The only difference is the fact accomplished in history. They, as we, have received the end of faith, which is the salvation of souls. "Of which salvation the prophets have inquired and searched diligently, who prophesied of the grace that should come unto you: searching what, or what manner of time the Spirit of Christ which was in them did signify, when it testified beforehand the sufferings of Christ, and the glory that should follow." Concerning the Old Testament saints and martyrs, the writer of the Book of Hebrews says, in chapter 11, verses 39 and 40, "And these all, having obtained a good report through faith, received not the promise: God having provided some better thing for us, that they without us should not be made perfect." Is there some category of Old Testament believers who were made perfect without the blood of Jesus Christ? There was never a man who was justified by the keeping of the Law. (Romans 3:30, Galatians 3:11).

In Romans 6:14 we read, "for we are not under the law, but under grace." If no one is justified by the law, then what does this mean? The law is divided into commandments, statutes, judgments, and ordinances. The ordinances were the law which was added at Mt. Sinai for the purpose of taking care of the sin problem of the people. Were not the other parts of the law already in existence? When God appeared to Isaac, he said, in Genesis 26:5, "because that Abraham obeyed my voice, and kept my charge, my commandments, my statutes, and my laws." This was four hundred years before Mt. Sinai. Was not the law from the beginning? Else why find fault with Cain for the murder of Abel? Was not the law which was added at Mt. Sinai (Galatians 3:19) the ordinances because of transgression of already existing laws?

Grace was in the beginning. Else why is it said in Genesis 6:8 that "Noah found grace in the eyes of the Lord"? Is not God's grace everlasting? Ephesians 2:8 says, "For by grace are ye saved through faith; and that not of yourselves: it is the gift of God." It is certain that the men of God in olden times had faith. That is the theme of the eleventh chapter of the Book of Hebrews. How can we question that their faith was not met with God's grace?

Still it may be said by some, "Well, I am not under the law, which has all those commandments". How many? Ten? In the Old Testament there are more than three hundred commandments. "Free from the Law, we sing. Are we free to steal, murder, and commit adultery? Done with commandments? In the New Testament there are more than six hundred commandments! Among them,"Love one another". And Jesus said, "If ye love me, keep my commandments."

When did the church begin? On the day of Pentecost? When Stephen made his defense before the council at Jerusalem, he spoke of "the church in the wilderness". What did he mean?

Our English word "congregation" is a translation of three different Hebrew words. One is MOED which means an appointed assembly, a festival or feast. Another is EDAH which means a company or multitude of people, a crowd. The third is QAHAL which means a called together assembly. Toward the end of the third century B.C., the Hebrew Old Testament was translated into Greek by a committee of seventy scholars. This Greek version of the Scriptures was called the Septuaguint, and was familiar to Jesus and his disciples. In this Greek version, the Hebrew word QAHAL was translated into Greek SUNAGOGE (Synagogue) about seventeen times, principally in the books of Exodus, Leviticus, and Numbers. However, beginning in Deuteronomy, the Hebrew word Qahal is translated into the Greek EKKLESIA more than fifty times throughout the Old Testament. This is identical with the New Testament EKKLESIA which we translate "church". Stephen was perfectly correct when he spoke of the church in the wilderness!

On the Day of Pentecost, according to Acts 2:41, "And the same day there were added unto them about three thousand souls." Nothing is said about the formation of a new group of believers. No new committee was appointed to draw up a constitution for a new organization. Then to what were they added? It had to be something already in existence!

Jesus said, "On this rock I will build my church", as if it were his intention to do something in the future. Yes, he used a simple future tense of the verb "to build". But what does this word "build" mean? The Greek word is OIKODOMEO, which is made up of OIKOS, meaning "house", and DOMA, meaning "housetop" or "roof". We got our word "dome" from the second one. The combination word then becomes "house-house-top" or "house-roof." When this is used in a verbal sense, it means to complete the building to the top, to finish the building. In Strong's concordance, the various forms of this compound word OIKODOMEO carry the connotation of "confirm" or "confirmation". It is frequently translated into English as "edify", which means to "build up", or "strengthen". It seems nowhere to mean "initiate" or "begin to build."

Who has ever been or ever will be saved except by the blood of Christ? The law was from the beginning. Grace was from the beginning. The Gospel was from the beginning. Can we not, also say that the church was from the beginning? Who would you leave out?

The new covenant is new with respect to what that is old? How can there be something new unless there is something old? Then what was old? The promises God made to Abraham? Never! In Galatians 3:17, we read, "And this I say, that the covenant, that was confirmed before of God in Christ, the law, which was four hundred and thirty years after, cannot disannul, that it should make the promise of none effect." Then the Old Covenant was the highly conditional covenant that God made with the people of Israel at Mt. Sinai which would in no way abrogate the unconditional promises God made to Abraham, Isaac, and Jacob. Christ did not confirm the Law; he confirmed the promises. In Ephesians 2:15, he "abolished in his flesh the law of commandments in ordinances", dealing with sin and atonement. By his atonement on the cross, he opened the doors of salvation to all who would believe, so that "ye being in the time past Gentiles in the flesh . . . who were without Christ, being aliens from the commonwealth of Israel, and strangers from the covenants of promise, having no hope, and without God in the world . . . are made nigh by the blood of Christ . . . who hath made both one, and hath broken down the middle wall of partition." This middle wall of partition was the wall which separated the people of Israel from the Gentiles, who had to remain outside. In Herod's temple, on this wall there was inscribed the following words: "Let no gentile enter inside of the barrier and the fence around the sanctuary. Anyone trespassing will bring death upon himself as a penalty." Christ died "that he might reconcile both unto God in one body by the cross, having slain the enmity thereby: and came and preached peace to you which were far off, and to them that were nigh. For through him we both have access by one spirit unto the Father." See Ephesians 2:11-22. See also Galatians 3:29, which reads, "And if ye be Christ's, then are ye Abraham's seed, and heirs according to the promise."

Some would say that such scriptures should not be taken in that literal sense. After all, the church is the spiritual progeny of Abraham and only the spiritual seed counts. The church has inherited all the promises made to Abraham according to their spiritual intent. The church has inherited all the Old Testament blessings. Then who inherited the curses? If the church has taken the place of Israel in God's scheme of things, than why, after 1900 years is there such a person as a Jew still in our midst? And since there is a Jew, then where is Israel? If the New Testament church has taken the place of Israel, then why does Paul, thirty years after Pentecost, take three chapters in the Book of Romans to talk about Israel of the flesh whom he does not call Jews? He writes of the Jews in chapters 2 and 3, but it is Israel which is the subject of chapters 9, 10, and 11. Only once in this passage, in Romans 9:24, does Paul refer to Jews. The literal rendition of this verse from the Greek reads, "Even us, whom he hath called not only from among Jews, but also from among Gentiles." Paul is making an application of a proposition he is developing to a current situation, but the proposition itself is far more comprehensive than the current situation.

Throughout the ninth chapter of Romans, several Old Testament passages are quoted, all of which were written before there were any Jews, and the quotation from Hosea was written to the northern people of Israel who were never called Jews.

It is the eleventh chapter of Romans to which we should give particular attention. It opens with Paul's claim to be of the tribe of Benjamin, an Israelite of the seed of Abraham. He is talking about the literal, biological descendants of Abraham. He claims that there exists in his day a "remnant according to the election of grace." In verse 7, he says, "Israel hath not obtained that which he seeketh for; but the election hath obtained it, and the rest were blinded." There is a part of Israel which is a faithful remnant: there is another part which is blinded; a simple but important division.

For the sake of clarity and emphasis, the proper name "Israel" will be substituted for the pronoun in several verses which follow. In verses 11 and 12 we then read, ". . . through Israel's fall salvation is come unto the Gentiles, for to provoke Israel to jealousy. Now if the fall of Israel be the riches of the world, and the diminishing of Israel the riches of the Gentiles; how much more Israel's fulness"? Remember what old Simeon said in Luke 2:34?

"This child is set for the fall and rising again of many in Israel." Paul is saying in Romans that God has not yet finished with Israel. He continues in verse 15, "For if the casting away of Israel be the reconciling of the world, what shall the receiving of Israel be but life from the dead"? It is promised in Hosea 6:2,"After two days will he revive us; in the third day he will raise us up, and we shall live in his sight." If a day is as a thousand years, then when shall that happen? Israel is to live again.

Continuing in Romans 11, Paul uses the figure of the olive tree and its branches. Now verse 17 is believed by some to read "And if all of the branches be broken off, and thou, being a wild olive tree, wert grafted in, in place of them, and instead of them partakest of the root and fatness of the olive tree." No! The word of God does not even imply that, much less say it! Listen! "And if SOME of the branches be broken off, and thou being a wild olive tree wert grafted in AMONG them, and WITH them partakest of the root and fatness of the olive tree. Boast not against the branches. But if thou boast, thou barest not the root, but the root thee."

The "thou" means "you Gentiles" (verse 13). The "them" must mean the natural seed of Israel, the remnant of whom, in verses 5 and 7, were those to whom the wild branches were added. Then the root would be Israel, covenant Israel, the Israel to whom the promises were made. Read again Ephesians 2:12, which says of the Gentiles "that at that time ye were wihout Christ, being aliens from the commonwealth of Israel, and strangers from the covenants of promise", and verse 19, which reads, "now therefore ye are no more strangers and foreigners, but fellow citizens with the saints and of the household of God." It would seem, therefore, that the Gentiles are added to Israel, are brought into Israel, and partake of the promises made to Israel.

How else could God's promise to Abraham that he would be a blessing to the Gentiles be fulfilled except this inclusion of Gentiles through the blood of Christ?

There is a warning in Romans 11:20,21, "Be not high minded, but fear: For if God spared not the natural branches, take heed lest he also spare not thee." Now read verse 23 with the noun in place of the pronoun: "And Israel also, if Israel abide not still in unbelief, shall be grafted in, for God is able to graft Israel in again." Further, in verse 24, "how much more shall these, which be the natural branches, be grafted into their own olive tree"? There is no hint in all this passage that the grafted-in Gentiles constitute a different category of believers in any way other than in the covenant people of all generations.

Now consider Romans 11:25, "For I would not, brethen, that ye should be ignorant of this mystery, lest ye should be wise in your own conceits; that blindness in part is happened to Israel, until the fulness of the Gentiles be come in." In verse 7, Paul speaks about a part of Israel which is a faithful remnant, and a part of Israel which is blinded. Then in verse 25, is Paul speaking about a partial blindness to all of Israel, including the remnants who were not blinded, or is he speaking about the part of Israel which is blinded? In verse 25 does the word "part" belong to the word "blindness" or to the word "Israel"? The latter makes for greater consistency of the entire passage. The RSV renders this phrase, "a hardening has come upon part of Israel." The Jerusalem Bible reads, "One section of Israel has become blind." The Amplified New Testament reads, "a hardening has befallen a part of Israel." The Synodale version of Le Nouveau Testament uses the phase, "c'est qu'une partie d' Israel", meaning "a part of Israel". In Thayer's Greek-English Lexicon, page 401, the meaning of the Greek construction of this phrase in Romans 11:25 is rendered, "as respects a part". Throughout Romans 11, Paul is discussing the relationship between a faithful part of Israel, a blinded part of Israel, and Gentiles who are grafted in for a time until their number is complete. In verses 25 and 26 he shows that the blinded part of Israel will come back in. "So all Israel shall be saved", then, refers to all parts of Israel, both the faithful remnant and the blinded part.

What is the contingency? "There shall come out of Zion the Deliverer and shall turn away ungodliness from Jacob: for this is my covenant unto them, when I shall take away their sins." In verses 30 and 31, we read, "For as ye (Gentiles) in times past have not believed God, yet have now obtained mercy through Isreal's unbelief: even so has Israel also now not believed, that through your mercy Israel also may obtain mercy. For God has concluded them all in unbelief, that he might have mercy upon all." Then Paul concludes this argument by breaking into a psalm of praise to God for his marvelous wisdom.

Again, what is the contingency? Has not the Deliverer come to take away the sins of God's people? Has he not completed the works of a high priest? Then what are we waiting for? Why is Israel not saved? Why is Israel not now in the one body of believers of all generations?

The Clock of Ages

XII Second Advent

I Israel

II Assyria

III Babylon

IV Medo-Persia

VI First Advent

VII Rome

VIII Dark Ages

IX Papacy

X Reformation

XI World-Missions

Chapter 10

The Clock of Ages

What time is it? An ordinary question, but one that is frequently asked by hurried people in our modern world. A more serious question to ask is "What is time?" This has bothered the philosophers and scholars for centuries, and no one has really developed a satisfactory answer. In terms of human life, time seems to be nothing more than the sequence of our experiences somewhat devoid of the concept or measurement of duration. It is certain that to students a lecture may seem to last forever, but on some fortunate occasions they might think, "Where did that hour go?" The differing reactions might be involved also in the responses to preaching, typing, or driving to work.

Psychologically, and subjectively, in terms of human experience, there is little or no duration to this thing we call time. Yet we do have some duration built into all of life because of the alternation of light and darkness, of daylight and night. This seems to be built into all life on this planet, except perhaps for the Eskimos who have only a few months of darkness in the year. The Astronauts travelling to the moon were in sunshine continuously, so they had to go to sleep by the clock back in Houston. Alternate periods of dormancy and activity seem to be built into everything that lives.

It is that biological clock that is disturbed when the President flies to some international meeting or the Secretary of State flies to the Middle East or an American tourist flies to the Greek Islands. People usually arrange to arrive a little early on such journeys in order to sleep awhile to get this biological clock readjusted to the new location. Why is all this? It is due simply to the rotation of the earth which marks out this natural unit of time we call the day.

For convenience we have divided the day into hours, minutes and seconds. The scientist divides the second into thousandths he calls milliseconds, into millionths he calls microseconds, and into billionths he calls nanoseconds. Some electronic gadgetry measures time in intervals even less than nanoseconds. For pragmatic expediency we take multiples of the day as weeks, months, and years. A month is determined by the revolution of the moon around the earth and a year is the time of the revolution of the earth around the sun. These form the natural measures of our time, because, physically, objectively, time is the measure of the motion of bodies of matter through space. If we measure the relative motion of two or more pieces of matter, then we can get an objective, physical measurement of time, and clocks become possible.

In Genesis 1:14 we read, "Let there be lights in the firmament of the heaven to divide the day from the night; and let them be for signs, and for seasons, and for days and for years." So it is these lights that we see up in the sky that mark out our time for us. We set our clocks to the rotation of the earth with respect to the sun, although we measure it by the rotation of the earth with respect to the stars because the sun does not cross our meridian in equal intervals of time.

Now how does God tell time? Or does He need to? Does He who formed the earth, the moon, the sun and the stars depend upon any of them for His counsel or purpose? This reminds us of a question we ask children, "Where is God?" and we teach them to reply, "God is everywhere." Are not all points of His material universe equally before him? A more provocative question might be "When is God?" Now if time is a measure of the relative motion of the objects of the physical world flung into space, then are not all points of time equally before him also? Therefore, God is every "when" at once. You can dump a lot of theological problems into that one. There is absolutely no time contingency in the counsels of God. The Scriptures use such phrases as "foreknowledge", "predestination", "before the foundation of the world", and others, but if all points of time are equally before Him, there is no time contingency with God. Everything is up to His wisdom and decision regardless of our experience in the time frame of our created world. Do not forget that time is a feature of the created, physical universe. There is no past, present, or future with God, just an eternal NOW. This was exemplified by Jesus when he said, "Before Abraham was, I am." There are many other scriptures that show God's continuing existence without regard to days, years, clocks, or calendars. With Him a day is as a thousand years, and a thousand years as a day.

Consider the week; where did it originate? Is there anything in the physical or astronomical world that corresponds to the week of seven days? If so, it is not very apparent. In six days God made the heavens and the earth and rested on the seventh day. Why did He not work eight days and rest on the ninth? Or three days and rest on the fourth? We are not told. God decreed the seventh day as the day of rest. The earth does not stop spinning on the seventh day or hesitiate in its travel about the sun. Stars in their courses continue their ceaseless journeys. There does not seem to be any recurring astronomical event or physical phenomenon which repeats itself in intervals of seven days. Perhaps we should look into the biological world for an answer. Perhaps, in addition to periods of sleep, we actually require additional rest every seven days in order to maintain our proper biological well being. Few of us can work seven days every week for months on end without suffering some deterioration in health. The seventh day of rest seems to be required.

The land also needs a rest. God commanded through Moses that the land should rest every seven years. The crop in the sixth year would be sufficient to last until the harvest of the eighth year. Even the economy needed a rest every seven years, because every seventh year was proclaimed as a year of release. All personal debts were to be cancelled and all indentured servants were to be set free. We still have the remains of that in our Statute of Limitations; Does not our Common Law come from the Bible? If someone lends Jimmie a hundred dollars, and he does not pay it back in seven years, then forget it. Most common laws will not allow anyone to collect it. Why? Because he will be better off, the lender will be better off, and everybody in society will be better off if it is not mentioned anymore. That is the law of release for every seven years. All debts are to be wiped out. If that seventh year is 1987, no one is to withhold any help to him in 1986 just because the following year is the year of release. The Bible tells us that we are not to regard the shortness of the time when we are helping our brother in need. In the Bible, God has ordained the law of the seventh, in days and in years, and even seven times seven years for the year of Jubilee when the land was returned to the original owner.

It is interesting to read the story of Jacob laboring for his wives in the 29th chapter of Genesis. Jacob served Laban for a period of seven years for each of Laban's daughters. He worked the first seven years for Leah, and another seven years for Rachel. Each of these seven year periods is called a week, or simply a seven, or seven days. In this case a period of seven days is a symbol for a period of seven years. In other words, a day represents a year.

When Joseph brought his father Jacob down into Egypt, he introduced him to Pharaoh. The Egyptians did not live to be old men. Here was this old man, perhaps white-headed and bearded, standing before Pharaoh; a rare spectacle. Pharaoh did not resist the temptation, so he asked Jacob, "How old are you?" Really, the language is more explicit. Pharaoh asked, "How many are the years of thy days?" Jacob answered, "The days of the years of my pilgrimage are a hundred and thirty years." Notice the reversal and the interchange of years and days in Pharaoh's question and Jacob's answer. Days and years are interchangeable in counting time.

When the Children of Israel were nearing the Promised land, Moses sent twelve spies into the land to find out what they could about the people, their cities, and the natural resources. Ten of the twelve spies brought back a very bad report, saying the people were giants and the land was not good. Caleb and Joshua were optimistic, saying that Israel could conquer the land and its inhabitants. The people chose to believe the ten spies, and became afraid and disobedient. God pronounced judgment upon them and consigned them to wander in the wilderness for their lack of faith. In Numbers 14:32-34 we read, "But as for you, your carcasses, they shall fall in this wilderness. And your children shall wander in the wilderness for forty years -- after the number of days in which you searched the land, even forty days, each day for a year, shall you bear your inquities, even forty years, and you shall know my breach of promise." This seems to be the scale according to which God measures out time to His people: a year for a day.

Yet again, this scale of representation of God's time in judgement is presented in the fourth chapter of Ezekiel. Ezekiel was asked to act out an object lesson. "Thou, also, son of man, take thee a tile, and lay it before thee, and portray upon it the city, even Jerusalem: and lay siege against it; set the camp also against it, and set battering rams against it round about. Morever, take unto thee an iron pan, and set it for a wall of iron between thee and the city: and set thy face against it, and it shall be besieged, and thou shall lay siege against it. This shall be a sign to the house of Israel. Lie thou also upon thy left side, and lay the iniquity of the house of Israel upon it; according to the number of days that thou shall lie upon it thou shalt bear their iniquity. For I have laid upon thee the years of their iniquity, according to the number of the days, three hundred and ninety days: so shalt thou bear the iniquity of the house of Israel. And when thou hast accomplished them, lie again on thy right side, and thou shalt bear the iniquity of the house of Judah forty days; I have appointed thee each day for a year."

Is this not very plain? Yet people who disagree with this line of thought refer to this Ezekiel passage as if it is the only passage of scripture dealing with it. We have already shown that the year-for-a-day scale was used before the time of Ezekiel, and Ezekiel is carrying on something that was already in practice in God's dealing with His people. The Word plainly states, "I have appointed thee each day for a year." God appointed this scale of representation of a day for a year when dealing with the question of time.

In the ninth chapter of Daniel, a time period is set forth called seventy weeks or simply seventy sevens. This is seven times the captivity period of one particular group of the people who were told by Jeremiah that they would be captives in Babylon for seventy years. This total of seventy weeks would include the time of restoration of the city of Jerusalem and the temple as well as the marvelous work of the Messiah as High Priest in the Sanctuary. Now many agree that this period is seventy times seven years or four hundred and ninety years, but there are various beliefs concerning which four hundred and ninety years in history fulfill this prophecy. Some of the most ardent opponents of the year for a day time scale admit its value in the case of the seventy weeks, but deny its application to all other prophetic times.

In the fourth chapter of Daniel there is an acount of a most extraordinary dream by Nebuchadnezzar and its interpretation by Daniel. The great king Nebuchadnezzar is debased and humiliated beyond measure. He is deprived of any reason and understanding for a period of seven times. Now Josephus tells us that Nebuchadnezzar was out of his mind for seven years. This would associate "seven times" with seven literal years, but there is more about it to be said than just this. Three times in this account of Nebuchadnezzar's debasement the expression occurs, "The Most High ruleth in the kingdom of men and giveth it to whomsoever He will." Daniel refers to this when he faces Belshazzar, the son or grandson of Nebuchadnezzar and applies it to Belshazzar. Nor did the kingdom of men cease with Belshazzar. Darius the Mede recognized God as the sovereign over his kingdom in Daniel 6:26,27. Cyrus the Persian proclaims "the Lord God of heaven has given me all the kingdoms of the earth" in Ezra 1:2. God later gave all these kingdoms to Alexander the Great, and it was God who subjected all these kingdoms to the Romans. Surely the Most High ruleth in the kingdom of men, and He did not stop with Nebuchadnezzar. He will continue until Jesus Christ comes as King of Kings and Lord of Lords; when the kingdoms of this world have become the kingdoms of our Lord and His Christ and He shall reign forever and ever. Is not Nebuchadnezzar a symbol of all subsequent kingdoms of earth until Jesus comes? When Daniel interpreted the dream of the great image to Nebuchadnezzar, Daniel said, "Thou art this head of gold," indicating that Nebuchadnezzar was symbolic of more than his own personal reign. Is not "Babylon" used in the Revelation as the symbol of the great world system which is destroyed by Christ at His coming? Read all of Isaiah 47 and all of Jeremiah 51 with Revelation 17 and 18.

Now if we apply this symbolic time scale to the Babylonian succession of world empires, we get some astonishing results. If we count "seven times" as seven years of years, we find a time period that spans centuries and encompasses most of the world's history as we know it.

The priests of Babylon kept a calendar of 360 days to the year. They would stick in five or six intercalary days to keep the calendar in line with the seasons. We do the same today by inserting one intercalary day every four years in leap years. The priests of Israel kept a lunar calendar with twelve lunar months of about 29 or 30 days, and added an intercalary month in some years. Seven of every nineteen years had thirteen months. Mohammedans keep the lunar calendar period of 354 and a fraction days, and a new year could come in any season of the year.

Calendar keeping is a mathematical science involving interrelationships of the exact numerical values of months and years as measured in days. Neither a month nor a year can be expressed in whole numbers of days. Nor can any fraction of a day, either common or decimal, be used to count out a whole number of days in any time period whatsoever. Such counting leads only to irrational numbers, numbers the multiples of which never come out whole numbers. One month equals 29.53059....days. One year equals 365.2422.....days. These numbers never repeat nor come out even.

The problem can be stated in the following manner. Suppose we have a full moon at midnight on December 31. That would place it on our meridian and near our zenith. Now, let the earth spin and the moon travel around the earth and both journey around the sun. How long will it be until we have a full moon again at midnight on December 31? Exactly? Never! The day, month, and year are mathematically incommensurable; they cannot be measured in terms of each other exactly.

In order to get a more practical answer that would be useful in calendar making, let us ask how long will it take for the moon to be full again within twelve hours of midnight on December 31. This would put it either side of midnight and could be counted as on the same calendar day as before. A rough approximation of such a period is nineteen years, and has been used since ancient times as an eclipse cycle. A longer, more exact period is 315 years, but it is little used in calendar making. However, eight times this period gives an amazing number of years which is 2520 years. It is amazing in the first place because 2520 is the lowest common multiple of all the digits, one through nine. If a "time" in the Bible is a year of 360 days, then on the scale of a year for a day, "seven times" is 2520 years. One half of 2520 is 1260, a number mentioned in both Daniel and Revelation. We can count 2520 lunar years of 354+ days each, 2520 calendar years of 360 days each, and 2520 solar years of 365+ days each, and consider their differences. These astronomical differences, when added to the 1260 years yield 1290 years and 1335 years, periods also found in Daniel, stated as days.

Another time period given in Daniel is 2300 days, which, if we understand to mean years, turns out to be a very exact astronomical time cycle. A period of 2300 literal days has no meaning at all astronomically, but 2300 years is a very accurate lunar-solar time cycle. Now the difference between 2300 and 1260 is 1040. A period of 1040 years is so precise that it was known to professional astronomers of the nineteenth century as the Daniel Cycle, but it is not mentioned in Scripture.

Thus we see that in Daniel and Revelation, we are dealing with time periods which, if taken literally, have absolutely no known physical or astronomical counterparts, yet when regarded as longer periods on the basis of a year for a day turn out to be very accurate lunar-solar time cycles of great precision and of definite physical and astronomical significance. It is amazing to note that careful research has not revealed any other such time periods of less than 10,000 years, and all of these mentioned are in the Bible. They are recorded in Daniel and Revelation and are all known to exist. They are all in there if we understand these numbers to apply to years, not days. To a mathematician who is an amateur astronomer, and to a physicist who is a Christian, these matters are of great significance.

There is still another passage of Scripture to examine. In the fifth chapter of Daniel we read the story of Belshazzar and his great feast. This was the occasion of the famous handwriting on the wall. After others failed, Daniel was brought in to interpret the handwriting. Daniel told Belshazzar and his lords the reason for the judgment the writing obviously portended. Then Daniel gave the content of the judgment pronounced by these cryptographic words on the wall. The words themselves were not strange, but the message they conveyed was the secret revealed by Daniel. The words were few: MENE, MENE, TEKEL, UPHARSIN. Daniel's messge of interpretation was brief, "MENE, MENE, God has numbered thy kingdom and finished it; TEKEL, Thou are weighed in the balances and art found wanting; and PERES or UPHARSIN, thy kingdom is divided and given to the Medes and Persians." These three words can be translated roughly as numbered, weighed, divided.

The three words themselves are nothing more than the Chaldee equivalent of the Hebrew words, MANEH, SHEKEL, and PARAS. Maneh and shekel are units of weight in the Hebrew system of measurements. Any good Bible dictionary will have a section of Weights and Measures in which you will find the values of the maneh and the shekel. The handwriting on the wall may as well have been POUND, POUND, OUNCE, HALF. Just ordinary words. There is no strangeness to the words themselves, but what in the world did they mean in the context of Belshazzar's feast? What is the value of these units of measure and what is their sum? The following scripture references will be of help: Ezekiel 45:12, Joshua 7;21, Leviticus 27:25, II Chronicles 3:9, II Samuel 24:24, and II Kings 15:20. One shekel equals 20 gerahs, very small units of weight. One maneh equals 60 shekels. Gold and silver were weighed by a different system. A maneh of gold or silver consisted of only 50 shekels. We do the same today, weighing precious metals by Troy weight, according to which there are twelve Troy ounces to the pound. We weigh beans and potatoes by sixteen ounces to the Avoirdupois pound. We have still a different system used by the pharmacist.

At Belshazzar's feast the gold and silver from the temple were being desecrated by the Babylonians, so which scale of measure is going to apply here? Naturally, the one dealing with gold and silver. A maneh of 50 shekels of gold would weigh a total of 1000 gerahs. Let us count up the value of the words as follows:

MENE	Maneh	1000 gerahs
MENE	Maneh	1000 gerahs
TEKEL	Shekel	20 gerahs
PERES	½Maneh	500 gerahs
		2520 gerahs

The numerical value of the handwriting on the wall is that wonderful number 2520!

The circumstances of its use involve the rise and fall of empires and the setting up putting down of kings and rulers. Literal days would have little meaning in such matters, since a single king could outlive such a short period of time. The value of 2520 used in judgment on the Gentile world powers is a valid, accurate and significant period of time if considered as 2520 years, but has no physical meaning at all if we consider them as literal days. How better to exemplify what God told us in Genesis 1:14 than that all these heavenly bodies are for times and for seasons, for days and years? So these inexorable motions of the earth, moon, and sun truly mark out our times on this celestial Clock of Ages.

These ideas are not new. The continuous development of history as fulfillment of prophecy without gaps or parentheses was a view held by nearly all the reformation teachers and martyrs. As soon as the Bible became available to the people of northern Europe, first from the hands of Wycliffe, and then Tyndale, the realities of history became understandable in terms of the year for a day scale used in the prophetic passages of the Bible. If there is a choice between agreeing with these stalwarts of the faith who laid down their lives for what they believed and more recent expositors of the prophecies, who aparently have a deep aversion to anything in the realm of mathematics and natural science, then the choice is not hard to make.

God knows all about arithmetic. He is no stranger to algebra, geometry, differential equations, exponential functions, group theory, computer circuitry, or any other mathematical concept that ever has been or ever will be thought of or devised by man. To claim that Biblical truth is totally unrelated to a realm of thought unfamiliar to a great many church leaders today is a presumption that puts a limit on God. Such a presumption also makes a judgment on those who have some understanding of these matters and whose faith and dedication are also valid. Christian leaders might protest that they have more important things to accomplish. The Gospel must be preached. They are right, but if they deal in prophetic time scales, as something of less importance then let them not enter into this domain without proper equipment and competence.

The question may be asked as to how all this might be applied to history as we know it. When Dr. Grattan Guinness in England saw that the Pope was stripped of all political power in 1870, he realized that an event had occurred which had deep prophetic meaning. He therefore undertook a study of these astronomical time cycles in relation to the progress of history. He wrote several books, one of which was *The Approaching End of the Age,* and another in 1887, *Light for the Last Days.* In the first he pointed out the declining power of the Turkish Empire, and in the second he made an outright prediction that the year 1917 should see the deliverance of Jerusalem from the Turks, nearly thirty years before the actual event took place. How was this possible? In his studies he showed the interrelationships between these lunar and solar time cycles and how they marked out some of the most important events of past history.

Nebuchadnezzar took Jerusalem the first time in 604 B.C. Since there is no year zero in our calendar, we must remember that December 31, 1 B.C. was just one day before January 1, 1 A.D., when we make calendar computations. Here is how we do it: Subtracting that 604 from 2520, we get 1916, but we must add 1 for no year zero, resulting in 1917. Therefore 1917 A.D. is 2520 years from 604 B.C.

Do you know the story of the miraculous deliverance of Jerusalem? General Allenby was driving up the Gaza coast for days and days against the Turkish army but was not making any headway. An American missionary went to him one night and showed from the Bible that Joshua had taken another route. Joshua led the Children of Israel around the east side of the Dead Sea, and crossed the Jordan from the East near Jericho. General Allenby did just that. He left enough of his troops to keep the Turks engaged but took a good army around the east of the Dead Sea. He crossed the Jordan near the place marked by the famous Allenby bridge today, came by Jericho, and got up on the Mount of Olives just East of Jerusalem, overlooking the city. The next morning a lone Turkish soldier rode out with a white flag, surrendering the city. All without a shot being fired. This story is now a matter of history.

Guinness recognized that the political power of the Pope had endured about 1260 years or about thirteen centuries. He also recognized that the Mohammedans had dominated the Middle East, including Palestine, for about thirteen centuries. His actual computations were far more detailed than these general statements, of course. When general Allenby received the surrender of the city of Jerusalem in 1917, he found the coins in use there bore the date 1335. It was the year 1335 on the Mohammedan calendar, which means it was 1335 years, using a lunar calendar, since 622 A.D., the year which begins all Mohammedan reckoning.

Twenty-five centuries after the setting up of the Babylonian succession of Gentile world powers, we see the breaking up of the old Holy Roman Empire in Europe through two world wars. Guinness traces many more pairs of events separated by this twenty-five century interval. Now these time cycles have almost run out. If so, what does that leave us for the future? Not much. Are we now in the time of the end when the coming of Christ is so near that no further chronological consideration is applicable? Who knows when the last human soul will be brought into the Body of Christ? That day and hour knoweth no man. But to believers it will not be unexpected. Read the fifth chapter of I Thessalonians. In the meantime, we patiently watch and pray, keeping our lamps well supplied and our wicks trimmed, because it is very late.

The men who died from the time of Wycliffe on believed they were living in prophetic history. They identified the apostate faith and the desolating Power. Read the notes on church history in Halley's Bible Handbook, or Halley's comments on the Book of Revelation, particularly the thirteenth chapter of Revelation. Halley claims that during a period of about 300 years, the "church" put to death 50 million martyrs. These men went gallantly, bravely, and faithfully to their death for the sake of the truth. These men believed they were living in prophetic times. Do we have that kind of faith today? Have you read Foxe's *Book of Martyrs?*

In the twelfth chapter of Ezekiel we read, beginning with the twenty-first verse, "And the word of the Lord came unto me, saying, Son of Man, what is that proverb that ye have in the land of Israel, saying, The days are prolonged and every vision faileth? Tell them therefore, Thus saith the Lord God; I will make this proverb to cease, and they shall no more use it as a proverb in Israel; but say unto them, The days are at hand, and the effect of every vision. For there shall be no more any vain vision nor flattering divination within the house of Israel. For I am the Lord: I will speak, and the word that I shall speak shall come to pass; it shall be no more prolonged: for in your days, O rebellious house, I will say the word, and will perform it, saith the Lord God. Again, the word of the Lord came unto me, saying Son of Man, behold, they of the house of Israel say, The vision that he seeth is for many days to come, and he prophesieth of the times that are far off. Therefore say unto them, thus saith the Lord God; There shall none of my words be prolonged anymore, but the word which I have spoken, shall be done, saith the Lord God."

We are not dealing with an imaginary future history. The Word of God deals with history NOW. We are in it. It is nearly midnight on God's Clock of Ages.

BIBLIOGRAPHY

1. Barton, Harold Edwin. *It's Here: The Time of the End.* New York. Exposition Press. 1963.
2. Guinness, H. Grattan. *Light for the Last Days.* London. Morgan and Scott, LTD. 1917.
3. Guinness, H. Grattan. *The Approaching End of the Age.* London. Marshal Morgan and Scott LTD. 1913.
4. Guinness, H. Grattan. *The Divine Plan of the Ages.* Brooklyn, New York. Dawn Publishers. 1937.

Chapter 11

Reformation: Part B

The Protestant Reformation was based upon two propositions:

I. The re-discovery of the foundation of salvation in God's grace which is justification by faith alone.

II. The identification of an apostate priesthood headed up by the Papacy as the subject powers described in the Bible by Daniel, Paul and John.

Associated with the first proposition is the totality of all the doctrinal disputes of the Reformation period. The Reformation leaders broke with the Roman church with respect to a great array of doctrinal issues. Included in the list would be the mediatorial position of the priesthood, the substance of the communion, the efficacy of baptism, the sale of indulgencies, auricular confessions, worship of relics, absolution, purgatory, prayers to the saints and the primacy of the Bishop of Rome. We used to hear of these doctrinal matters in sermons delivered from the pulpits of the land when our churches observed Reformation Sunday. Few observe it any longer. The debates, writings, public speeches, pleadings, and testimonies of men like Wycliff, Luther, Calvin, Knox, and a host of others, stalwarts of the true faith, resulted in open hostilities and persecutions. These more familiar aspects of the struggle may be designated as Reformation: Part A.

Now Reformation: Part B is another matter. It is less familiar. It includes the understanding of the Reformers regarding the Prophetic Scriptures. John Wycliff's translation of the Bible from the Latin Vulgate into vernacular English touched off an explosion of knowledge unparalleled in human history. Never before did the common people have such access to the Word of God. This access to the Holy Scriptures by the laity was bitterly opposed by the entrenched priestly establishment who considered itself as the sole guardian of the Bible which was not to fall into the hands of the unenlightened populace. But into the hands of the people it fell, through the studious efforts of Wycliff, Tyndale, Luther, Coverdale, King James and others.

The first book of the Bible translated by Wycliff was the Book of Revelation. In his studies, Wycliff recognized certain parallels or correspondences between the words of the Scriptures and the events of Wycliff's own times. He noticed the description of the great whore of Babylon and the Beast upon which she rode, and realized that the unbridled apostate ecclesiastical system ruling in Rome fitted this description. There was correspondence also with the Little Horn of Daniel and the Man of Sin of Paul in II Thessalonians. He applied the name Antichrist to all the Popes collectively.

A word of explanation concerning the term "Antichrist". It has been used for many centuries. Its only Biblical use is in the first two Epistles of John. In I John 2:18, the writer says "Ye have heard that (the) Antichrist shall come, even now there are many antichrists; whereby we know that it is the last time." Where did anybody ever hear anything about any antichrist? Christ himself did not use the term. Neither did Paul, not even once. John also wrote the Book of Revelation, but we look in vain for the term in that Book. It is not there.

The concept seems to have originated in the dualism in Zoroastrianism, the religion of Persia. Zoroaster, in about the 6th century B.C., taught that the world is in conflict due to the everlasting cosmic battle going on between good and evil. The god of evil is coeternal with and equal in power to the god of good, and this dualism accounts for the conflicts of human existence. It appealed to the popular mind as an explanation of human nature and human struggles. This belief was probably absorbed by the Jewish captives in Babylon and Persia, and was reinforced by the incursion of the Parsees into middle Eastern countries about the 3rd century B.C. It became part of Rabinnical teaching in about the 2nd century B.C. and was already wide spread in early Christian times. It is well known that the Roman church applied Christian terminology to deep-rooted or long standing popular but pagan beliefs.

Now John says, if we might paraphrase, "You have heard about this Antichrist business, but let me tell you something. There are a lot of them. I know because they left us. They denied that Jesus is the Christ, so that makes them antichrists." (vs 22) He was trying to dispel a popular myth by using a bad name to identify the numerous opposers of the true Gospel. The term is used again in I John 4:3 and II John:17, and nowhere else in the entire Bible!

The application of the term "the Antichrist" to Daniel's "Little Horn", Paul's "Man of Sin", or the 2nd beast of Rev. 13, is nothing more than conjecture or inference in the mind of some readers. It is not based upon any explicit statement of Scripture.

However, the damage has been done, and the term has been used in all the centuries of Christian history with scarcely a challenge. The Reformers were almost unanimous in their application of the name "Antichrist" to the succession of popes referred to collectively as the Papacy. The short history of the popes in Halley's Bible Handbook (early editions) will show the Reformers were justified.

According to Halley, the popes indulged themselves in immorality of unimaginable depravity. When they were challenged, opponents were quickly disposed of by the subservient secular authorities who were totally dependent upon the priesthood. The succession of popes occupying the seat of universal authority in Rome was recognized as the apostate remnant of the last of the chain of empires foretold by Daniel and John. The correspondence between prophecy as prediction and history as fulfillment was inescapable.

Wycliff, Luther, Knox, and others accused the Papacy of all the wrongs and excesses of the Man of Sin in II Thessalonians. The reason this identification could not have been made in earlier centuries was simple. The historical events portrayed by the prophet had not happened yet. By the time of Luther, 1400 years had passed since the end of the age of the Apostles. Much had happened in those intervening centuries. The mighty worldwide Roman empire had fallen. Out of its fragmented debris another world power had arisen, claiming supreme authority over nations, kings, and priests. This new power had grown corrupt. Its leaders even gave Christian labels to many of the persistent practices and beliefs carried over from a pagan polytheistic past.

Luther nailed his 95 propositions to the door of the church in Wittenberg. Calvin elevated theology to the realm of sublime truth beyond the limit of human experience. Knox thundered his denunciation of papal impieties and became precipitated into a position of leadership in a struggle for a return to Biblical Christianity. The excesses of papal immorality became scandalous. The popes were openly accused of sin and infidelity. Churchman after churchman indicted them. One pope was driven from Rome by an angry populace. Dr. Edwin Froom, in his four volume work, *The Prophetic Faith of Our Fathers,* gives many examples from the writings of the Reformation leaders. In the following citations, all from Volume II, only page numbers will be noted.

Martin Luther's comment on Daniel 12.4 concerning the sealing of the book, said, "This is the work which we are doing at the present time. And as formerly stated, prophecies can only be perfectly understood after they have been fulfilled." (page 272)

Luther commented on the papacy in a family letter in 1540, saying, "Oh, Christ, my Lord, look down upon us and bring upon us thy day of judgment, and destroy the brood of Satan in Rome. There sits the man, of whom the Apostle Paul wrote that he will oppose and exalt himself above all that is called God, that Man of Sins, that Son of Perdition. What else is papal power but sin and corruption? It leads souls to destruction under thine own name. O Lord! ... I hope the day of judgment is soon to dawn." (page 281)

Nicolaus von Amsdorf, a companion of Luther, wrote concerning the beast in Revelation, "The beast we know is the Roman Empire, which carries and supports the red Babylonian whore, which is the Papacy. The mark of the beast is the canons, the decrees and ceremonies of the Pope, and all the ecclesiastical traditions concerning food, drink, and dress, singing, reading, and other childish things which have nothing to do with, nor belong to, the Kingdom of God, which is true Christianity." (page 306)

John Bale, a bishop in Ireland, wrote in the sixteenth century, "The great antichrist of Europe is the king of faces, the prince of hypocrisy, the man of sin, the father of errors, and the master of lies, the Romish pope." Again, Bale wrote,"No abomination nor mystery of iniquity, as Paul calleth it, was ever found in these kingdoms, but now reigneth manifold in the detestable papacy or monstrous kingdom of antichrist, as all the world may see." (pages 598-599)

After Archbishop Thomas Cranmer was condemned to death by fire, he repented of the recantations he had written, and with firmness he wrote, "And forasmuch as my hand offended, writing contrary to my heart, my hand shall first be punished therefore: for, may I come to the fire, it shall be first burned. ... And as for the pope, I refuse him as Christ's enemy, and antichrist with all his false doctrine." (pages 390-391)

Throughout Tyndale's writings there is frequent reference to the papacy as the whore of Babylon. In his *Obedience of Christian Man,* Volume I, page 191, we read"And they have set up that great idol, the whore of Babylon, antichrist of Rome, whom they call pope; and have conspired against all commonwealths, and have made them a several kingdom, wherein it is lawful, unpunished, to work all abomination." (page 356)

John Foxe, who wrote the Book of Martyrs, applied the prophecy of the second beast of Revelation 13 to the bishop of Rome when he wrote "The description of this second beast being well viewed, it cannot be avoided, but needs must be applied to the Bishop of Rome, and to none other; as by History, and order of times is evident to be proved. For who else representeth the horns of the Lamb of God which taketh away the sins of the world, but only he? Who speaketh with the voice of the Dragon so proudly as he?" (page 416)

Edwin Sandys, archbishop of York, toward the end of the sixteenth century, wrote a scathing denunciation of the papacy. "This is our apostasy. We have foresaken him who has forsaken

God, and whom God hath forsaken: we have left that man of sin, that rose-colored harlot with whom the kings of the earth have committed fornication, that triple-crowned beast, that double-sworded tyrant, that thief and murderer, who hath robbed so many souls of salvation, and sucked so much innocent blood of christian martyrs, that adversary unto Christ, that pretensed vicar, who hath displaced the person, not only taking upon him Christ's room and office, but also boasting himself as if he were a god, and being content of his parasites so to be called. Daniel in his prophecies, Paul in his epistles, and John in his revelations, have most lively described and pointed him forth even as it were with the finger." (page 420)

John Knox, drawn into a dispute in which he defended the position of John Rough, made a public declaration concerning the church at Rome. Knox declared in part, "As for your Roman Church, as it is now corrupted, and the Authority thereof, wherein stands the hope of your Victory, I no more doubt but that it is the synagogue of Satan; and the head thereof, called the Pope to be that man of sin of whom the Apostle speaketh, then that I doubt that Jesus Christ suffered by the procurement of the visible Church of Jerusalem. Yea, I offer myself by work or writing, to prove the Roman Church this day farther to degenerate from the purity which was in the days of the Apostles." (page 452)

The answer of the Roman church was vigorous. It consisted of several parts.

1. The Society of Jesus, or the Order of the Jesuits, organized by Ignatius Loyola, was formally recognized in 1540 as the teaching and preaching arm of the Roman Church. The Jesuits were able scholars who dedicated their efforts to the maintenance of the Roman Church as the only authority to be obeyed.
2. The decrees of the Council of Trent, concluded in 1563, established the doctrinal statements which have remained the unyielding positions of the Roman Church since.
3. The introduction of the two interpretations of the prophecies of the Bible which pointed away from the Papacy as the ful-

fillment of certain prophecies.

4. The establishment of the Index which proscribed all books and publications containing any accusations regarding the papacy in all writings of scholars among the clergy.
5. The establishment of the Holy Office, or Inquisition, as the prosecuting arm of the Roman Church against all heretics. This effort accounted for the slaughter of 50 million martyrs over a period of about 300 years. See Halley.

Thus a counterreformation was relentlessly pursued by ecclesiastical Rome to put down this rebellion of the Protestants. The preaching of the Jesuits, the Council of Trent, and the Index properly belong to the doctrinal controversy we have called Reformation: Part A. The alternate prophetic interpretations are the essential elements of Reformation: Part B, and the persecutions resulting from the Inquisition properly belong to both parts.

One of the ingredients of the prophetic teaching of the Reformers was the insistence that the time periods stated in the prophecies of the Bible were themselves evidence that the historical occurrences of their day were indeed the subject of the revelation of sacred writings. This argument rested upon the recognition that the time periods of the prophecies were presented in symbolic form according to which one day in prophecy is equivalent to one year of actual history. Thus the 1260 days of prophecy would stand for 1260 years of history. More than 30 of the Reformation scholars agreed with this interpretation, including Wycliff, Brute, de Cusa, Luther, Bulinger, Foxe, Napier, Brightman, Mede and Isaac Newton. This thesis was used to fortify the identification of the evil powers of the prophets with the apostate church.

The two alternate interpretations of the prophecies of the Bible were designed to eliminate the happenings of current history from any consideration whatever. The first, proposed by the Jesuit Alcazar, claimed that the historical events discussed by the prophets were already past; they were completed in the persecutions of the Christians by the Roman Emperors during the early centuries of the church. It was all accomplished; finished. It was past history. This is known as the Preterist interpretation of prophecy.

The second theory, developed by another Jesuit, Ribera, proposed that the events foretold by the prophets were still in the future. They would not occur until a short period of time just before the Second Advent of Christ. Instead of looking for fulfillment in the then current affairs of the church, the prophecies spoke of a time yet to come. Cardinal Bellarmine in the late 16th century, took these ideas of Ribera, and wove them into a complete system of prophetic interpretation known today as Futurism. This view regards the time periods as literal days and calls for a seven year period of world trouble immediately preceding the Second Coming of Christ. This view is widely held by evangelical Christians today who are not aware of its historic origins in the Roman church.

If you were to write the Christian History of the World, what would you select as the significant highlights of the history of Western Civilization during the past four or five centuries?

First was the Reformation itself. The Reformation occurred primarily among the northern tribes and nations of Europe. Multitudes of people became Christians under the preaching of the defenders of apostolic faith. Bibles proliferated. Marytrs suffered death. Kings were enthroned and dethroned. Battles were fought. Europe was in turmoil. In the end, northern Europe was christianized, but outside the Roman church. The Bible, not some ecclesiastical despot, became accepted as the final authority and arbiter of the affairs of faith and practice.

The Reformation affected the political, social, and religious life of Norway, Sweden, Denmark, Germany, Holland, Switzerland, England and Scotland. Thus the Reformation was political and racial as well as religious. In retrospect, the Reformation was an ethnic rebellion against a corrupt Mediterranean civilization. The fair-haired, blue-eyed barbarians of the northern forests, who had once been Roman slaves, had conquered. It was culture against culture, race against race, and nation against a super national authority. It was the coming into being of a religious community of believers with a common faith and trust in the Holy Bible. True, there were continuing disputes, but the elements of community have always existed among these kindred people. Rome exercised political control over some of these countries for intervals of time afterward, but in the main, northern Europe is not Roman today.

Another significant outcome of the Reformation was the multiplication of Christian literature. Sermons, books, and commentaries became increasingly available. The first translations of the Bible were handwritten, but the printing press made possible the spread of ideas throughout all Europe. The Bible became sought after as the pinnacle of all learning. Protestant Theology became the dominant public philosophy which shaped the lives of men and nations.

The world was exploding. The leading nations of Europe sent out fleets of ships to explore new lands, new frontiers, new colonies. North and South America offered the most promising and profitable opportunities.

The Spaniards came with a sword, looking for gold. The French came with their traps, looking for furs. The English came with a rifle, an axe, a hoe, a package of garden seed, a Bible, and a pregnant wife. They came to stay. They were looking for the Kingdom of God. They said so. This story is told in ***The Light and The Glory,*** written by Peter Marshall and David Manuel.

In South America, Christianity accompanied or followed the sword. It was established by coercion and declaration. The authoritarianism of the Roman church could account for much of what we see throughout South and Central America today.

On the other hand, it was Biblical Christianity which accompanied the Pilgrims and Puritans who settled the shores of North America. It was the Bible which gave to the English settlements of New England and Virginia their concepts of law and freedom. It was the teachings of the English Christian philosophers which inspired them to perform the impossible. The United States of

America arose as a new nation on the earth, "conceived in liberty and dedicated to the proposition that all men are created equal."

In the late 18th Century, William Carey enlisted as a missionary to go out as an evangelist to foreign lands. This marked the beginning of the modern world wide missionary effort of Protestant churches which continues to this day. As teeming millions multiply, so do the efforts of mission boards and evangelists, but the efforts stem from those countries in which Protestant Christianity prevails.

Bibliography

1. Clouse, Robert G. *The Meaning of the Millennium.* Downers Grove, Illinois. Inter Varsity Press. 1977.
2. D'Aubinge, J. H. Merle. *History of the Reformation* (in four volumes). New York. American Tract Society. 1848.
3. Froom, LeRoy Edwin. *The Prophetic Faith of Our Fathers* (in four volumes). Washington. Review and Herald Publishing Association. 1950.
4. King, Marie Genert. *Foxe's Book of Martyrs.* Old Tappan, New Jersey. Fleming H. Revell Company. 1968.
5. Waddington, George. *A History of the Church.* New York. Harper and Brothers. 1878.

Chapter 12
The Treasures of Joseph

Joseph is one of the most remarkable men in all of Holy Scripture. His character is unimpeachable. The story of his life reads like a fairy tale or a Horatio Alger book. He lived from humble beginnings to become the second in office to the ruler of a powerful nation. His wisdom averted a great natural catastrophe. He is remembered as a great provider of the people.

There are many analogies between the life of Joseph and the life of Jesus. In the old Scofield Bible we find the following seven analogies:

1. Joseph and Jesus were each the objects of a father's special love. Genesis 37:3 and John 5:20.
2. They were both hated by their brothers. Genesis 37:4 and John 15:25.
3. Each made claims which were rejected by their brothers. Genesis 37:8 and Matthew 21:37-39.
4. Their brothers conspired to kill them. Genesis 37:18 and Matthew 26:3,4.
5. They were both killed by their own brothers (in figure). Genesis 37:24 and Matthew 26:63-66.
6. Each became a blessing to Gentiles. Genesis 41:1-45 and Acts 15:14.
7. Each reconciled their brothers to himself and provided for their future. Genesis 45:1-15 and Hebrews 2:17

To those seven can be added a list of an additional seven:

1. Both sojourned in a foreign land. Genesis 39 through Genesis 50 and Phillippians 2:5-8
2. Both were the first born of a favorite wife. Genesis 30:24 and Revelation 12:1-3
3. Both went from humility to great glory and honor. Genesis 41:41-43 and Hebrews 2:9.
4. Both announced his own death. Genesis 50:24 and Mark 9:31.

5. Both died in Egypt. Genesis 50:26 and Revelation 11:8. ("Egypt, where also our Lord was crucified")
6. Both had many descendants. Genesis 48:15,16, and Romans 8:29.
7. Their descendents received a rich inheritance. Genesis 49:22-26 and 1 Peter 1:4.

By these comparisons, we see that Joseph was a savior to his own people; but in a far greater measure Jesus was a savior to his people. The salvation wrought by Jesus differed in kind and extent than that wrought by Joseph. Thus Joseph was a mere type of Christ and is not to be compared to Christ as an equal.

The story of Joseph really begins with the story of the courtship of his father, Jacob. When Jacob went back into the East county to obtain a wife from among his own kind of people, he saw and fell in love with Rachel, the daughter of his uncle Laban. Jacob worked seven years for his uncle in order to obtain Rachel for a bride. However, when the expected moment came Laban provided Leah, the elder sister of Rachel, with the excuse that it was the custom that the elder sister should marry first. Jacob loved Rachel so much that he worked an additional seven years in order to obtain her also. It was Leah who gave birth to six sons of Jacob, but Rachel was barren. Following these six, there were two sons born by Rachel's hand-maid, Bilhah, and then two sons born by Leah's hand-maid, Zilpah. After these ten sons were born, God remembered Rachel and she conceived and gave birth to Joseph, who became Jacob's favorite son. When Jacob returned to the land of Caanan, Rachel died when she gave birth to Benjamin as they came to Bethlehem. Thus Jacob had twelve sons, only two of which were Rachel's.

Jacob loved Joseph more than any of his other children and his preferential treatment of Joseph provoked the other sons to jealousy. We read the story in Genesis 37.

There are several significant events in the life of Joseph. He developed an ability to interpret dreams. His brothers sold him as a slave in Egypt. He was falsely accused of wrong doing by his master's wife and thrown into jail. Joseph had an opportunity to interpret the dreams of two of his fellow prisoners and accurately predict their fate. One was restored to his position as butler to Pharaoh. When Pharaoh became troubled by a dream, the butler remembered Joseph and Pharaoh called for Joseph to interpret his dream. Joseph's interpretation predicted seven years of plenty and seven years of famine and suggested to Pharaoh that he prepare for the famine by storing food during the years of plenty. Pharaoh agreed and gave Joseph the job of administering this program. Joseph was elevated in position and became second only to Pharaoh in all of Egypt.

Into this situation Joseph's family re-enters the story. The famine extended into the land of Canaan. Jacob heard of the food available in Egypt and sent ten of his sons to Egypt to buy grain. They had to deal with Joseph, who recognized them, but concealed his own identity from them. After several emotion-laden encounters with them, he revealed himself to them and persuaded them to bring his father Jacob into Egypt where Joseph could care for them throughout the remainder of the famine.

Jacob recognized that Joseph could never again become a member of the family because of his exalted position in Egypt. In the place of Joseph, Jacob adopted the two sons of Joseph into the family as full-fledged sons. This was a private affair, between Jacob and Joseph, and we read the account of this transaction in Chapter 48 of Genesis. It was not necessary that the boys be present. In this act of adoption, Jacob made mention of the promises of the land and of the multiplicity of decendants. Also, by this act of adoption, Jacob had thirteen sons, counting Ephraim and Manasseh as full sons in the place of Joseph.

In the latter half of this same chapter, a wonderful ceremony is recorded. Joseph presented his two sons to Jacob who proceeded to bless them. This is a very special blessing, and it is to be noted that the name Israel is used on this occasion for Joseph's-father. Therefore, this blessing is of covenant significance.

The blessing was in two parts. First, there was a blessing pronounced on Ephraim and Manasseh together, with a mention of Abraham and Isaac and the promise of a multitude of children.

Then there was a blessing pronounced upon Ephraim and Manasseh separately, with the pre-eminence given to Ephraim the younger brother. To Ephraim, Israel gave the blessing of a multitude of nations and to Manasseh the blessing of a great nation. How can these blessings ever be realized by a small group of people in the land of Palestine today?

Jacob, knowing that he was about to die, called all his sons together and orally gave his last will and testament. God had appeared personally to Abraham, Isaac and Jacob. He did not appear to the sons of Jacob. Therefore, this formal statement by Jacob constituted the official transfer of the promises of the Fathers to the sons of Jacob. In Genesis 49:1,2 we read, "And Jacob called unto his sons, and said, gather yourselves together, that I may tell you that which shall befall you in the last days. Gather yourselves together, and hear, ye sons of Jacob; and hearken unto Israel your father." Beginning with Reuben, the eldest son, Jacob prophesied what is to be the destiny of each of his twelve sons. Some of these statements are mixed blessings and trials, others are blessings of historical significance.

To Judah was passed the right to rule, in keeping with God's promise to Abraham that "kings shall be of thee," in Genesis 17:6. "The scepter shall not depart from Judah, nor a lawgiver from between his feet, until Shiloh come" are the words that Israel used in Genesis 49:10. The most prominent of these blessings is that given to Joseph in verses 22-26. We read, "Joseph is a fruitful bough, even a fruitful bough by a well; whose branches run over the wall." The blessing to Joseph thus begins with the blessing of a multitude of children; which had already been passed on to Ephraim and Manasseh the sons of Joseph in the previous chapter. The blessing of Joseph continues in verse 23, "The archers have sorely grieved him, and shot at him, and hated him: But his bow abode in strength, and the arms of his hands were made strong by the hands of the mighty God of Jacob; from thence is the shepherd, the stone of Israel: Even by the God of thy father who shall help thee." This portion of the blessing speaks of conflict or military activity in which the people of

Joseph would be aided by the Almighty. Continuing in verse 25, we read "And by the Almighty, who shall bless thee with the blessings of heaven above, blessings of the deep that lieth under, blessings of the breasts, and of the womb." This certainly speaks of a favorable environment of land and sea in which the people would flourish and produce many offspring, fulfilling the promise of a multitude of seed.

The next verse is of particular importance. Jacob said, in verse 26, "The blessings of thy father have prevailed above the blessings of my progenitors unto the utmost bound of the everlasting hills: they shall be on the head of Joseph, and on the crown of the head of him that was separate from his brethren." Who is "thy father?" It is Jacob himself who is speaking. Who are "my progenitors?" They are Isaac and Abraham, Jacob's father and grandfather. What does "prevail above" mean? Strong's concordance lists "exceed, make stronger, and confirm" as connotatons of this word "prevail". Thus this verse could be rendered, "The blessings that I, myself, now pronounce on you, Joseph, are greater, or greatly exceed, the blessings I received from my father Isaac and my grandfather Abraham." What a blessing! A blessing greater than that bestowed upon any of the other sons of Jacob. A blessing greater that Jacob himself had ever received. This puts Joseph and none other in the the main stream of the line through whom God is operating throughout history to fulfill God's program and purpose. Certainly, the promise of the one seed, the king, was given to Judah, but the greater portion of the "promises to the fathers" involving the many seed and material well-being went to Joseph.

In I Chronicles 5:1 there begins an enumeration of the families of Israel, beginning with Reuben, the eldest son. We read, "Now the sons of Reuben the first born of Israel, for he was the first born; but, forasmuch as he defiled his father's bed, his birthright was given unto the sons of Joseph, the son of Israel." Reuben had disqualified himself from the birthright, the right of the eldest son to inherit his father's estate, by having an affair with Bilhah, his father's concubine, who was the mother of Dan and

Naphtali, two half-brothers of Reuben. Since the eldest was disqualified, it would be natural to suppose that the right of inheritance would pass to the second son of Leah, who would be Simeon. Jacob decreed otherwise. The birthright passed from Reuben, the first born of Leah, to Joseph, the first born of Rachel, Jacob's favorite wife. The passage in I Chronicles 5 continues: "The genealogy is not to be reckoned after the birthright. For Judah prevailed above his brethren, and of him came the chief ruler; but the birthright was Joseph's." Here is a clear distinction between the scepter and the birthright. We should never expect to find the promises of either fulfilled in the other. These two parts of the promises made to the fathers should never be confused.

Neither should we confuse the birthright and the blessing. Esau, the elder brother of Jacob, inherited the birthright which was a legal matter. The birthright was his to have and to hold. It was also his to sell, which he did to his brother Jacob for a bowl of stew. However, the blessing was something for the father to bestow upon the sons of his choice. It was Isaac's wish to bestow this blessing upon Esau, whom he favored above Jacob, but Rebekah contrived for Jacob to disguise himself as Esau in order to obtain this blessing. When Isaac pronounced his blessing upon Jacob, it was irrevocable. He could not withdraw it and give it again to Esau. See Genesis 27:26-42.

Joseph was the eldest son of Rachel, Jacob's beloved wife and to him was assigned the birthright. The blessing given to Joseph by Jacob was in addition to the birthright, and Jacob pronounced these covenant blessings upon Joseph in the verses we have been considering in Genesis 49. Remember that the scepter, the birthright, and the blessings are three distinct aspects of the promises God gave to Abraham, Isaac, and Jacob. Although all the sons of Jacob share in a general way the benefits of the promises, Judah and Joseph are selected for special functions in God's program.

Let it be repeated and emphasized that Jacob's blessings upon his sons and grandsons took place several centuries before the old covenant at Mt. Sinai and a thousand years before there was a Jew!

We encounter a similar situation again in Deuteronomy 33, when Moses blessed the tribes of Israel when they were ready to enter the promised land after their wilderness years. By this time, the theocracy had been established and the tribe of Levi was selected as the servant tribe for the operation of the nation. Therefore, Levi is given some special attention on this occasion, but this was to be temporary as the Book of Hebrews explains.

Again, as in Genesis 49, Joseph is prominent. In Deuteronomy 33:13 we begin to read, "And of Joseph, he said, Blessed of the Lord be his land, for the precious things of heaven, for the dew, and for the deep that coucheth beneath, and for the precious fruits brought forth by the sun, and for the precious things put forth by the moon, and for the chief things of the ancient mountains, and for the precious things of the lasting hills, and for the precious things of the earth and fulness thereof." All these are promises of great material abundance, involving wealth from sea, sky, and land. Great agricultual wealth and great mineral wealth are here promised.

The blessing of Moses continues in verse 16. "And for the good will of him that dwelt in the bush." This may refer to good relationship with less fortunate peoples in distant lands. We read on, in verse 16, "Let the blessing come upon the head of Joseph and upon the top of the head of him that was separated from his brethren." This repeats the words in the blessing pronounced upon Joseph by his father Jacob, showing the favored position of Joseph in the distribution of the promised blessings.

In verse 17, we read, "His glory is like the firstling of his bullock, and his horns are like the horns of unicorns: with them he shall push the people to the ends of the earth." The word for "unicorn" is RAME, which is a very large wild bull, second only to the elephant in size, which became extinct in parts of Asia Minor long ago. It was noted for its ferocity and strength. The word does not refer to the unicorn of mythology. This passage symbolizes an aggressive, expanding, military power which subdues many weaker people throughout the earth.

Finally, in verse 17, we read, "And they are the ten thousands of Ephraim and they are the thousands of Manasseh." This much repeats the blessing of the multitude of seed which was transferred to Joseph and through him to his sons as mentioned before in Genesis 48.

It is interesting to observe that in this blessing of the tribes by Moses, the promise of kingship is not repeated to Judah, although there is no mention of any repeal. On the other hand, there is an indication in verse 7 that Judah will be in some kind of trouble and be in need of rejoining his kindred.

In this study it has been shown that the great and wonderful promises made by Almighty God to Abraham, Isaac, and Jacob were divided among the sons of Jacob and as a consequence distributed among the tribes of Israel. The promises pertaining to the scepter the king, the chief ruler, the lawgiver, and the one seed through whom all the nations of the earth were to be blessed where all given to Judah. See Genesis 22:18 and Galatians 3:16. The promises pertaining to material prosperity, military strength, and the multitude of seed who were to be the servant people to bring the blessing to the nations were all given to Joseph.

These two main streams of covenant blessings provided the natural cleavage in later years which became the basis for the division of the kingdom following the death of Solomon into the House of Israel and the House of Judah. This division was no accident of history nor was it solely the failure of men to live amicably with one another. In I Kings 12:24, we read, "For this thing is from me". God ordained this division of the people into two groups according to the division of the blessings of Judah and Joseph in order to work out his purpose in history. These two groups have different histories, different promises, different functions, and different destinies.

"But the birthright was Joseph's," we read. Not only the birthright, but great and wonderful promises of blessings were given to Joseph. Promises of greatness and wealth. Promises of strength and power. Promises of abundance and treasure. Since the people of Joseph are never called Jews in the Bible, then how can we expect that these promises can ever be fulfilled by a people to whom they were never given?

The last verse in the Book of Genesis reads, "So Joseph died, being a hundred and ten years old: and they embalmed him, and he was put in a coffin in Egypt." This is where the majority of Christians leave him: dead, in a coffin in Egypt. We shall see.

Chapter 13

O, Rachel, Don't You Weep!

When the ten brothers of Joseph came to Egypt to buy grain, they faced Joseph without recognizing him. Perhaps he now wore a beard, or wore an Egyptian mask or headdress which covered his face. It is said that he made himself strange to them. Joseph certainly recognized them and accused them of being spies.

They protested, saying, in Genesis 42:13, "Thy servants are twelve brethren, the sons of one man in the land of Canaan; and behold, the youngest is this day with our father, and one is not." The youngest would be Benjamin who was still at home with their father Jacob. The one who was not, was Joseph, standing before them. They thought he had disappeared into slavery, and they would never see him again. Their claim to be twelve reflects the strong family bonds amongst kindred in those days. Joseph was very much alive and in a position to help them. After several emotional encounters with his brothers, Joseph revealed himself to them and effected a complete family reunion.

In the Gospel of Matthew, when King Herod ordered the slaughter of the infants in Bethlehem, Matthew quotes a passage from Jeremiah concerning the children of Rachel. This quotation includes the words, "Rachel weeping for her children, and would not be comforted, because they are not." Turning to Jeremiah 31:15, we read, "Thus saith the Lord, a voice was heard in Ramah, lamentation, and bitter weeping; Rachel weeping for her children refused to be comforted for her children, because they were not."

What does this have to do with Bethlehem? Ramah was a town in the tribal territory of Benjamin. Benjamin was born at Bethlehem when Rachel died. It was Rachel, not her children, who died at Bethlehem. Rachel died where David was born, and Rachel died where Jesus was born.

What about Rachel's children? Rachel's children were Joseph and Benjamin. What does it mean to say "they were not"? What did it mean when Joseph's brothers said, "and one is not"? These expressions have the connotation of appearances, of the obvious, and not necessarily the reality. Certainly, in the case of Joseph, the reality was that Joseph was standing there in front of them. Then what about the case of Rachel's children?

When we turn to the source of the quotation in Jeremiah 31:15 and continue reading, we find, in verses 16 and 17, "Thus saith the Lord, Refrain thy voice from weeping, and thine eyes from tears; for thy work shall be rewarded, saith the Lord; and they shall come again to their own border." This does not sound as if Rachel's children would cease to exist, but merely that their existence would be unrecognized for a time.

This passage in Jeremiah continues, speaking of Ephraim as the "dear son" of the Lord and yet to be restored along with Judah. For a time, God will sow them in the earth before he restores them to their land. Ephraim is the name used in this passage to denote the people of Israel other than those of Judah. The Bible frequently uses the name Joseph and Ephraim when it speaks about the northern people; not on every page nor in every breath, but enough to show they are synonymous. All of Hosea is a message addressed to the people of the northern tribes under the name "Ephraim".

How did God "sow them in the earth"? He scattered them among the nations. He covered them as seed is covered. He sowed them where they would remain undetected until the coming forth of the green leaf. Although Israel disappeared from the pages of history, Israel was never lost. God hid them. They were lost to public view, but always known to God. To the world, "they were not".

There never was a tribe of Joseph. The expression is used once in the Bible, in Numbers 13:11, which reads, "of the tribe of Joseph, namely, of the tribe of Manasseh, Gaddi the son of Susi". In this listing of the spies sent into Canaan, the tribe of Ephraim was mentioned earlier in verse 8. A similar expression is used in

Numbers 1:32, which says, "of the children of Joseph, namely, of the children of Ephraim." Because Jacob had adopted Ephraim and Manasseh as sons in the place of Joseph, then Joseph was represented among the tribes of Israel by the tribe of Ephraim and the tribe of Manasseh.

There was, however, the House of Joseph. This name was used for the tribes of Joseph's sons together, but in the latter history of the people of Israel in Canaan, the House of Joseph came to mean all the tribes of Israel other than Judah and Levi. Perhaps this came about because of the growing strength of the tribe of Ephraim, which was the dominant leader of the people in the northern tribes of Israel. Within the term "House of Joseph" all the other eleven tribes were included. Read the story of Shimei of the tribe of Benjamin who identified himself as belonging to the House of Joseph in 2 Samuel 15 and 16. In I Kings 11 and 12, we are told of the revolt led by Jeroboam which resulted in ten of the eleven tribes of the House of Joseph splitting away from Judah, the tribe of King Rehoboam. Benjamin was the only tribe of the eleven which remained loyal to Judah.

In many Old Testament passages it can be seen that Joseph-Israel or Ephraim-Israel came into the blessings made to the fathers, but usually in some limited way.

True, they had two kings of the line of Judah, namely, David and Solomon. However, from the death of Solomon until the Assyrian captivity no king of David reigned in the north. It is true, also, that David's kingdom extended from the Euphrates to the River of Egypt. This last is not a reference to the Nile, but to a smaller stream which separates Gaza from the Sinai peninsula. It is true that the tribe of Ephraim became very numerous and dominant among the people.

It is also true that when the people disobeyed God, worshipped other gods, and fell into idolatry, the punishment meted out involved these specific items of the covenant blessings. In Amos 4:6-10, we read, "And I also have given you cleanness of teeth in all your cities, and want of bread in all your places: yet have ye not returned unto me, saith the Lord. And also I have withholden the rain from you. I have simtten you with blasting and mildew: when your gardens and your vineyards and your fig trees and your olive trees increased, the palmer worm devoured them: yet have ye not returned unto me, saith the Lord. I have sent among you the pestilence after the manner of Egypt; your young men have I slain with the sword."

In Isaiah 24:3-6, we read, "The land shall be utterly emptied, and utterly spoiled for the Lord hath spoken this word. The earth mourneth and fadeth away, the haughty people of the earth do languish. The earth also is defiled under the inhabitants thereof; because they have transgressed the laws, changed the ordinances, broken the everlasting covenant. Therefore hath the curse devoured the earth, and they that dwell therein are desolate: therefore the inhabitants of the earth are burned, and few men left." Surely, the blessings upon the land were taken away.

In Hosea 9:13, 14, we read, "Ephraim--is planted in a pleasant place; but Ephraim shall bring forth his children to the murderer. Give them, O Lord, what wilt thou give? Give them a miscarrying womb and dry breasts." And in verse 16, "Yea, though they bring forth, yet will I slay even the beloved fruit of their womb." In Isaiah 1:9, we read, "Except the Lord of Hosts had left unto us a very small remnant, we should have been as Sodom, and we should have been like unto Gomorrah." In all these messages we see that God's punishment involved judgment with respect to the specific blessing of the multiplicity of seed. Did not Moses warn the people in Leviticus 26 that God would punish them when they disobeyed Him?

Just as emphatic as were the prophets in denouncing the people for their sins, so were they emphatic in their message of redemption and restoration. Not only emphatic, but exultant in their proclamation of God's final consumation of his purpose in Israel and Israel's glorious restoration. Paul tells us in Galatians 3:17, "And this I say that the covenant, that was confirmed before of God in Christ, the law, which was four hundred and thirty years after, cannot disannul, that it should make the promise of none effect." Although the Law would not hinder nor set aside the fulfillment of the promises, it is the Cross which makes fulfillment possible.

Jesus came to confirm the promises according to New Testament scripture. Romans 15:8 says, "Now I say that Jesus Christ was a minister of the circumcision for the truth of God to confirm the promises made unto the fathers." In Luke 1:54,55 we read, "He hath holpen his servant Israel in remembrance of his mercy; as he spoke to our fathers, to Abraham, and to his seed forever." Also, Zacharias exclaimed, in Luke 1:72, "To perform the mercy promised to our fathers, and to remember his holy covenant; the oath which he sware to our father Abraham." The coming of Jesus Christ, the "one seed" of Genesis 22:18 and Galatians 3:16, is the most essential part of the promises which God gave to Abraham. The entire program of redemption hinges upon the Cross.

During the period of history when Israel was entering the long-term punishment for their sins, the prophets, in addition to their indictment of the sinful people, almost in the same breath, proclaimed a bright future in which the promises would be realized. In Hosea 1:10, we read, "Yet the number of the children of Israel shall be as the sand of the sea, which cannot be measured nor numbered; and it shall come to pass, that in the place where it was said unto them, Ye are not my people, there is shall be said unto them, Ye are the sons of the living God."

In Isaiah 54:2,3 we read, "Enlarge the place of thy tent and let them stretch forth the curtains of thy habitations: spare not, lengthen thy cords and strengthen thy stakes; for thou shalt break forth on the right hand and on the left; and thy seed shall inherit the Gentiles, and make the desolate cities to be inhabited."

In Deuteronomy 32:8, we are told, "When the most high gave the nations their inheritance, when he separated the children of men, he set the bounds of the people according to the number of the children of Israel." And remember, this promise of the multiplicity of seed was given to Joseph and his sons Ephraim and Manasseh. Since the prophets speak of it as yet future, then in no way can we say this promise was fulfilled in Old Testament times.

The aggressiveness of the people of Israel, and of Joseph in particular, is to be one of their characteristics. In Numbers 23:24, Balaam prophecies, "Behold the people riseth up as a lion--he shall not lie down until he eat of the prey and drink the blood of the slain." Again, in Number 24:8, Balaam says, "He hath as it were the strength of a wild ox and he shall eat up the nations his adversaries, and break their bones in pieces and smite them through with arrows." The wild ox was the particular symbol for Joseph, and such military prowess is in the future of the people of Joseph. In Jeremiah 51:20, we read, "Thou art my battle axe and weapons of war."

The land will be restored. Because of the sins of the people, God put a curse on the land. Look at Jeremiah 44:22, "So that the Lord could no longer bear, because of the evil of your doings, and because of the abominations which ye have committed; therefore is your land a desolation, and an astonishment, and a curse, without an inhabitant, as at this day." In contrast to this, we read a song of joy when the land is restored. Isaiah 62:4 says, "Thou shalt no more be termed Forsaken: neither shall thy land any more be termed desolate: but thou shalt be called Hephzibah (my delight is in her), and thy land Beulah (married): for the Lord delighteth in thee, and thy land shall be married."

These examples involving people, power, and land show that God is not through with his people regarding the promises to the fathers. The people are yet to become a multitude of nations and people. They are still to become a strong force in the earth. And the very land given to Abraham by promise and confirmed by an oath of death in Genesis 15:17 shall yet be restored.

When?

When shall these promised blessings fall upon Israel, and upon the people of Joseph in particular? What further condition or contingency is necessarily required? God has done all he can do to take care of the sin and disobedience of his people. By his death on the cross he not only made atonement for sin, but as Husband-Redeemer, his death set free from the law his adulterous wife allowing her to remarry him in righteousness and newness of life. He came to save his people from their sin (Matthew 1:21). Why, then, are they not saved? Since "there remaineth no more sacrifice for sin" (Hebrews 10:26), then God has done all he can do to bring salvation and righteousness to his people.

The problem of the timing of the blessings upon the children of Israel was settled by Israel himself when he said, in Genesis 49:1, "that I may tell you that which shall befall you in the last days." The warning of Moses In Deuteronomy 4:27-31 includes the words, "And the Lord shall scatter you among the nations--but if from thence thou shalt seek the Lord thy God, thou shalt find him--when thou art in tribulation, and all these things are come upon thee, even in the latter days, if thou turn to the Lord thy God, and shalt be obedient unto his voice--He will not forsake thee--nor forget the covenant of thy fathers which he sware unto them." There are other Old Testament passages that speak of the "latter days" and the "last days" as the time for restoration of God's people Israel.

When are the "latter days" and the "last days"? The term "last days" is used in 2 Timothy 3:1, Hebrews 1:2, and 1 Peter 1:20, all referring to the time Christ was made manifest. The terms "last days" and "last time" are used in 2 Peter 3:3,4, 1 John 2:18 and Jude 18 to refer to still future events of the time of writing. Then the "latter days" or "last days" must refer to this present age between the two advents of Christ.

The people of Israel are to be called the Sons of God. Christians today are called the Sons of God. Then is Israel to be found among Christians? Why not? What is there to hinder?

The promised blessings of material well-being and power do not pertain to a millennial age of bliss and peace. We should see some fulfillment of them, therefore, in this present age. Neither are we to look for their fulfillment in the life of the people known as Jews in the world today. There is a vast difference between what Jewish scholars write and what Jewish politicians say about these matters. Beginning with Ezra and Nehemiah, then Josephus, and including the scholars who wrote the Jewish Encycolpedia, all agree that the Jews did not include the ten tribes of the House of Joseph. Ezekiel, in Chapter 37, prophesies the eventual reunion of the House of Joseph and the House of Judah. Since God divided them after the death of Solomon, then it will be God who will unite them under the King and Shepherd of Israel, even Christ. This reunion did not, nor will it ever, occur in some obscure or secret fashion. Concerning Ezekiel's vision of the two sticks, C.E. Scofield once wrote, "it is impossible seriously to pretend that this prophecy has ever been fulfilled in any sense." In The Pulpit Commentary, Volume 12, page 267, we find, "that Israel has never yet been made one nation upon the mountains of Israel, is incontestable."

In summary, the House of Joseph should receive its inheritance in this present age.

Joseph, in terms of his own life and in terms of the wonderful promises given to him, is a type or foreshadowing of what the people of Joseph are to be, are to do, and are to have. We should expect to find the people of Joseph in this right relationship to God, in a position of authority and power among the nations of the world, with surpluses and plenty, rich in natural resources, strong in military power, expanding throughout the earth, having appeared from out of a wilderness, with an obscure history and without traceable parentage, establishing themselves in a land of their own, an"appointed place", as God told David. There are the things that we might expect on the basis of our Bible study to characterize the people of Joseph in the "latter days".

Now there is such a people. There is a people in the world today whose past history is lost in considerable obscurity. There is a people who have such great agricultural wealth that the rest of the world is in poverty by comparison. There is a people that well-nigh have a monopoly on the mineral wealth of North America, South America, Europe, and Africa, leaving only Asia and the Far East to others. There is a people whose military might is greater than that of all other armies of all other nations in all of recorded history. There is such a people. There is a people who are Christian and are known to the rest of the world as Christian. There is a people whose destiny has been to bear witness of the

Christian faith to the rest of the world. There is a people blessed of God above all measure, more than all other people on the face of the earth. Blessed with natural resources, blessed with wealth, blessed with power, and blessed with faith.

Did you ever wonder who these people are? Well, did you ever look in the mirror? To show the relationship of scripture to history, what better hypothesis can we set forth to defend than that we are that people? We have been involved in a westward movement for centuries and centuries, starting in Media, the place where Israel was taken into captivity, sweeping across the northern shores of the Black Sea, up the Danube Valley, through the forests of Eastern Europe, skirting the fringes of the Roman Empire, converging on one little island in wave after wave, and later moving out from that spot to the whole world. We have spied out a vast new land, established a great civilization in what had been a wilderness. We have established in this land the greatest agricultural prosperity the world has ever known, and this great abundance is being produced by only 3 percent of our population. We have taken from the ground more mineral wealth in coal, oil, metals, and other valuable materials than all other peoples in all of history put together. These things were promised to the people of Joseph. If we are not these people, then why do we have these blessings?

We are a people who have unimaginable military might. Twice in this century we have rescued the world from evil men. Even in this generation we are pushing at the heathen in the ends of the earth in order that some men might have freedom. In none of our efforts have we sought territorial gain or the punishment of conquered people. The benign treatment we have given our enemies following military victory is unheard of in the annals of history. Our effort has been in behalf of freedom.

We are a people in whose heart is the law of God. It is built into our national life because it was in the hearts of those men who founded our nation. It has set the standards of our private and corporate behavior. This law of God is the touchstone by which we judge the increasing evil and lawlessness of our times.

This law of God is the mortar which holds the stones of our social structure together. It is our public philosophy.

We are a people whose land is filled with churches. It has been so from the beginning. We are a church-going people. We are known the world around as the people of the Book. Other people consider Christianity as the religion of a particular race of people, just as we would consider Buddhism as the religion of Asiatics. Nowhere in the Bible is it said that the Gentiles are to be converted in such large numbers that there would be an equitable distribution of populations of all races in the church. The Bible does say that in the latter days the people of Israel shall return and seek the Lord.

In the providence of God it has been our destiny to be a witness to the world, to proclaim that the Lord God is God, and that his mighty work through Jesus Christ is the way whereby men must be saved and live as children of God. It has been said that 98% of all Christian literature and 95% of all Christian missionaries, outside the Roman church, have come from this one particular group of people, namely, the English speaking people and their kinsmen in northern Europe. We have witnessed to the world, and this witness has gone to every nation. Some governmental repesentative of every soul on the face of the earth in this generation has heard the Gospel message. Not every individual, but the political and social leaders who represent every person in the world have heard it. Why this drive to evangelize the world? It just comes with us; it has been our burning desire since Reformation days, and God has provided the material means in the form of transportation, communication, and printing to enable us to carry out the Great Commission.

We are a people whose history is consonant with the fortunes of the people of Israel as told in the Bible. We have returned to God, and God has blessed us mightily. Do you realize just what it means that we as a people have practically encircled the whole world since the time we first began our westward trek? We have gone nearly all the way around the world; westward, westward, always westward. Why did Paul go west? Why did God call him to

Macedonia? Why did he not go into Africa, or India or China? Did you ever consider what fortunes of history were involved in the selection of a direction for the main thrust of the Gospel? There must have been a purpose in it, for in God's history, nothing is left to chance. Could it be that the people whom God intended should receive the Gospel were already in northern Europe?

These are the promises, and these are the facts. We have looked in the mirror of history. What is the explanation? Who are we? Make no mistake, we need to be explained. There is just a tremendous amount to be explained to account for our place in history. Whatever scheme of interpretation of scripture we adopt must include an explanation of our own people in the world today.

What are the alternatives? If we are not literally, historically, and corporately the people of the Book, then just who are we?

It might be said that all these blessings have come upon us because as any other Christian people we enjoy the blessings which God showers upon his children in any age. This is contrary to the teachings of scriptures to the effect that as Christians in this age we are to expect suffering. The blessings we enjoy are of the specific kind given to the House of Joseph as the descendants of Abraham, not to Christian gentiles, although the condition for the restoration to the place of blessing is contingent upon the people of Joseph becoming Christian.

It might be said that all the blessings we enjoy are but small in comparison to the extent of the promised blessings to be enjoyed during the millennial reign of Christ. How would any group of people have such blessings exclusively during the millennium? Furthermore, is it not incongruous that any people would enjoy as a blessing the war-like, aggressive, military strength promised to Joseph during the millennium? These blessings are for the latter days, which began at Christ's first advent, not the millennium of peace.

Perhaps we are the revived and last phase of the fourth great beast empire of Rome that will persecute Christians at the end of time. Are not Christians to be persecuted regardless of national origin in the end of time? Are not Christians being persecuted now? More Christians have been martyred in this generation than in any previous generation. You might expect that our missionaries think this is tribulation. What more can evil men do to a Christian beyond torturing him to death? No; if we are Rome, we are certainly seeing a strange behavior in the area of Christian persecution. Besides, our historical posture has been distinctly anti-Roman.

Many people have been led to believe that the people we know in the world today as the Jews are to fulfill all the prophecies relating to Israel and enjoy the blessings promised to the fathers. But the Jews do not qualify. They cannot qualify. They cannot qualify because they are not the whole of Israel. The Bible says much about the separation of the people of Abraham into distinctive groups each with its own part to play in the story; and the Jews are only one part. To Judah went the promise of the king, the place of the sanctuary, the lawgiver, the scepter, the throne, and the Messiah; but the people, under the name of Joseph, were given the promises of many seed, the material prosperity, and the work of witnessing throughout the world. The Jews were never given these latter promises. The people of Joseph were driven into captivity before there were any remaining who could even be called Jews.

If we think that at some time the Jews are to fulfill the promises made to the fathers, why not more rightly think that the people to whom the promises were made would fulfill them? The Jews are not that people. They say so. Yet Christian people go on assigning to them this role without question. For too long we have ascribed the fulfillment of many promises to the wrong group of people, promises specifically assigned to the people of Joseph and Ephraim. The Jews nowhere have ever admitted that they are those people; in fact, they themselves disclaim it, completely and explicitly, in the statements of their scholars and by their prayers for the future restoration of their brethren of the house of Joseph.

Why do you think it strange that God would select a real people in a real time to do a real job? Is it possible that we are doing something of which the prophets had no knowledge? Did God forget to tell them? Are we doing something apart from revelation? Did we slip up on God when he was looking the other way? We are the mightiest nation ever on the face of the earth; do you think we are not in the scriptures at all? Is this an oversight on God's part? Is this a piece of ignorance on the part of the prophets? Why were they never told? What is really going on here in the world today? Whatever history happens, is it not God's history?

Now this is not a doctrinal matter. It is primarily a question of who we are. Christians who were brought up to believe that all these wonderful things in some far off future time would happen to the people we know as the Jews, should re-examine their understanding. If the Jews are a real people who are to do real things in a real time, then why not Israel? Why should a question of this importance be swept off into some dark corner as if it were sacrilegious or unworthy of consideration? The time has come in the history of the world when God's people are going to know who they are.

Well, just who do you think they are?

Is it possible that any who accept Christ could be assigned to this group of God's people? Yes. In Galatians 3:29, "If we are Christ's then are we Abraham's seed and heirs according to the promise." Of course, any Christian is adopted into the body of God's people. In our studies we have shown that adoption itself is not enough to fulfill the requirements that the children of Abraham receive the promises. Else we need no Old Testament promises at all. All we need is to begin with Jesus Christ, and he needs nothing prior to Himself. If the Old Testament promises mean anything at all, it is that the children of Abraham will share in this provision that God makes through Jesus Christ. If not, why choose an Abraham? If it is just a question of adoption, then why not the Chinese? Or the tribes of Africa, or the South Americans? There is still a great deal to explain if we are no more than adopted gentiles.

The churches have traditionally taught that the church in a spiritual sense has inherited all the promises made to the Old Testament people, and that in a spiritual sense the church today is the Israel of God. If this were true, then why, after nineteen hundred years, is there still a people identified as the Jews? And if Judah is yet here, then why not Israel? A lot of straining is being done today to make this Jewish venture in Palestine fit prophecy, and it just will not fit. The events in Palestine may fit the scriptures pertaining to Judah, but not all of Israel. The prophets speak much of Judah being at Jerusalem at the last time, but of Israel as being in far off places.

This proposition explains our history as a people, our present position in the world, and our entire missionary witness. We are known corporately as a Christian people; whether we think we are or not, to the outside world, we are. And we are in the land to which multitudes wish to come. What better rationale of history can we find?

O Rachel, don't you weep! Joseph is alive!

Bibliography

1. Brooks, Pat. Hear, *O Israel.* Fletcher, North Carolina. New Puritan Library. 1981.
2. Bruce, F. F. *The Spreading Flame.* Grand Rapids. William B. Eerdmans Publishing Company. 1958.
3. Raymond, E. Capt. *Missing Links Discovered.* Thousand Oaks, California. Artisan Sales.
4. Du Chaillu, Paul B. *The Viking Age.* New York. Charles Scribner's Sons. 1889.
5. Elder, Isabel Hill. *Celt, Druid, and Culdee.* London. The Covenant Publishing Company, LTD. 1978.
6. Potts, W. E. *America's Destiny.* Florence, South Carolina.

Chapter 14
The Ecstasy of Pride

The assault on the Papacy by the Reformation leaders was two-fold. There was a revolt against the doctrinal positions of the Roman church with regard to such matters as the substance of the Mass, the sale of indulgences, auricular confessions, the supremacy of tradition over scripture, and an intermediary priesthood. The second prong of attack was in the realm of prophecy, and this phase of the attack came from a reading of the Bible which for the first time became a book open to all believers.

The identification of the Papacy with the Little Horn of Daniel 7, the Man of Sin of II Thessalonians 2, the second beast of Revelations 13, and the great whore of Revelations 17, was a dominant theme of the majority of the Reformers. The acceptance of the year-day prophetic time scale was a basic premise of this position. The proposition was simple: the history which was happening before their own eyes must be in keeping with history as pre-written by the prophets. History is but the world's answer to the divine call of prophecy.

Just as the attack was two-fold, so the counterattack was two-fold. The answer to the accusations of the reformers regarding doctrine was formulated at the Council of Trent. This Council, meeting in 1545, was largely Italian in character and under tight control of the Papacy. It met for nearly 20 years, and concluded with the issuance of a Papal Bull signed by Pius IV in 1564. The conclusions of the Council of Trent became the binding law of the Catholic church and have remained so until this day. Only two significant additions have been made since: the doctrine of the Immaculate Conception (of Mary) in 1854 and the doctrine of the infallibility of the pope in 1870.

After the Council of Trent, there remained the problem of prophetic interpretation. In these matters, the counterreformation moved more slowly and with greater care. It was easier to deal with the IDEAS of doctrine than with the FACTS of history.

The application of the prophetic scriptures to the then current history was denied by Roman scholars in two ways. The first was by claiming the completed fulfillment of the prophecies in the days of the Roman emperors when Christians suffered great persecution. This first view was promulgated by Alcazar, a Spanish Jesuit, about 1614, and is better known as the Preterest interpretation of Prophecy. The second was by postponing the realization of the prophecies until a short period of time in the closing days of the age just prior to the return of Christ.

The second view, put forth by Francisco Ribera, a Jesuit of Salamanca, Spain, sought to postpone the fulfillment of the prophecies to a future time. Ribera taught that the world would be ruled by a single man, the Antichrist, for a literal three and one half years just before the second advent of Christ. He taught that this Antichrist would rebuild a physical temple in Jerusalem, be acknowledged by the Jews, and conquer the world, all in the brief span of three and a half literal years.

However, it was Robert Bellarmine who systematized this Antichrist interpretation of prophecy. Over a period of years in the later 16th century he lectured and wrote concerning his answer to the protestants. Bellarmine's assault on the protestant interpretation of the prophecies centered on the year-day scale of representing prophetic time. He argued that the church fathers had always considered a literal rather than a symbolic application of these time cycles. He took advantage of disagreements among the many Protestant scholars. He assigned the prophecies as belonging to past history or future history but not to the then current history. Bellarmine claimed that the Antichrist is to be an individual Jew, and not of an apostate Christian system. Therefore the duration of his reign would be a literal 1260 days (3 ½ years) and not 1260 years. His arguments were potent and convincing. The results of his lectures and publications were but a deepening of the rift between the Papal south and the Protestant north, with pockets of each within territories of the other throughout Europe. The stand-off continued for more than 200 years.

Early in the nineteenth century, in the 1820's, Samuel R.-Maitland led a pro-Romanist movement from within the church of England. He published many pamphlets, including one which set forth Ribera's Futurist interpretation in an attempt to show that the popes were not such evil men, after all. This view was adopted by John Nelson Darby, who was a leader in the Brethren movement in Dublin and Plymouth.

The High Church Oxford movement, which only lasted about twelve years, was an attempt to persuade the Protestants of their errors and urge them to rejoin Rome. The thrust was chiefly in terms of prophetic interpretations of the two schools of thought. Writers of the Oxford Church movement published a total of 90 so-called "Tracts for the Times" in about eight years. One of the chief writers was John Henry Newman who was converted to Roman Catholicism and eventually became a cardinal. Newman derived his teachings from Dr. James H. Todd, Professor of Hebrew at the University of Dublin. Also, Newman openly claimed to be a follower of S.R. Maitland. Todd claimed that the Protestants were in error in declaring that the leaders of the Roman Church were the Antichrist of Scripture. He likewise opposed other teachings of the Reformation leaders and espoused the Futurism of Ribera as the proper alternative. In his writings, Todd gives credit to Maitland.

J.N. Darby, associated closely with the Brethren movement in Plymouth and Dublin, quickly accepted the teachings of S.R. Maitland and became a convincing lecturer on prophetic topics. By 1840, he began to include in his teaching the idea of a rapture of the saints of the world before the day of trouble at the end of the Age. A pre-Tribulation rapture became an integral part of the Futurist interpretation of the prophecies. In all this we see that in the early part of the nineteenth century the teachings of Ribera calling for a postponement of the fulfillment of the prophecies to some future time were adopted by some protestant leaders, principally in England.

Following these early successes, there was a long list of teachers, preachers, evangelists, and scholars who adopted this viewpoint in both England and America. In America there was a succession of prophetic conferences throughout the late nineteenth and early twentieth centuries which taught and promoted the Futurist interpretations. Many godly teachers and preachers accepted and promoted it. The culmination of this success was the publication of the Scofield Reference Bible with notes written by Dr. C.I. Scofield. The original Futurist scheme was by then enhanced by the teaching of a pretribulation rapture of believers and a scheme of interpretations by which God ordered his dealings with men in different ages called Dispensations. This dispensationalism, from the time of the Scofield Bible, became an essential part of Futurism in modern times.

By the time of World War I, the Protestant viewpoint of prophetic interpretation with its emphasis upon all history as the unfolding work of God had practically disappeared from the pulpit and platform. Of all the major groups of Christian churches, only the Seventh Day Adventists kept the Protestant Historical interpretation alive. How do we account for this overwhelming success of Futurism which had its most significant formulations as a Romanist doctrine set forth as an integral part of the counterreformation? What is the appeal? Why did so many protestant and evangelical men accept it so readily and teach it as the only scheme of the prophetic scriptures? First, let us take a look at the principle teachings of Futurism.

Foremost is the teaching that the fulfillment of all the prophetic scripture in both the Old Testament and New Testament not accomplished by the time of the destruction of Jerusalem in 70 A.D. is being postponed until a future short period of time at the end of the age. In this short period of seven literal years, the purposes of God regarding the Church, the Jews, and the world will be accomplished in order to bring in the millennium reign of Christ. There is now an indefinite period of time which is like a huge gap or parenthesis in history during which prophetic time is not counted. The only significant events are those concerning the preaching of the Gospel and the establishment of a Gentile church. This is the crux of the whole matter. Is God in control of the whole world or is he a stranger in a forest whose chief concern is the protection of his own small family against the wolves of adversity which surrounds them?

In Daniel 4:17, we read, "to the intent that the living may know that the most high ruleth in the kingdom of men and giveth it to whomsoever he will, and setteth up over it the basest of men". This would account for all the world leaders of history including the Roman Emperors, the popes, a Napoleon, George Washington, Hitler, Stalin, Richard Nixon,. and Ronald Reagan. God not only knows history, he directs history. He is still in charge of human affairs, and through the prophets, he told us what he was going to do. Either God controls history, or He, Himself, is the victim of historical circumstances, which is unthinkable. Are you one of those who say, "I don't see any meaning to history, and since God would not do anything I can't understand, then history has no meaning."? Read the Bible! Read the Prophets! Read Matthew 24! Sometimes these scriptures are important for what they do not say.

Second, another tenet of the Futurist school of interpretation is that the church had its beginning on the Day of Pentecost. There is no mention in Acts 2 of the beginning of a new entity called the church. There is an account of a new and powerful manifestation of the Holy Spirit upon God's people. It is stated that 3000 souls were added to the body of believers, this implying that such a body already existed. These and other problems are discussed in the chapter "ALL ONE BODY WE".

Third, there is a claim by the Futurists that the Church is Gentile and the Kingdom is Jewish. This view belittles the fact that the Apostles, including Paul, were of Israel. In addition to the twelve, there were the 120 of Acts 1:15, the 5000 of Acts 4:4, the great company of priests in Jerusalem of Acts 6:7, and the numerous converts to Christ from among the Jews to whom Paul preached in cities throughout the Roman Empire. Moreover, is it not an inconsistency that the very people who claim that the Church is exclusively Gentile give such ardent support to the modern missionary effort to convert Jews today? To bring them into a Gentile Church? How does this help to achieve their supposed destiny as a kingdom people separate from the Gentile Christian Church?

Fourth, the Futurists claim that the Church is the Gentile Bride of Christ. Nowhere in scripture is it stated that the Church is the Bride of Christ. Paul never uses the word for "bride". Not even once! Repeatedly, the New Testament says that the Church is the BODY of Christ and that Christ is the Head of that Body, (Romans 12:4,5, 1 Corinthians 6:15, 1 Corinthians 12:12, Ephesians 1:22,23, Ephesians 5:29,30, Colossians 1:18, Colossians 2:19). How does a head marry its own body?

No, there is another group known as the Bride in Scripture. It is Israel. Read again the chapter *"WHY CHRIST DIED"*. In Revelation 21, there is a description of the Bride, the holy city. Is this the Gentile Church? In verse 12 we read of the twelve gates to the city which bear the names of the twelve tribes of Israel. How did these slip into a Gentile Church? Supposedly, the twelve tribes are not in the Church which is exclusively Gentile. It is adulterous Israel who is the bride, as we find in Isaiah 62:5, "For as a young man marrieth a virgin, so shall thy sons marry thee, and as the bridegroom rejoiceth over the bride, so shall thy God rejoice over thee.". In Isaiah 61:10, we read, "I will greatly rejoice in the Lord, my soul shall be joyful in my God; for he hath clothed me with the garments of salvation, he hath covered me with the robe of righteousness, as a bridegroom decketh himself with ornaments, and as a bride adorneth herself with jewels."

"Thou shalt call his name Jesus, for he shall save his people from their sins." Well, did he? or has he?

Fifth, perhaps the most popular of the teachings of the modern Futurists is the belief that the rapture of the Church occurs before any day of trouble arrives. So much so that a widespread expression of leavetaking is "I'll see you in the Rapture." The origin of this idea is no earlier than about 1830 A.D., according to Dave MacPherson, who wrote several books on the subject, including *The Incredible Cover-Up*, and *The Great Rapture Hoax.*

The expectation of leaving the earth before any period of

tribulation begins is based partly on the claim that we will not suffer the wrath of God that is poured out on the earth during a period. Wrath is one thing, but what about chastisement? In Hebrews 12:5, we begin to read, "And ye have forgotten the exhortation which speaketh unto you as unto children, My son, despise not thou the chastening of the Lord, nor faint when thou art rebuked of him: for whom the Lord loveth he chasteneth and scourgeth every son whom he receiveth."

Not only chastisement, but tribulation itself. Did not our Lord ordain us to tribulation when he said, "In the world ye shall have tribulation: but be of good cheer; I have overcome the world," in John 16:33? Are those who hope in a rapture of the saints before a time of trouble also hoping to escape "the fellowship of his sufferings" mentioned in Philippians 3:10?

Corrie Ten Boon set us straight on this point. She upbraided American Christians for trusting in a rapture while Christians in other lands are suffering and dying for their faith in Christ. Millions of Chinese Christians were unprepared for the Communist takeover because they had been taught by American missionaries that they would never see trouble. How tragic.

Following the roll call of the heroes of faith in Hebrews 11, there is an account of the kinds of suffering they endured. To this list we could add the sufferings of early Christian Martyrs during the persecutions by the Romans. Also the sufferings of Christians during the several centuries of the Inquisition. In Halley's Bible Handbook, we read in Halley's comments on Revelation 13, that 50,000,000 martyrs suffered under the rule of the Papacy. A number of these are accounted for in Foxe's Book of Martyrs. One such was Anne Askew, a young mother of two children, who, at about age 25, defied the authority of the Roman Church. She was stretched on the rack until every joint in her body was separated. Enduring such exquisite pain, she still refused to conform to the demands of her torturers. She kept a diary from which Foxe quotes. In her last signed statement she refused the doctrine of transubstantiation of the mass, and claimed the Bible superior in authority to the traditions of the

Church. She concluded by praying for her persecutors. Anne Askew was then led out and, with other Christians, burned at the stake, offering her body as a flaming sacrifice to her Lord and Savior. Such is the faith of martyrs.

When you get to heaven and see Anne Askew, will you say to her, "Well, I am sorry about that, but Christ loved me so much he excused me from any such trouble"? To what heights of self-righteousness will our spiritual vanity take us?

Just what is tribulation? Is it necessary for some soldier to take you from your home and slit your tongue or cut off your hand before you would admit to tribulation? Is not tribulation possible in the mental and spiritual realms as well as the physical?

"We wrestle not against flesh and blood, but against principalities, against powers, against the rulers of the darkness of this world, against spiritual wickedness in high places." (Ephesians 6:12). While we exclaim "Rapture", is not Satan stealing our children through the false philosophy of humanism in our schools, through the appeal to sensuality in our entertainment media, and through the false moral values in the many religions on the New Age Movement? Christians, wake up! Are we not losing the psychopolitical and spiritual battle of our own age because of a false sense of spiritual security? Tribulation? How much more will we tolerate before we fall on our knees and cry out to God to help us. Yes, millions are coming to Christ for salvation but, after enlistment, are they getting the proper armor for the great spiritual battle in which we find ourselves?

World events will force Christian leaders, Godly men, to change their minds on various issues. The pretribulation rapture of the Church is one of the first to go. An Australian minister, Alexander Reese, was one of the first to abandon the popular Rapture Theory. His book, *The Approaching Advent of Christ* gives a rather complete critique of the Darby teachings on the subject. This was followed by *The Return of Christ in Glory* by Alexander Fraser in America. In 1956, George Ladd of the Fuller Theological Seminary, published *The Blessed Hope* in which he shows that a pretribulation rapture is based upon inferences and is not the explicit teaching of scripture. These men are Futurists who have seen the non-scriptual basis for their false hope.

Our hope is Resurrection, not Rapture. Did all our Christian forebearers die in hopelessness because they did not live to experience the Rapture? Let's get our priorities in order.

For a detailed word study on this subject, please read *"Three Little Words"* in Appendix E. This study is patterned somewhat after a part of the discussions of Ladd's *Blessed Hope.*

Sixth, can Christ come at any time? Many say yes, because Jesus said, in Mark 13:32,33, "But of that day and that hour knoweth no man, no, not the angels which are in heaven, neither the son, but the Father. Take ye heed, watch and pray: for ye know not when the time is." This does not mean that the Father has not determined the time, but only that men do not yet know it. The idea that Christ may return at any time is known as the doctrine of the imminence of Christ's return. If Christ can come at any moment, then he could have come at any moment, else the doctrine has no meaning to Christians in former generations. He could have come two hundred years ago. If he had come two hundred years ago, then the history of the past two hundred years has no meaning. This includes the missionary efforts to evangelize the world throughout the past two centuries which would then have become meaningless and irrelevant. The great commission would have been thwarted.

God can do anything He pleases. He pleased to tell us through the prophets what he intended to do. Certainly, the gospel must be preached first, because Jesus said, Matthew 24:14, "And this gospel of the kingdom shall be preached in all the world for a witness unto all nations; and then shall the end come." This is a forthright statement of a contingency, and this one statement should demolish the any moment theory. In Matthew 24, you will not find any mention of a gap in history, any mention of a rapture before tribulation, or any mention of an antichrist.

If we cast aside the assumption of a pretribulation rapture, we are forced to consider other contingencies. In Matthew 24:29,30, we are told that it is after the tribulation that the sign of the Son of Man in heaven shall appear and the elect gathered. Then tribulation is a contingency. Paul tells us in II Thessalonians 2 that the day of Christ will not come until after an apostasy and the appearing of the man of sin, which make two more contingencies. In Matthew 24, Jesus adds others, such as the days of Noah, the appearance of the false Christs, and signs in the sun and moon.

Thus we see that the time of the return of Christ is highly conditional, and the conditions are known and determined by the Father. In 1 Thessalonians 5, Paul tells us that the time comes as a thief in the night to the unbelieving world, but believers should not be surprised. In verse 4, we read, "But ye, brethren, are not in darkness, that that day should overtake you as a thief. Ye are all children of light, and the children of the day." This message would seem to indicate that believers, not knowing the day or the hour, would be able to discern the historical setting at the time of his return.

Shortly after World War II, there was a film produced which showed all the plays in a football game in two and one half minutes. Every play from the snap of the ball to the down of the ball was shown. Talk about fast action! Everything was shown at about forty times the normal speed.

In early America, it took about one hundred fifty years to move from Plymouth Rock to the Revolution. Other historical developments move ponderously slow, yet the Futurists expect the major portion of the Book of Revelations to be fulfilled in the short space of 7 literal years. This would call for world events to come to pass 365 times as fast as they ordinarily occur. Throughout all this accelerated activity, our Futurist friends won't even be on earth. In their teachings they share great concern about events on earth that will be of no concern at all to them. They also assert that the Holy Spirit will be absent from the earth during this seven year period. Yet there will be millions saved during this time, including the Jews. How? At this point they make unclear sounds regarding the basis of salvation. No church to witness, and no Holy Spirit to convict of sin, calls for a rather strange doctrine of salvation.

The Bible provides us with a test for the prophets. In Deuteronomy 18:21,22, we read, "And if thou say in thy heart, How shall we know the word which the Lord hath not spoken. When a prophet speaketh in the name of the Lord, and if the thing follow not, nor come to pass, that is the thing which the Lord hath not spoken, but the prophet hath spoken it presumptuously: thou shalt not be afraid of him." Then in Jeremiah 28:9, we read, "The prophet which prophesieth of peace, when the word of the prophet shall come to pass, then shall the prophet be known, that the Lord hath truly sent him." From these words we conclude that history is the test of prophecy. If none of God's people are around to apply the test, of what use is this criterion? Have the Futurists placed themselves beyond this Biblical test by claiming they will be separated from history in the Rapture?

In the first chapter of this book there is a short outline of four systems of interpretation of the prophetic scriptures. There is the group which accepts only the spiritual value of prophecy which has no relevance to actual history. The Preterist claims the prophecies were fulfilled in times past during the persecutions of the Roman Empire. The Futurists claim fulfillment at some future time at the close of this age and in relation to Christ's second coming. The Historicist maintains that fulfillment is occurring throughout history all of which is described in the prophecies. Let us resort to baseball parlance and ask, "Who's on first?".

The spiritual or symbolic interpreter says, "Who cares?. It is just a make-believe game anyway." The Preterist exclaims, "Stupid, the game is over.". The Futurist protests, "Hey, wait. It's not our inning yet." The Historicist yells, "Why don't you look and see!" Clearly the advantage is with the Historicist, who is the only realist in the bunch. Look at history and study what the Bible says. If there is no correspondence, then can we not ask, "Is God really in control"?

The Reformers saw the corrupt power of an apostate papacy, and, in faith in the Word of God, resisted unto death. Since the Reformation, the world has been explored and enlarged and expanded until it has become a very small dot. There is now no more space on planet Earth to which a small group of Christians can flee and make a new beginning as was done on this continent during the seventeenth century. Now the world must stand and face itself. Moreover, it must face its Maker. The two principle events since the Reformation are the world missionary enterprise and the development of the American civilization which made this missionary activity possible in the twentieth century. Do you see this in prophecy? If not, perhaps some more homework is in order.

Bibliography

1. Andrews, Samuel J. *Christianity and Anti-Christianity.* Chicago. The Bible Institute Colportage Association. 1898.
2. English, E. Schuyler. *Re-Thinking the Rature.* Neptune, New Jersey. Loizeaux Brothers. 1954.
3. Fraser, Alexander. *The Return of Christ in Glory.* Scottsdale, Pennsylvania. The Evangelical Fellowship. 1957.
4. Katterjohn, Arthur. *The Tribulation People.* Carol Stream, Illinois. Creation House. 1976.
5. Ladd, George E. *The Blessed Hope.* Grand Rapids. William B. Eerdmans Publishing Company. 1956.
6. Lindsey, Hal. *The Late Great Planet Earth.* Grand Rapids. Zondervan Publishing House. 1970.
7. MacPherson, Dave. *The Great Rapture Hoax.* Fletcher, North Carolina. New Puritan Press. 1983.
8. MacPherson, Dave. *The Incredible Cover-Up.* Plainfield, New Jersey. Logos International. 1975.
9. Pit, Jan. *Persecution: It Will Never Happen Here?* Orange, California. Open Doors With Brother Andrew 1981.
10. Reese, Alexander. *The Approaching Advent of Christ.* London. Marshall, Morgan, and Scott LTD.
11. Ryrie, Charles Caldwell. *Dispensationalism Today.* Chicago. Moody Press. 1978.
12. Tombler, John W. and Funk, Hubert J. *The Raptured East.* Orange, New Jersey. Trumpet Press, Inc. 1977.
13. Walvoord, John F. *The Return of the Lord.* Grand Rapids. Zondervan Publishing House. 1971.

Chapter15
The Man of Kerioth

Who is the man of Kerioth? What in the world is Kerioth? Kerioth is a city. We read of it first in the Bible in Joshua 15:25 in a list of cities conquered by Joshua when the children of Israel came up out of Egypt and entered the Promised Land. This list is introduced in Joshua 15:1 as "the uttermost cities of the tribe of the children of Judah toward the coast of Edom southward . . ." More familiar cities in this area were Hebron and Beersheba.

There were other cities which used the name Kerioth, a word which means "city". There was Kerioth-Arba, a name for Hebron. There were others, which used the name in combination, the English spelling varying, such as Kerioth or Kirjath.

However, the one in Joshua was known as Kerioth-Sepher or Debir, the city of letters. It was located north of Beersheba and southwest of Hebron. It has an interesting history in that it was finally occupied by the Edomites.

Originally, the Edomites lived in the territory southeast of the Dead Sea, south of the country of Moab. The descendants of Amalek, the grandson of Edom, occupied the region southwest of the Dead Sea. It was the Amalekites who blocked the passage of the children of Israel from Egypt to the Promised Land. There is an account of a great battle between Israel and Amalek in the seventeenth chapter of the Book of Exodus which ends with the words, "The Lord hath sworn that the Lord will have war with Amalek from generation to generation." Neither would Edom allow the children of Israel to pass through their land, as related in Numbers 20:14-21. Israel had to march east of Edom and Moab in order to reach the Jordan River near Jericho.

These people and other descendants of Esau harassed Israel throughout the Old Testament period. During the days of Samuel, King Saul was instructed to smite the Amalekites, but he would not finish the conquest. He chose instead to spare the life of Agag their king, and take much booty. Samuel told Saul, in I Samuel 15:23, "Because thou hast rejected the word of the Lord, he hath also rejected thee from being king."

Both David and Solomon had trouble with the Edomites. The prophet Obadiah tells of the actions of the Edomites when the Babylonians captured Jerusalem. Among other acts, Obadiah says that the Edomites cast lots upon Jerusalem even before it fell; they prevented the children of Judah from escaping; they delivered the fleeing people of Judah to their enemies; and entered and looted the city. Obadiah's words are harsh, in verse 16, "For thy violence against thy brother Jacob shame shall cover thee, and thou shalt be cut off forever." In verse 15, "As thou hast done, it shall be done unto thee: thy reward shall return upon thine own head." In verse 21, "And saviors shall come up on mount Zion to judge the mount of Esau; and the kingdom shall be the Lord's."

After the destruction of Jerusalem by Babylon, the prophet Ezekiel says of Edom in Ezekiel 25:12-14, "Thus saith the Lord God, because that Edom hath dealt against the house of Judah by taking vengeance, and hath greatly offended, and revenged himself upon them, therefore thus saith the Lord God; I will also stretch out mine hand upon Edom . . . and I will lay my vengeance upon Edom by the hand of my people Israel: and they shall do in Edom according to mine anger and according to my fury; and they shall know my vengeance, saith the Lord God." In a prophecy concerning God's judgment of the nations in Isaiah 34:5-6, we read, "For my sword shall be bathed in heaven: behold it shall come down upon Idumea, and upon the people of my curse. The sword of the Lord is filled with blood, . . . for the Lord hath a sacrifice in Bozrah, and a great slaughter in the land of Idumea." And in verse 8, "For it is the day of the Lord's vengeance, and the year of recompenses for the controversy of Zion."

Idumea is but the Greek name for the country of Edom. Bozrah was the capital city of the Edomites. Remember that Edom is Esau.

When the Lord returns to take vengeance on his enemies, on

whom will he pour out his anger? In Isaiah 63:1-6, there is a clear statement concerning the object of his displeasure. There is a presentation of this action in the form of a question and answer revelation.

> **Question:** Who is this that cometh from Edom, with dyed garments from Bozrah? This that is glorious in his apparel, traveling in the greatness of his strength?
>
> **Answer:** I that speak in righteousness, mighty to save.
>
> **Question:** Wherefore art thou red in thine apparel, and thy garments like him that treadeth in the winevat?
>
> **Answer:** I have trodden the winepress alone; and of the people, there was none with me: for I will tread them in my anger, and trample them in my fury; and their blood will be sprinkled upon my garments, and I will stain all my raiment. For the day of vengeance is in my heart, and the year of my redeemed is come. And I looked, and there was none to help; and I wondered that there was none to uphold: therefore mine own arm brought salvation unto me; and my fury, it upheld me. And I will tread down the people in mine anger and make them drunk in my fury, and I will bring down their strength to the earth.

At the last end of the Old Testament, in Malachi 1:1-4, we read, "I loved you, saith the Lord. Yet ye say, Wherein hast thou loved us? Was not Esau Jacob's brother? saith the Lord: yet I loved Jacob, and I hated Esau, and laid his mountain and his heritage waste for the dragons of the wilderness. Whereas Esau saith, we are impoverished, but we will return and build the desolate places; thus saith the Lord of hosts, They shall build, but I will throw down; and they shall call them, the border of wickedness, *and the people against whom the Lord hath indignation forever.* And your eyes shall see, and ye shall say, The Lord will be magnified from the border of Israel."

Thus, throughout the Old Testament, from Genesis to Malachi, Esau-Edom is presented to us as the adversary of God's people and of God Himself. We wonder about God's intention to use evil men to further his purposes in world affairs. Paul discusses this problem of our understanding in Romans 9. In verse 10 we read, "But when Rebecca also had conceived by one, even by our father Isaac; For the children being not yet born, neither having done any good or evil, that the purpose of God according to election might stand, not of works, but of him that calleth; it was said unto her, The elder shall serve the younger. As it is written, Jacob have I loved, and Esau have I hated." Paul then asks, "Is there any unrighteousness with God?" and continues to give Old Testament examples of God's sovereign will. Again, Paul asks "Why doth he yet find fault? For who hath resisted his will? Nay but, O man, who art thou that repliest against God? Shall the thing formed say to him that formed it Why hast thou made me thus? Hath not the potter power over the clay, of the same lump to make one vessel unto honor, and another unto dishonor?"

Another example of this thought is found in Daniel 4:17, where Daniel tells Nebuchadnezzar, "that the living may know that the most high ruleth in the kingdom of men, and giveth it to whomsoever He will, and setteth up over it the basest of men". This concept will account for such men as Lincoln, Washington, Luther, Columbus, but also for Nero, Napoleon, Hitler, and Stalin. Remember that God always makes use of sinful men in his program. Is there any other kind standing around that he can use? We can only bow before his sovereign will and praise him for his mercy. To summarize, God chose Edom for a special role in his program.

There is some interesting history concerning Edom in the centuries between the Old and New Testaments. Following the conquest of Jerusalem by Babylon, a number of Edomites moved into the vacated regions of southern Judah. There were additional migrations of Edomites into this territory when the Nabateans moved against the Edomites from the east. By the time of the Greek occupation of the country, this territory in southern Judea was called Idumea, the country of the Edomites. At one time it included the city of Hebron, not far south of Jerusalem. It certainly included Kerioth, which was south of Hebron.

The following is taken from The Cambridge Ancient History,

Volume III, page 479. "The investigation of the actual history of these southern immigrants and that of the passages which directly or indirectly concern them here converge. From the Judean genealogies in 1 Chronicles 2 and 4, it has long been seen that the tribe of Judah after suffering heavy losses, ostensibly before the monarchy, was built up again through Calebite and other clans of south Palestinian and Edomite affinity. These became genuinely "Israelite" and finally (presumably during the Exile) moved northward to the neighborhood of Jerusalem; indeed, as late as the days of Nehemiah, traces of Calebites can be found among the leading men who helped to rebuild the walls of Jerusalem. The evidence, on the face of it, might seem to point naturally to a Judah of semi-Edomite origin, the creation of David, in whose early days these clans had an independent existence in the south of Judah (I Samuel 26:31). It is quite in agreement with this perspective of history that the Chronicler, after describing the singularly mixed constituents of the new Judah (Benjamin can also be included) proceeds to represent a temple service inaugurated by David, where the names of prominent Levites are appreciably of semi-Edomite, south Palestinian, and non-Israelite origin. Hence, it is possible to trace a close connection between (a) the southern clans who became Judean, (b) the temple personnel, and (c) the families of the scribes."

During this period of history, the Jews enjoyed intervals of independence, but no king of the House of David ruled over them. The High Priest in Jerusalem was accepted as their leader in all matters political and military. One such high priest was John Hyrcanus, who, in about 125 B.C., conquered Idumea, forced the men to undergo circumcision and to adopt the Jewish laws. Josephus says of them that thereafter they became none other than Jews. The entire community of Edomites became proselyte Jews.

Herod the Great was such an Edomite Jew. He was appointed King of the Jews by the Romans. When the wise men came to Jerusalem and asked "Where is he that is born King of the Jews?" is there any wonder at the outburst of Herod who felt threatened and ordered the slaughter of the infants in Bethlehem? It was in the character of an Edomite to be an adversary on the occasion of the birth of the Savior. The descendants of Esau had played this role throughout Old Testament times. Always the hinderer. Would it not also be appropriate for Esau to have a hand in the events surrounding the death of the Savior? We return to the original question: Who is the man of Kerioth? The Hebrew word for man is ISH. Therefore the man of Kerioth can be written as ISH KERIOTH. In the Hebrew language as well as the Greek there is no letter H. Instead, there is a breathing indicated. More accurately, then, the expression becomes IS KERIOT. ISCARIOT! JUDAS, THE MAN OF KERIOTH! Judas as Edomite? Why not? He certainly was no Galilean: he is never called a Judean. He is always indentified as Iscariot or Judas the son of Simon Iscariot. A family of the town of Kerioth.

How appropriate for an Edomite to have a hand in the death of Jesus in the light of the long history of the Edomites as the opposer of Israel. In most Bibles, in the account of the betrayal of Jesus, there is in the margin a cross reference to Psalm 41.9, which reads, "Yea, mine own familiar friend in whom I trusted, which did eat of my bread, hath lifted up his heel against me." Whose heel? Esau's heel! Remember when the twins were born to Rebecca that Jacob took hold of Esau's heel? Lifting up the heel was a sign of contempt or disdain. The phrase in Psalm 41 literally reads, "He has shown me the bottom of his foot."

If Edom was on hand at the birth of Jesus in the person of Herod, then it is fitting that Edom was on hand at the death of Jesus in the person of Judas. Edomites, the people against whom the Lord has indignation forever (Malachi 1:4).

Were there others? During his life Jesus taught repeatedly concerning his enemies. In John chapter 8, the Pharisees encountered him in the temple. In verse 33, they claimed "We be Abraham's seed, and were never in bondage to any man." In verse 37, Jesus said, "I know ye are Abraham's seed, but ye seek to kill me", but in verse 39, he said, "if ye were Abraham's children, ye would do the works of Abraham." How could they be Abraham's seed and not Abraham's children? And how can they claim never to have been in bondage? These statements can be reconciled if we consider that the covenant line came through Jacob and not Esau, that the children of Israel (Jacob) were the covenant children of Abraham and that the seed of Esau (Edom) were not. Furthermore, the Edomites were not in bondage to Egypt when Israel was, nor were they carried into captivity by Assyria or Babylon. Although proselyte Jews, the Edomites, living in the south of Judea, had their own army and entered Jerusalem for a time during the siege of the city in 70 A.D. This was at the invitation of the Zealots who held the city hostage necessitating the actions of the Romans.

We are not told just who the enemies of Jesus were. In John 10:26, Jesus said, "But ye believe not, because ye are not of my sheep, as I said unto you." Who are his sheep? Was not Jesus using a figure from the Old Testament known to his listeners? In Psalm 78:52 we read, "But made his own people to go forth like sheep, and guided them in the wilderness like a flock." There are other similar references in the Old Testament.

> **Psalm 79:13.** "So we thy people and sheep of thy pasture will give thee thanks forever."
>
> **Psalm 95:7.** "For he is our God; and we are the people of his pasture, and the sheep of his hand."
>
> **Psalm 100:3.** "Know ye that the Lord he is God: it is he that hath made us, and not we ourselves; we are his people, and the sheep of his pasture."

In Jeremiah 23 and Ezekiel 34, it is plain that the children of Israel were considered God's sheep. Then in John 10:26, is Jesus speaking to men not of Israel?

In Matthew 21:33-46, Jesus tells the parable of the wicked husbandmen. The parable speaks of the mistreatment of God's messengers over a considerable period of time, so it must have applications to Old Testament days. Then, in verse 37-38, we read, "But last of all he sent unto them his son, saying, they will reverence my son. But when the husbandmen saw the son, they said among themselves, this is the heir, come, let us kill him, and let us seize upon his inheritance." Just what is the inheritance of the son? Is it not all the kingdoms of the world? Psalm 82:8 reads, "Arise, O God, judge the earth: for thou shalt inherit all nations." Also, in Isaiah 65:9, we read, "And I will bring forth a seed out of Jacob, and out of Judah an inheritor of my mountains: and mine elect shall inherit it, and my servants shall dwell there." Psalm 22:28 states that "For the kingdom is the Lord's", and in Revelation 11:15, the great voices in heaven say, "the kingdoms of this world are become the kingdoms of our Lord, and of his Christ; and he shall reign forever and ever." All this and more is the inheritance of the son.

Jesus is teaching that the right of inheritance is challenged by unfaithful and wicked men. Who are they? In Matthew 21:45, we read, "And when the chief priests and Pharisees had heard his parables, they perceived that He spake of them.". In Matthew 23:13, Jesus utters these words to His detractors, "But, woe unto you, Scribes and Pharisees, hypocrites! for ye shut up the kingdom of heaven against men: for ye neither go in yourselves, neither suffer ye them that are entering to go in." Hinderers and obstructionists.

In Matthew 23:29-36, Jesus spoke concerning His parable of the wicked husbandmen we find in Matthew 21. Jesus described the activities of those anti-God pretenders, and spoke of their continued opposition to the messengers of God in generations yet to come. The Book of Acts reveals the zeal with which the opponents of the Gospel pursued the Apostle Paul throughout the cities of the Roman Empire.

In the parable of the pounds in Luke 19, Jesus referred to citizens who hated Him and sent a message to Him, saying, "We will not have this man to reign over us." At the conclusion of the parable, in verse 27, Jesus said, "But those mine enemies, which would not that I should reign over them, bring hither and slay them before me." The gentle, loving Jesus said that. Here, Jesus is speaking of judgment, not of the gospel of persuasion, "Shall not the judge of all the earth do right?" (Genesis 18:25). Also see Romans 9:18-22.

It was the high priest John Hyrcanus who made the Edomites to become proselyte Jews in the late second century B.C. Immediately following the death of Hyrcanus, the Pharisees became the dominant sect within Judaism. The two movements then grew together until New Testament times. We do not know how many of the Edomite proselytes became Pharisees but the antichrist nature of both is evident. In 1 John 4:3, we read, "And every spirit that confesseth not that Jesus Christ is come in the flesh in not of God: and this is that spirit of antichrist, whereof ye have heard that it should come; and even now already is it in the world."

Jesus was in continual conflict with the chief priests, scribes, and Pharisees. He was challenged by them on the basis of their own legalistic interpretation of the Law, the system of interpretation Jesus calls the traditions of the fathers. This was not a reference to the Old Testament teachers and prophets, but rather to the oral tradition of teachers known as Rabbis which developed after the return of the Jews from Babylon, during the period between the Old and New Testaments. These teachings became the basis for the teachings of the Pharisees of New Testament times.

In the latter part of Matthew 5, Jesus countered the restriction of the letter of the Law as taught by the Pharisees by the wider and more spiritual intent of the Law. In verse 20, he said, "For I say unto you, that except your righteousness shall exceed the righteousness of the scribes and Pharisees, ye shall in no case enter into the kingdom of heaven." In Matthew 15, the scribes and Pharisees from Jerusalem asked, "Why do thy disciples transgress the tradition of the elders?" Jesus counters with, "Why do ye also transgress the commandment of God by your tradition?" He gives them a quotation from Isaiah which closes with, "But in vain they do worship me, teaching for doctrines the commandments of men."

In Matthew 16:5-12, Jesus taught his disicples a lesson concerning bread, which concluded with, "Then understood them how that he bade them not beware of the leaven of bread, but of the doctrine of the Pharisees and of the Sadducees."

There was little in common between the messages of Jesus and the teachings of Judaism of his day. It is questionable to ever use the phrase, "Our Judeo-Christian" heritage or tradition or culture. The late Stephen S. Wise, chief Rabbi of America, said, "The return from Babylon, and the adoption of the Babylonian Talmud, marks the end of Hebrewism, and the beginning of Judaism." The article on JUDAISM in the *New Bible Dictionary* edited by Dr. J.D. Douglas, begins with, "Judaism is the religion of the Jews in contrast to that of the Old Testament. While in any full study of it, it would be natural to start with the call of Abraham, this would be solely as an indispensable introduction. Judaism should be regarded as beginning with the Babylonian exile." The Rabbi, Synagogue, Talmud system was certainly not the Priest, Levite, Temple system. Yes, we have an exceedingly rich heritage in our Hebrew-Christian tradition which teaches us about life, but the term Judeo-Christian is a misnomer.

The Talmud is the written collection of the teachings of leaders of the Jews from the time of their Babylonian captivity. Some of the early written traditions were made an integral part of the Law of Moses and together known as the Torah, "Instruction".

After 70 A.D., the Jews continued to offer resistance to the Romans wherever Jews were in any sizable number in the cities near Palestine. This opposition became very disruptive of civil order in many places, so much so that the Roman Emperor Hadrian, in 135 A.D., forcibly deported Palestinian Jews to cities further west in the Roman Empire. There was already a large Jewish enclave at Alexandria in Egypt, and several lesser ones in the cities of Asia Minor. A large group of these deportees were settled in Spain, known as Sepharad. These Sephardim, or Spanish Jews, became the nucleus of Judaism in western European countries for some centuries to come. They used a short version of the Talmud, known as the Jerusalem Talmud. The Jews in eastern Mediterranean countries continued their scholarly pursuits, and by the sixth century A.D. had added a great amount of material to their version of the Talmud, known as the

Babylonian Talmud.

While western Europe lay sleeping during the dark ages, events were happening in the region north of the Black Sea which would bring great changes in the subsequent history of the Jews. A sizable kingdom developed in this region which has been largely ignored by Western historians. The people of this Khazar kingdom were related to the Huns, Bulgars, Magyars, and Turks. In their legends about their origins there are repeated references to Gog and Magog, Togarmah and Japheth. They cannot be considered of Mediterranean origin by any serious student. They were certainly not of the stock of Abraham nor even Semitic.

When the Mohammedans swept the world in the seventh and eighth centuries, the Khazars, who were a pagan people, were faced with a dilemma. They were being pressured by two strong religious movements; Christianity from Byzantium and Islam from the South. Somewhat as a polictical expediency, in the middle of the eighth century, the king of the Khazars chose Judaism as a state religion as a ploy to fend off the onslaught of the two more aggressive religious parties. Jewish Rabbis were brought in from Asia Minor to teach a whole nation a new religion. The story is told in the first article, CHAZARS, in Volume IV of the 1905 edition of *The Jewish Encyclopedia.* It is told in greater detail in a book entitled *"The Thirteenth Tribe"* written by Arthur Koestler, a well-known Jewish author, published in 1978.

The Khazars flourished for a few short centuries. Their kingdom was finally destroyed by the Rus and other invaders from the North. By the late 12th century, the Mongols were moving in and very little was left of Khazar culture. Great numbers of the Khazar Jews had moved into Poland and later into East Germany, which the Khazars called Ashkenaz. These eastern European Jews subsequently have been known as Ashkenazim.

A quotation from Koestler's book is appropriate. On page 181, he writes:

> "The Jews of our times fall into two main divisions, Sephardim and Ashkenazim. The Sepharadim are descendants of the Jews who since antiquity have lived in Spain until they were

> expelled and settled in the countries bordering the Mediterranean... In the 1960's the number of Sepharadim was estimated at 500,000. The Ashkenazim, at the same period numbered about eleven million. Thus, in common parlance, Jew is practically synonymous with Ashkenazim Jew... There is no other term to refer to the non-Sephardim majority of contemporary Jewry."

The Khazar Jews were well taught by their Rabbinical mentors whose scriptures were the Babylonian Talmud. The fine shades of legalistic morality, the concept of a people set apart, and the expectation of eventual world dominance were all parts of a religious system transmitted by the Pharisees to the Khazar proselytes.

The Jews in political control in the state of Israel today are the Ashkenazim from eastern European countries. The Sephardim in Israel today have difficulty in finding jobs, in getting land or housing, and having adequate representation in political affairs. Yet the Sephardim are the only Jews who have any historical ties to the Jews of the Bible. The Japhetic Ashkenazim have been particularly harsh in their treatment of Semitic Arabs who are the descendants of Abraham and his son Ishmael. The most oppressed and forgotten people in Israel today are the Palestinian Christians who have been almost totally ignored by western Christians.

Do the plans and aspirations of the Ashkenazim extend beyond the borders of the state of Israel, or even of world Jewry?

Just what is the attitude of Jews toward the Christian West? A great number of Jews have lived and prospered in Christian countries. They have become assimilated with our more tolerant Christian cultures. These Jews are largely anti-Zionists. Some, however, have been and are today disdainful of Christianity and oppose it in many ways. Let men speak for themselves.

"We Jews, we, the destroyers, will remain destroyers forever. Nothing that you will do will meet our needs and demands. We will forever destroy because we need a world of our own."

-Maurice Samuel
You Gentiles p. 155

"You have not begun to appreciate the depth of our guilt. We are intruders. We are subverters. We have taken your natural world, your ideals, your destiny, and played havoc with them. We have been at the bottom of not merely the latest great war, but of every other major revolution in your history. We have brought discord and confusion and frustration into your personal and public life. We are still doing it. No one can tell how long we will go on doing it. Who knows what great and glorious destiny might have been yours if we had left you alone."

-Marcus Eli Ravage *Century Magazine* February, 1928

"The Jewish people as a whole will be its own Messiah. It will attain world dominion by the dissolution of other races, by the abolition of frontiers, the annihilation of monarchy, and by the establishment of a world republic in which the Jews will everywhere exercise the privilege of citizenship. In this new world order the Children of Israel will furnish all the leaders without encountering opposition. The governments of the different peoples forming the world republic will fall without difficulty into the hands of the Jews. It will then be possible for the Jewish rulers to abolish private property, and everywhere to make use of the resources of the state. Thus will the promise of the Talmud be fulfilled, in which is said that when the Messianic time is come, the Jews will have all the property of the whole world in their hands."

-Baruch Levy, Letter to Karl Marx *La Revue de Paris* p. 574 June 1, 1928

"I am devoting my lecture in this seminar to discussion of the possibility that we are now entering a Jewish century, a time when the spirit of the community, the non-idealogical blend of the emotional and rational and the resistance to categories and forms will emerge through the forces of anti-nationalism to provide us with a new kind of society. I call this process the Judaization of Christianity because Christianity will be the vehicle through which this society becomes Jewish."

-Rabbi Martin Siegel *New York Magazine* p. 32 Jan. 18, 1972

"I believe that the active Jews of today have a tendency to

think that the Christians have organized and set up and run the world of injustice, unfairness, cruelty, misery. I am not taking any part in this, but I have heard it expressed, and I believe they feel it that way. Jews have lived for the past 2000 years and developed in a Christian world. They are a part of that Christian world even when they suffer from it or be in opposition with it, and they cannot dissociate themselves from this Christian world and from what it has done. And I think that the Jews are bumptious enough to think that perhaps some form of Jewish solution to THE problems of the world could be found which would be better, which would be an improvement. It is up to them to find a Jewish answer to THE problems of the world, the problems of today."

-Baron Guy de Rothschild NBC-TV *The Remnant* August 18,1974

Is this not evidence of a plan to take over the control of all wealth and all nations? Is this not the plan to seize upon the inheritance of the Son of God? Is this not the scheme of usurpers and pretenders of authority in the affairs of men? Much has been written, too much to be included here. Reference is made to the Appendix for publications relating to these subjects.

How powerful is this influence? Senator Fulbright of Arkansas said publicly, "The Zionists can count on 75 or 80 senators to give them any thing they want." Fulbright was never re-elected. Congressman Rarick from Louisiana introduced a bill requiring the United States to buy back the Federal Reserve Bank. Rarick was never re-elected. President Truman was pressured into recognizing the new state of Israel in May 1948 within minutes of its claim to independence, leaving our representatives in the United Nations red-faced for two weeks waiting for our State Department to come up with a rationalization for a complete reversal of policy. The list could go on and on.

How strong is this connection that goes back through time to its origins? From Zionism through the Ashkenasim, Khazars, Asiatics, Rabbinical teachers, Pharisees, and Edomites; all the way back to the Old Testament false teachers and prophets? If not biological, at least in spirit this connection is there amongst the opposers of God and his Christ. How can the prophecy of Isaiah 63 ever be fulfilled unless these contenders against the kingdom are here on earth when the Lord comes to take vengeance on his enemies? Remember, Edom is in Jewry. In Isaiah 34:5,6, we read, "For my sword shall be bathed in heaven: behold, it shall come down upon Idumea, and upon the people of my curse to judgment . . . . For the Lord hath a sacrifice in Bozrah, and a great slaughter in the land of Idumea." Finally, then, retribution shall come to the Man of Kerioth.

Bibliography

1. Forest, A. C. *The Unholy Land.* Old Greenwich Connecticut. The Devin-Adair Company. 1972
2. Friedman, Benjamin H. *Facts and Facts.* New York. Personal Letter. 1954.
3. Graham, O. J. *The Six-Pointed Star.* Fletcher, North Carolina. New Puritan Library. 1984.
4. Koestler, Arthur. *The Thiteenth Tribe.* New York. Random House. 1976.
5. Lilienthal, Alfred. *The Zionist Connection.* New York. Middle East Perspective. 1978.
6. Manhattan, Avro. *The Vatican Moscow Washington Alliance.* Chino, California. Chick Publications. 1982.
7. North, Gary. *Call It Conspiracy.* Seattle. Double A Publications. 1985.
8. Reed, Douglas. *The Controversy of Zion.* Durban, S. H. Dolphin Press. 1978.
9. Robison, John. *Proofs of a Conspiracy.* Boston. Western Islands. Original. 1798
10. Robnett, George W. *Conquest Through Immigration.* Pasadena. Institute for Special Research. 1968.
11. Saxon, William Norman. *The Mask of Edom.* Merrimac, Mass. Destiny Publishers. 1985.

Chapter 16
The Woman in the Sun

In the twelfth chapter of the book of Revelation there is, in highly symbolic form, a picture of the struggle of God's people against their arch enemy Satan throughout much of history. The scene is both propositional and historical.

The first of these symbols is a woman clothed with the sun, with the moon under her feet and wearing a crown of twelve stars. She travailed to bring forth a man child who is to rule all nations with a rod of iron. There is a prevelant interpretation which makes of the woman the church and Jesus the man child. Those who teach this are some of the very ones who claim that the church began on the day of Pentecost. They want to have their cake and eat it too. This interpretaton is inconsistent within itself. The church did not bring forth the Christ child, but rather, Jesus said, "On this rock I will build my church." The church did not produce Jesus, but rather, Jesus produced the church. This popular interpretation would have the man child produce his own mother!

There is only one other place in the Bible where the symbol of the sun, moon, and stars, is used for God's people. It is found in the story of Joseph, in Genesis 37:9, as a symbol in Joseph's dream. Since, in the dream, Joseph's brethren are symbolized by stars, Joseph being the twelfth one, then the sun and moon would be their parents, Jacob and his wives. Therefore the symbol of the woman in Revelation 12 is the symbol for the people of Israel in their corporate historical entity.

In great travail, the people of Israel brought forth the man child, even Jesus Christ. The travail came as a consequence of the punishments of the people for their disobedience of God's commandments and laws. The travail took the form of adverse weather conditions, idolatry, compromise with alien elements, the country paying tribute to foreign kings. The final blow was the military conquest by foreign governments; first the Assyrian captivity of Israel and then the Babylonian captivity of Judah. It was the struggling residue of Judah which returned from Babylon, and later, under the travail of Roman rule, brought forth the man child Jesus Christ. It was Herod, an Edomite Jew under Roman rule, who stood ready "to devour the man child as soon as it was born."

Continuing the symbolism, the woman fled into a "wilderness where she hath a place prepared of God." Israel went through a wilderness when Israel was led out of Egypt, but the wilderness in Revelation 12:6 is another one. It was yet future when Hosea wrote, "Therefore, I will allure her and bring her into the wilderness, and speak comfortably unto her." (Hosea 2:14) It is also yet future when Jeremiah wrote in Jeremiah 31:1-2, "I will be the God of all the families of Israel, and they shall be my people. Thus saith the Lord, the people which were left of the sword found grace in the wilderness; even Israel, when I went to cause him to rest." There are other references to a future wilderness experience. In fact, there seems to be more than one wilderness in view. Reading the passages indicated under the word "wilderness" in a good concordance will confirm this.

Herodotus wrote at the time of the Greek-Persian wars. He describes a nomadic people living north of the Black Sea who obstructed the advance of the Persians. The country was known as Scythia, and whoever lived in these regions at any time were called Scythians by the Greeks. Herodotus describes several groups of Scythians, all of whom had stories of their origin in Media. Media, of course, was the country into which the tribes of Israel were taken captive by the Assyrians just a few centuries earlier.

The Scythians of the time of Herodotus, under the pressure of the advancing Persians, left that country, going northward into what Herodotus describes in several passages in his history as a wilderness wherein no man dwelt. They lived for several centuries in the regions east of the Danube and were known to the Romans as the fair-haired barbarians of the north.

When the Roman empire waned, these so-called barbarians swept across Europe as the Vandals, Goths, Heruli, and farther north, as the Vikings in the Baltic regions. They had been virtually unknown to historians for about thirteen centuries since their departure from Media; hence the 1260 days, and the time, times and half time of Revelation 12:6 and 12:14. The rest is well known history. Like arctic terns finding their nesting place after a journey of 10,000 miles over a chartless sea, so now these people of the chartless north assembled in one place, in wave after wave of Angles, Jutes, Danes, Saxons, and Normans, coming together in the Isles we call Britian.

Since the Normans, or North men, no other foreign invader has ever gained a foothold in these islands. Neither the Spanish Armada, nor Napoleon, nor Kaiser Wilhelm, nor Hitler, were ever successful in their attempts to subdue Britain, but a more insidious foe was successful for a time. The great whore of Rome dominated the life of the people of the isles for several centuries until the time of the English reformation. England was harassed by the Catholic countries of the continent and was continually under the dominance of the Catholic hierarchy until the time of Henry VIII. Soon the northern countries were Christian and Protestant.

The Papal reprisals against the Protestants were devastating. The inquisition was truly deadly. In the notes on the thirteenth chapter of Revelation in Halley's Bible Handbook it is stated that there were 50,000,000 martyrs. The heroism and utter devotion of such large numbers of saints who suffered and died for their faith in Christ are unmatched anywhere in all of history unless it was during the persecutions by Imperial Rome. Surely during the dark days of the Inquisitors, Satan was persecuting the woman who had brought forth the man child.

The earth then opened up to swallow the adversaries of God's people. World exploration got under way. North America was discovered. Although the Spaniards had arrived earlier in the South, it was the Protestants who came to North America. The Spaniards came with a sword, looking for gold. The French came with their traps, looking for furs. The English came with a rifle, an axe, a hoe, a package of garden seed, a Bible, and a pregnant wife. They meant to stay. According to their own testimony, they came looking to build the Kingdom of God.

And build something they did. They built a country which won its independence as a sovereign nation in 1776. They built churches and schools everywhere they went. They built cities and highways. They built industries and manufacturing. They expanded inland from the eastern shores. The wagons rolled again, westward, always westward. The men rode on horses; the women and children in covered wagons, just as their ancestors had moved northward from ancient Scythia. Everywhere they settled, they built churches until spires pointing heavenward dotted the landscape from sea to shining sea. There has never been another venture like it. Not only the English, but the Germans, the Dutch, the Scots, the Irish, and the Scandinavians came and built. They shared a common ancestry and common faith. They created a nation, a culture, and a civilization which became the envy of the world.

Then that other world came. The opportunists, the unbelievers, the freeloaders, the destroyers, and the detractors came in large numbers in the latter years of the nineteenth century. In a hundred years, our heritage has been stripped from our history books, prayers have been outlawed from our schools, the ten commandments have been replaced by the ten plagues, and our laws have been reinterpreted to favor the lawless. Our babies are executed while still in their mother's womb just for being there, and our young men are made to believe it is morally wrong to defend our country against its declared foes.

The nation's young people have been taught a science with no soul, a philosophy with no purpose, a peace with no righteousness, an art with no beauty, a music with no melody, and a love with no sacrifice. Their most popular entertainers sing with a snarl instead of a smile. They are not super kids; they are not smart enough to invent any new heresy nor wicked enough to invent any new sin. They have not yet learned that it has all been said and done before. Satan's lie is an ancient one.

Surely an enemy has done this. In Revelation 12:17, we read, "And the dragon was wroth with the woman, and went to make war with the remnant of her seed, which keep the commandments of God, and have the testimony of Jesus Christ." This is a very apt description of our present situation today. We are experiencing the most vicious spiritual warfare the world has ever known. It seems that Satan is making every possible effort to control the minds, the hearts, the souls of men in an effort to thwart the return of Christ. "For we wrestle not against flesh and blood, but against principalities, against powers, against the rulers of the darkness of this world, against spiritual wickedness in high places." (Ephesians 6:12). Against these we need the whole armor of God. The warfare is in the realm of psychopolitics and philosophical subtleties with which average church members are ill prepared to contend.

Such is the story of the woman in the sun, the Israel of God. How different from the imaginary story of some hypothetical entity of believers put together outside the body of Christ, without the ministry of the Holy Spirit, in some supposed location of persecution in a future short period of time! Reality has a way of eventually imposing itself upon our consciousness.

In Revelation 12, the story is left unfinished. And so we leave it here. The last verse of the chapter so closely describes our present situation that neither pen nor tongue could more accurately summarize the current spiritual warfare being waged against us.

The Woman in the Sun is experiencing a cloudy day indeed, but there is bright hope for tomorrow. Someday, the Son of Righteousness will surely burst through the clouds bringing light and life to those who are his. We are nowhere told the exact schedule of events surrounding his appearing, but come He will, and come He must. He alone is our hope.

Bibliography

1. Hunt, Dave and McMahan, T.A. *The Seduction of Christianity.* Eugene, Oregon. Harvest House Publishers. 1985.
2. Noebel, David A. *The Marxist Minstrels.* Tulsa. American Christian College Press. 1974.
3. Williams, Lindsey. *To Seduce A Nation.* Worth Publishing Company. 1984.

Chapter 17

The City of Chaos

Babylon is the name of a city. Actually, Babylon is the name of several cities.

The first use of the name is in the eleventh chapter of the book of Genesis. After the flood, men built a city in the plains of Shinar, in the valley of the Euphrates river. In this city they built a very high tower which served as a monument to themselves, their own importance and their own accomplishments. The Lord God came down to the people and pronounced judgement upon them. He scattered them abroad upon the earth and confounded their speech so they could not understand one another. The name of the city became Babel, or Babylon, which means "confusion".

Ancient Babylon, or Babel, was more than the place of the scattering of the people and the confusion of languages. It was also the home of Nimrod, the mighty hunter, and grandson of Ham. There is a brief account of Nimrod in Genesis 10:6-10.

The classic treatment of the history of this early culture is found in Alexander Hislop's "The Two Babylons". In this book we find that the mother of Nimrod was Semeramis. The two of them were worshipped as gods, and this worship was a perversion of the promise in Genesis 3:15 concerning "the seed of the woman."

Semeramis, called th Mother of the gods, was the chief object of worship, although she derived her power from the son. According to Genesis 10:8, the father of Nimrod was Cush, who was also known as Bel, "the confounder" or the "god of confusion." When the inhabitants of this ancient city of confusion were scattered abroad and their language confounded, they took with them their religious beliefs. Thus Semeramis and Nimrod appear in many ancient cultures of the East in all the variant forms of mother goddess worship. In India they were known as Iswira and

Isi. In Egypt, they were known as Isis and Osiris; in Greece as Ceres and Dionysius or Bacchus; and in Rome as Fortuna and Jupiter. There is scarcely an ancient culture where this worship of mother and child cannot be found.

In the Bible, reference is made to the mother as Ashtaroth, the queen of heaven, and to Tammuz, the son. The queen of heaven was called by the Phoenicians Astarte, and Ishtu by the Assyrians.

In all the variant forms of the worship of the mother goddess, there can be found in the religious practices of the people a common element of sexual promiscuity and perversion. Fertility rites, orgies of many varieties, public prostitution, and sodomy were normal practices in the religious life of the people. Throughout the Old Testament there are continual condemnations of these practices from the voices of priests and prophets. In the New Testament Paul exhorts the Corinthians to abandon their former practices and live as Christ would have them live. At Ephesus, the worship of Diana was the chief obstacle to the preaching of Paul. Diana has been depicted as a many-breasted queen wearing a miniature turreted stone tower as a crown on her head.

Tourists in Rome today are shown the ruins of ancient temples to the many gods and goddesses of the divine hierarchy. The high priest of all these religious systems was Caesar or the Emperor. His title became "Pontifex Maximus," or High Priest, and was himself the object of worship, which was given by all his loyal subjects. When Romans became Christians they carried with them many of their earlier beliefs. Rather than attempt to eradicate these beliefs completely, they became Christianized by the rulers. An example is the worship of the sun when it began its northern motion again at the time of the winter solstice, about December 22. This was declared to be not only the rebirth of the Sun, but the birth of the Son, and so Christmas was born.

Another ancient practice that was Christianized by the Latin church was the worship of the mother and son. The elevation of the Madonna and child as a central symbol of worship followed. The mother of the gods became the mother of God. Although it is recognized that the power is in the son, our only access to that power is through the mother. Therefore, our prayers should be directed to her. The doctrine of the Immaculate Conception, adopted by the Roman church in 1854, declares that Mary herself was conceived and lived without sin. The belief in the Assumption of Mary is that Mary ascended directly into heaven without suffering a normal death. Michelangelo's magnificent sculpture Pieta depicts Mary holding the body of Jesus in her lap. These and other practices indicate the veneration of the Mother above the Son.

It is the nature of man to worship. Lacking gods outside of himself to worship, he worships himself. Man becomes the only god man needs. The supernatural is denied. This is the essence of the secular humanism which is fast becoming the public philosophy of America and much of the civilized world. It is a philosophical Tower of Babel which men are erecting in our modern times. It is an outgrowth of a naturalistic view of man based upon a belief in man's evolutionary development. Having begun with something less than an amoeba, he has now progressed to the point at which he can command his own future development. Man is now lord of himself, all nature, and the heavens above. Man is God. What a pity!

When we look into the religious practices of secular men, we find that having abandoned the moral restraints of our traditional culture they seek to indulge themselves in every available pleasurable pursuit. This hedonistic approach to personal and public behavior has opened the flood gates of antimoral teaching in our schools and our public entertainment media. It has resulted in the return of an open acceptance of cultism and even witchcraft. It has become the protagonist of every variant sexual deviation imaginable. Since nothing is immoral, anything is permissible. Any attempt to impose moral or legal restraints is antisocial and an invasion of personal rights.

When two people meet together, there are three mental entities at work. Each of the two think individually, as well as in concert. When three people meet and act together, the three thinking and acting together make one entity, and the three acting as individuals take three more. However, there can also be three pairs of individuals, making for a total of seven possible combinations of mental entities operating. There is a mathematical equation which enables us to calculate the possible combinations of relationships in a total group. For a group of 4 there is a total of 15 possible combinations of operations. For a group of 5 there is a total of 31 combinations. The number of possible combinations increases much faster than the number in the group.

Instead of five, suppose there are five billion human individuals in the group. How many combinations of relationships or interactions within such a group, which is the total population of the earth? The number would be unimaginable! Yet that is the possible total mental and spiritual entities operating in the world today. This is a concept developed by Thomas E. Bearden in his book *"The Excalibur Briefing"*, in which he calls this monstrous mental influence ZARG. However, because it is so fragmental, ZARG is insane.

As Christians, we know that the total mind-set of humanity is anti-God because of sin. In Romans 8:7-8, we read, "Because the carnal mind is enmity against God: for it is not subject to the law of God, neither indeed can be. So then they that are in the flesh cannot please God." And in Isaiah 59:2, we read, "But your iniquities have separated between you and your God, and your sins have hid his face from you, that he will not hear." Thus Zarg is not only insane, it is evil.

When a person becomes a Christian, he also becomes a dropout from the world system. "Therefore if any man be in Christ, he is a new creation: old things are passed away; behold, all things are become new." (IICorinthians 5:17). Christians constitute another assemblage of mental and spiritual communities. We are in the world, but not of the world. In Ephesians 2:19, we read, "Now therefore ye are no more strangers and foreigners, but fellow citizens with the saints, and of the household of God." In our new communities of prayer, we are aided by the Holy Spirit who is present in any group of believers, and enables us to communicate with the Father. Jesus said in Matthew 18:20, "Where two or three are gathered together in my name, there am I in the midst of them." Jesus, then, is a member of any spiritual group of believers.

The organized religions of the world represent man's attempt to find God, to be God-like, or to become God. Theology has been replaced by a man-centered social philosophy. This secular humanism has become the religion of men who reject the God of creation and who seek to create a God in their own image. Thus man strives to become the God of ZARG, which is both insane and evil. Surely, this is Babel reborn, the Babylon of man's self-esteem and rebellion.

In the second chapter of the Book of Daniel there is an account of Nebuchadnezzar, king of Babylon, having a strange dream. Daniel was enabled, through divine revelations, to tell the king both the substance and the meaning of the dream.

The dream was of a great image in the likeness of a man, having a head of gold, chest and arms of silver, thighs of brass, legs of iron, and feet part iron and part clay. There was also a stone which grew and smote the image upon his feet so that the entire image was broken to pieces.

Daniel then gave an interpretaton. Babylon, symbolized by Nebuchadnezzar, was the head of gold. After Babylon, there would be three other kingdoms which would rule over the men of earth. Notice in this passage, Daniel 2:36-44, the words king and kingdom are used interchangeably. Daniel explains that the stone represents an everlasting Kingdom which would be set up by God himself and which would destroy all the kingdoms represented by the great image. Nebuchadnezzar recognizes that Daniel's interpretation is true and gives the God of Daniel honor for the revelation given to Daniel. The king then gives Daniel a position of high honor in his kingdom.

There are two sequels to this story. The first, in the third chapter of Daniel, is that Nebuchadnezzar attempts to make the dream a physical reality by building a great image like that in his dream, requiring men to worship it. Daniel's three Hebrew companions refuse, and are cast into a fiery furnace, from which they are miraculously saved. The second sequel, told in the fourth chapter of Daniel, concerns the pride of Nebuchadnezzar. Again, it involves a dream. The dream is of a great tree which is cut down and the stump left to the ravages of time and weather.

Just as Daniel addressed Nebuchadnezzar following his first dream by declaring "Thou art this head of gold", so now Daniel declares to the king regarding the great tree "It is thou, O King, that art grown and become strong," (Daniel 4:22). Then in verses 24-26 Daniel gives the meaning of the dream. "This is the interpretation, O King, and this is the decree of the most High, which is come upon my lord the king. That they shall drive thee from men, and thy dwelling shall be with the beasts of the field, and they shall make thee to eat grass as oxen and they shall wet thee with the dew of heaven, and seven times shall pass over thee, till thou know that the most High ruleth in the kingdom of men, and giveth it to whomsoever he will. And whereas they commanded to leave the stump of the tree roots; thy kingdom shall be sure unto thee, after that thou shalt have known that the heavens do rule."

Twelve months after this vision. Nebuchadnezzar was viewing his palace and the city, and boasted, "Is not this great Babylon, that I have built for the house of the kingdom by the might of my power, and for the honor of my majesty?" In the same hour the king was stricken, and he was incapable of ruling for the seven times. Josephus tells us that Nebuchadnezzar was out of his mind for seven years. As a consequence of his humiliation, Nebuchadnezzar declared his recognition of the King of heaven who is the sovereign ruler of all kings and kingdoms.

Nebuchadnezzar not only represented his kingdom of Babylon, but the entire succession of gentile world powers who would rule for the seven times. On the basis of a year for a day, this seven times would be seven years of days or 2520 days, which represent 2520 years of historical time. This is a prime example of the year-day principle. Nebuchadnezzar first took Jeruselem in 604 B.C. In

1917 A.D., General Allenby took Jerusalem from the Turks exactly 2520 years after Jerusalem was taken by the king of Babylon, and the world has not been the same since.

The four political empires represented by the great image of Nebuchadnezzar's dream are considered to be the same four as represented by the four great beasts of Daniel's vision in chapter seven. These four are Babylon, Medo-Persia, Greece, and Rome. There are many theories concerning the final course of events involving the end of the fourth empire. The Reformation leaders were of one voice in declaring that the Papacy succeeded political Rome. It is interesting to note that Daniel gives a short summary of the history of the world from his own time to the end of the age in Daniel 2:44, "And in the days of these kings shall the God of heaven set up a kingdom which shall never be destroyed: and the kingdom shall not be left to other people, but it shall break in pieces and consume all these kingdoms, and it shall stand forever." Again, in Daniel 7:17,18 we read, "These great beasts, which are four, are four kings (kingdoms) which shall arise out of the earth, but the saints of the most High shall take (receive) the kingdom, and possess the kingdom forever, even for ever and ever." The message is the same in both summaries. There is no room in history for a fifth world power between the fourth and the Kingdom of God's people.

Why just four? Could it be that these four are the very gentile world powers of concern to God's people Israel? Read Hosea 13:4-9, "Yet I am the Lord thy God from the land of Egypt, and thou shalt know no god but me: for there is no saviour beside me. I did know thee in the wilderness, in the land of great drought. According to their pasture, so were they filled, and their heart was exalted; therefore have they forgotten me. Therefore I will be unto them as a lion: as a leopard by the way will I observe them; I will meet them as a bear that is bereaved of her whelps, and I will rend the caul of their heart, and there will I devour them like a lion; the wild beast shall tear them. O Israel, thou hast destroyed thyself; but in me is thine help."

The message is to Ephraim-Israel, the Israel of the ten tribes, not Judah. They are to be present with, and harassed by the four great powers; Babylon, Medo-Persia, Greece, and Rome; neither China nor India nor any civilization in South America, but these four well known in history. These four are called the Babylonian succession of empires because Babylon was their head.

The fourth empire, Rome, was followed by the Papacy, which set up the Holy Roman Empire, made up of the divided countries of Europe. The leader of this assemblage was Germany under Charlemagne. Now look at history. Has this assorted assemblage of nations been broken up? In vain the Futurist look for a strong union of ten European countries. Daniel's interpretation of Nebuchadnezzar's dream image speaks only of progressive weakening; it does not indicate a revival of strength in the feet and toes of the image.

Who has broken up the remnants of political Rome? Was it not Britain who surpassed Spain? Was it not Britain who defeated Napoleon? Was it not America who brought Germany to its knees twice in the twentieth century? What remains of the weakened feet, made of iron and miry clay? Does this mean that Britain and America are the stone kingdom of the saints?

The kingdom is not the church. Nor is the kingdom some ephemeral ghost-like, vaporous sphere of disembodied spirits. The kingdom is a real historical domain of flesh and blood people; God's people. There is evil in the kingdom which cannot be said of the body of Christ, the church. In Matthew 13, the tares grow in the field of the kingdom. The bad fish are caught in the net of the kingdom. The time will come, according to Matthew 13:41, when the Son of Man will send his angels to gather out of his kingdom all things that offend and them that do iniquity. Therefore these things must be in the kingdom until the cleansing takes place.

There was a time when it was said "The sun never sets on the British Empire." Now it can be said that the sun never sets on an American soldier. It can also be said that the sun never sets on an American missionary. Deny history if you will and you will come up empty.

Does this mean that we are the stone kingdom? Why not? Our presence is felt throughout the entire world, and we are certainly not Roman in our national origin. For more on the stone as a symbol in our national life, read "The History of the Great Seal" in the Appendix.

Now we find that the Camp of the Saints is besieged from within and without by men of alien faiths. They demand the benefits of our age long struggle, but deny the Author of our liberties. In vain, men have gathered together into a United Nations which denies the Lord of Nations and of history. Nobly conceived by men of high principles, it has deteriorated into a clamorous cacophony of selfish national demands. Every tribal chieftan now has equal vote with the mightiest of nations simply by declaring his small enclave a national entity.

Surely, we have returned to Babel in our confusion. We have erected a political tower that depends upon man's intelligence as the solution to all our international problems. Secular humanism has become the operational public philosophy of most nations of the world community. In the Meditation Room at the United Nations building in New York, any delegate may worship whatsoever or whomsoever he will, but on the public floor only man is recognized. The God who created men and governs nations is ignored. "Except the Lord build the house, they labor in vain that build it." (Psalm 127:1)

In Revelation 16:19, we read, "And the great city was divided into three parts and the cities of the nations fell and great Babylon came in remembrance before God, to give unto her the cup of the wine of the fierceness of his wrath." In the two following chapters, 17 and 18, there is set forth the judgment of God on these three parts: the religious, the political and the financial aspects of the great city, which has become the three aspects of the entire world system called Babylon.

When a farmer plants seed in the ground, he hopes for a crop which will not only replace his seed but supply him food for his family. He is a capitalist, expecting a gain from his efforts. He recognized that the gain depends upon his own labor which he invests and also upon the life giving processes of nature over which he has little control, such as the weather. He has become an investment capitalist, taking the risk that all his efforts may come to nought. This is the system whereby wealth is produced and accumulated or lost. This is venture capitalism which made America a wealthy nation.

In the eighteenth chapter of the book of Revelation there is another type of capitalism described, which may be called monopoly capitalsm. Just as there is a religious Babylon and a political Babylon, so is there a financial Babylon. The temples of Babylon were the safest place for the people to keep their silver and gold. When the precious metals were brought to the temple, the priests would write a receipt or certificate of deposit which the holder could return to obtain possession of his silver or gold. This certificate of deposit became transferrable, and the people learned they could use these certificates of deposit to purchase goods and services from the merchants who in turn could collect the silver and gold at the temple. Thus paper money was invented. It became so desirable that the people were willing to even pay interest to the priests for the convenience of using the substitute for the real store of value in the temple.

Then the priests made a startling discovery. Not many people asked for their precious metals, so the wily priests began to issue as loans more certificates than there was gold on deposit. They knew full well that all the people would not clamor for their gold and silver at the same time. Of course, if a lot of people did ask for their gold and silver at the same time, the priests were in trouble.

The Jews who were in captivity in Babylon learned their lessons well. When the Jews returned to Jerusalem under the leadership of Ezra and Nehemiah, their primary concern was the rebuilding of the temple and the wall of the city. No one had time to farm. No wealth was produced from the soil. It was a consuming society, not a producing one.

Because human nature is not automated, there came about inequalities in the economic well being of the citizens who made up the work force. The less agressive and the more indolent among the people soon had to borrow from the more industrious. The process continued until the majority of the people were in debt to a few who held mortgages on their houses, their lands, their goods, and even the labor of their sons and daughters. The people complained bitterly to Nehemiah who called a council and made a decision. The story is in the fifth chapter of the book of Nehemiah. In verses 9-11, Nehemiah said, "It is not good that ye do: ought ye not to walk in the fear of our God because of the reproach of the heathen our enemies? I likewise and my brethren and my servants, might exact of them money and corn: I pray you, let us leave off this usury. Restore, I pray you, to them even this day, their land and their vineyards, their oliveyards, and their houses."

Usury was strictly forbidden by the law of Moses which defines usury as any increase whatever of money or goods of any description. Nehemiah's small society proved the reason why. Debt cannot increase wealth, it only channels it into the hands of the lenders.

North America is rich in natural resources. Our people through their labors, have produced the greatest wealth of any nation in the history of the world. Through agriculture, forestry, mining and manufacturing, we have become the wealthiest people ever. Now we face the prospect of losing so much of it because of our debt money economy. Every dollar bill is a certificate of indebtedness on which we pay interest. Our total debt, national, corporate, state, and personal, now runs into the trillions of dollars. While America was growing, the land produced enough to give us an increase in wealth and pay the interest on our debts. This may not be true any longer. Our debts are catching up on us just as in Nehemiah's time. Perhaps our productivity is slowing down to the point where we can no longer live the good life and pay our debts with what we produce. We have moved from an agricultural and industrial economy to a service economy. It is a sure thing that we cannot create wealth by taking in each other's washing. Somebody has to produce.

One of the Rothchilds is reported to have said, "Let me control the money of a nation and I care not who makes it's laws." The imposition of our interest bearing debt money system on a nation has only one consequence, which is the transfer of the wealth of a people into the hands of the few who control our money through the banks.

A few years ago Mr. Robert McNamara retired as head of the World Bank. At a dinner in his honor in Washington, Mr. David Rockefeller made the following revealing statement:

"The world which we have worked to construct is threatened. The gravity of this moment, when Mr. McNamara and others are about to leave their posts while a new administration re-examines American foreign aid policy, is great. If we are going to save the international institutions we have put in place, the moment is now or never, for the struggle between the old guard and the new is going to go far beyond the reduction of capital appropriations. It is going to endanger the new world order which we have based on the alliance between Wall Street and Washington. While we men of firms and banks organize international channels of economy and raw materials, the government is now building its own diplomatic and economic bridges between Washington and foreign governments. By our methods, our governments contribute to the stability and economic growth of the world, our multinationals benefit, and when it is necessary, they contribute their political support. Now radical conservatives are attempting to destroy all that in seeking first and foremost to serve the national interests of the United States."

Notice such phrases as "international institutions we have put in place," " new world order which we have based on the the alliance between Wall Street and Washington," and the last sentence which castigates those who seek to serve the national interests of the United States. In the face of a statement like this, can there be any lingering doubts that there exists a financial superstructure over the governments of the world which is international, multinational and supranational in scope?

The judgment on such a scheme as this is vividly portrayed in the eighteenth chapter of the book of Revelation. All nations are involved. In verse 3 notice that the kings and merchants of the earth are singled out. The cry goes out to "come out of her, my people, that ye be not partakers of her sins". How is this possible, since the system is worldwide? Get out of debt! Do not pay any interest to that crowd! Not even on credit card accounts. That may mean adopting a standard of living that is affordable. Why not?

The judgment is sure. In verse 8 we read, "Therefore shall her plagues come in one day, death and mourning, and famine; and she shall utterly be burned with fire: for strong is the Lord God who judgeth her". The judgment is upon three groups. First are the kings of the earth which would include all rulers. Next, in verses 11-16, are the merchants of the earth who have accumulated great treasures and are rich by trading in them. Thirdly, are the shipmasters and traders of the earth, in verse 17-19. The cry is the same from all, "Alas, Alas that great city, for in one hour is thy judgment come, so great riches is brought to nought and she is made desolate."

When this great worldwide city of finance and riches is brought to judgment, God's people are to rejoice! They will no longer be slaves to this interest-bearing debt system.

Notice that nowhere in this passage is agriculture or manufacturing condemned. There is nothing wrong with the production of wealth. Among the promised blessings to God's people is wealth but not riches. It is the financial superstructure exercising unbridled control over the wealth producing activities of man which is condemned. It has to go.

Babylon is the world system of man's effort to control his own destiny. Babylon is divided into three channels of activity on man's part; the religious, the political, and the economic. The total endeavor of man will fail, because it is godless. It is judged of God, and destroyed. This is the message of Revelation 17 and 18.

In the twelfth chapter of the gospel of John, Jesus declares a principle which may apply here. In John 12:24, he says, "Except a corn of wheat fall into the ground and die, it abideth alone: but if it die, it bringeth forth much fruit." What he seems to be saying is that death precedes life. He was speaking of his own imminent death. The principle also applies to us when we are born again. We die unto self in order to live unto Christ. In Galatians 2:20, we read, "I am crucified with Christ: nevertheless I live". In Romans 6:6, Paul says, "Knowing this, that our old man is crucified with him, that the body of sin might be destroyed, that henceforth we should not serve sin. For he that is dead is freed from sin. Now if we be dead with Christ, we believe that we shall also live with him."

If this is such a strong principle in the life of the individual, cannot it also apply to society as a whole? If so, then it can be said that this civilization must die in order for the Kingdom of God to live. In our present world order, neither man nor society is evolving into the kingdom of God on earth. It is not within us to accomplish any such goal. If we could, then we are vain enough to give ourselves the credit for our own accomplishments. No, the salvation of man and society is the work of God. "For the Lord shall judge his people, and repent himself for his servants, when he sees that their power is gone." (Deuteronomy 32:36) Only God himself can save us. And He will!

In Jeremiah 51, in verses 6-8, we read, "Flee out of the midst of Babylon and deliver every man his soul: be not cut off in her iniquity; for this is the time of the Lord's vengeance; he will render unto her a recompense. Babylon hath been a golden cup in the Lord's hand, that made all the earth drunken: the nations have drunken of her wine; therefore the nations are mad. Babylon is suddenly fallen and destroyed," and in verse 13, "O thou that dwellest upon many waters, abundant in treasures, thine end is come." In Revelation 18:20,21 we find, "Rejoice over her, thou heaven, and ye holy apostles and prophets; for God hath avenged you on her. And a mighty angel took up a stone like a great millstone, and cast it into the sea, saying, "Thus with violence shall that great city Babylon be thrown down, and shall be found no more at all."

Babylon, the great city, the city of confusion and chaos, the city of religious power, political power, and financial power, the Babel of man's efforts to rule himself without God, the city which is the building of this world's vanity, shall be no more.

"And it shall be said in that day, Lo, this is our God; we have waited for Him, and He will save us: this is the Lord; we have waited for Him, we will be glad and rejoice in his salvation!"

Amen!

Bibliography

1. Bearden, Thomas E. *Excalibur Briefing.* San Francisco. Strawberry Hill Press. 1980.
2. Hislop, Alexander. *The Two Babylons.* London. Partridge. 1929.
3. LaHaye, Tim. *The Battle for the Mind.* Old Tappan, New Jersey. Fleming H. Revell Company. 1980.
4. Panker, C.F. *Moses the Economist.* London. Covenant Publishing Company. 1947.
5. The Club of Rome. *The Limits to Growth.* New York. New American Library. 1972.
6. Woodrow, Ralph. *Babylon Mystery Religion.* Riverside, California. Ralph Woodrow Evangelistic Association. 1981.

Chapter 18
Mobtown

In the thirty-eighth and thirty-ninth chapters of Ezekiel there is described a great war. This war is to involve a people called Gog, the chief prince of Meshech and Tubal and their associates. God is against them. Who are these people?

The ethnic origin of the various nations mentioned in the Bible can be found in the tenth chapter of the book of Genesis. In Genesis 10:2-5, we find first the progeny of Japheth, one of the three sons of Noah. Among these names, the following occur in both Genesis 10 and Ezekiel 38: Gomer, Magog, Tubal, Meshech, and Togarmah. Ezekiel, then, is plainly writing about the family of Japheth.

In Ezekiel 38:5, three other allies are mentioned: Persia, Ethiopia, and Libya. Persia is considered by some to be the same as Elam, a country just east of the Euphrates river. However, a careful study will show there was both an Elam and a Persia. Persia was situated further to the east, bordering upon the Caspian Sea, the Persians having migrated from what is now southern Russia. They were probably Japhetic.

Ethiopia is ancient Cush, and Libya was known as Phut. In Genesis 10, Cush and Phut are among the sons of Ham. Thus in Ezekiel 38, we see an alliance between the descendants of Japheth and the descendants of Ham. It is interesting that the transliteration of "chief prince" in verse 2 is Nasi Rosh. The NASV reads, "the prince of Rosh, Meshech, and Tubal."

In Ezekiel 38:2, we read, "I am against thee", and in verse 4 "I will turn thee back, and put hooks into thy jaws, and I will bring thee forth." So it is God himself who directs the events described in this important passage. Does this mean that Gog will act prematurely, willy-nilly, ahead of schedule, forced to do so by some unforeseen adverse set of events beyond control? What constitutes the "hooks in thy jaws"?

This great array will have many horses, and be equipped with weapons more primitive than those used in modern warfare, unless the language is merely symbolic of more advanced weapons.

In verse 8, the invaders come to "the land that is brought back from the sword." The sword has been used as a symbol of Mohammedanism or Islam. The land of Palestine was set free from the rule of Turkey, a Mohammedan empire, in 1917 when General Allenby took Jerusalem. The time of this release could certainly be called "in the latter years."

The Israelis of this past generation have come from many people brought forth out of many nations. They are trying very hard to turn the land from a waste to a productive land, even by means of irrigation rather than natural rainfall.

The attack is by a multitude of men, "who shall ascend and come like a storm, thou shall be like a cloud to cover the land." Is this a massive air strike?

Throughout the twentieth century, it has been the concensus of prophetic expositors that this chapter refers to Russia, the colossus of the North, and its allies. The names Rosh, Meshech, and Tubal, would be equivalent of Russia, Moscow, and Tobolsk.

Now look carefully at verse 10. "Thus saith the Lord God: It shall also come to pass, that at the same time shall things come into thy mind, and thou shall think an evil thought." This is a break in thought. Verses 8 and 9 indicate an attack upon the land brought back from the sword, but verse 10 introduces an additional thought. In both the Hebrew and Greek rendition of "that at the same time" the words used are emphatic, and the phrase could be rendered "even on that very same day."

The cry is heard, "Oh, when Russia invades Palestine!"

They wouldn't dare!

The reality of history is that Russia has a strong adversary in the world; namely, the United States of America. Russia would not dare move against Palestine unless the United States had already been made powerless or unless Russia decides to attack both at the same time. Never before in history has the stage been set for such a conflict. If it does not occur now as the culmination of world movements over the past several centuries, then it could take several more centuries or a thousand years for a situation to develop that would be as likely to place national antagonists in the position for the final resolution of world contention. How many times will planet earth be ripe for a harvest? The Bible indicates only once. The description of the land invaded by Gog in verses 11-13 is not a description of the land of the Israelis today. What is described is a very wealthy land. Whatever prosperity there is in Palestine today is due to the irrigation by water taken from the Jordan above Galilee and to the largess of the American taxpayer as funneled through our foreign aid program.

It is Sheba and Dedan, descendants of Abraham through Ishmael, who challenge the invaders, "Have you come to take a great spoil?"

The invaders come from the north, a mighty army, with much cavalry. It is interesting to note that an official Russian postage stamp of 1929 shows all of Asia covered with a huge cloud in which there are horsemen, four of them, charging to the North and East. Do they know who they are?

In Ezekiel 38:17, we read, "Art thou he of whom I have spoken in old time by my servants the prophets of Israel, which prophesied in those days many years that I would bring thee against them?" In other words, "This is the war I have been talking about through my prophets." What do these prophets say about some final conflict?

Isaiah says, in 34:1-3, "come near, ye nations, to hear; and hearken ye people: let the earth hear, and all that is therein; the world, and all things that come forth of it. For the indignation of the Lord is upon all nations, and his fury upon all their armies: he hath utterly destroyed them, he hath delivered them to the slaughter. Their slain also shall be cast out, and their stink shall come up out of their carcasses, and the mountains shall be melted with their blood." Again, Isaiah says, in 66:15-16, "For, behold, the Lord will come with fire, and with his chariots like a whirlwind, to render his anger with fury, and his rebuke with flames of fire, For by fire and by his sword will the Lord plead with all flesh: and the slain of the Lord shall be many."

In Jeremiah 25:31-33 we read, "A noise shall come even to the ends of the earth; for the Lord hath a controversy with the nations, he will plead with all flesh; he will give them that are wicked to the sword, saith the Lord. Thus saith the Lord of hosts, behold, evil shall go forth from nation to nation, and a great whirlwind shall be raised up from the coasts of the earth. And the slain of the Lord shall be at that day from one end of the earth even unto the other end of the earth: they shall not be lamented, neither gathered, nor buried; they shall be dung upon the ground."

In Joel 3:2, we find, "I will also gather all nations, and will bring them down into the valley of Jehoshaphat, and will plead with them there for my people and for my heritage Israel, whom they have scattered among the nations, and parted my land." Again, in verses 9-12, "Proclaim ye this among the Gentiles; prepare war, wake up the mighty men, let all the men of war draw near; let them come up: beat your plow shares into swords, and your pruninghooks into spears: let the weak say, I am strong, assemble yourselves and come, all ye heathen, and gather yourselves together round about: hither cause thy mighty ones to come down, O Lord. Let the heathen be wakened, and come up to the valley of Jehoshaphat: for there will I sit to judge all the heathen round about."

The story of Jehoshaphat, the king of Judah, is found in II Chronicles Chapter 20. Word was brought to the king that a large army of Ammonites and Moabites had appeared on the west side of the Dead Sea at Engedi, in the territory of Judah. This news greatly disturbed Jehoshaphat. He called the people of Judah together, and prayed to the Lord for guidance and protection. The answer came through a young Levite who advised the king to march against the invaders.

The counterattack was organized and the next morning King Jehoshaphat's forces began their march toward the Dead Sea. At the head of the march, instead of the best bowmen or charioteers, was the choir, praising "the beauty of Holiness" and singing

"Praise the Lord: His mercy endureth forever."

Word soon reached Jehoshaphat that the Ammonites and Moabites were fighting the Edomites from Mt. Seir who had joined the battle. All the army of Judah had to do was to take the spoils of war from the enemy dead, a task which required three days.

This story is told in some detail to illustrate the point that in desperate circumstances the people of God who trust in their God should have no fear in the day of battle. The valley of Jehoshaphat becomes, then, a symbol of a situation in which God's people are in grave danger from their enemies, a situation in which God's sovereignty prevails. Joel uses the symbol in this sense, and in Joel 3:14, we read, "Multitudes, multitudes in the valley of decision: for the day of the Lord is near in the valley of decision." Since in verse 2 mention is made of all nations, then is not Joel speaking of the final showdown between God and the heathen nations who are in rebellion against him?

Returning to Ezekiel 38, in verse 21 we read, regarding Gog, "And I will call for a sword against him throughout all my mountains, saith the Lord God: every man's sword shall be against his brother. And I will plead against him with pestilence and with blood; and I will rain upon him, and upon his bands, and upon the many people that are with him, an overflowing rain, and great hailstones, fire and brimstone. Thus will I magnify myself, and sanctify myself; and I will be known in the eyes of many nations, and they shall know that I am the Lord."

The destruction of the northern armies is complete. In Ezekiel 39:2 we read that only the sixth part will survive, that is, five-sixths will be destroyed. God uses the forces of nature and induces confusion and madness among the armies who turn against each other. They fall in the open field and are given to the birds of prey and wild beasts who feast upon their dead bodies. In Ezekiel 39:7,8 we read, "So will I make my holy name known in the midst of my people Israel; and I will not let them pollute my holy name any more; and the heathen shall know that I am the Lord, the Holy One in Israel. Behold, it is come, and it is done, saith the Lord God; this is the day whereof I have spoken."

This certainly sounds as if God has appointed a time when his controversy with the heathen will be consummated, and when there will be a great unveiling of his purpose in history. In Revelation 16:13,14, we find, "And I saw three unclean spirits like frogs come out of the mouth of the dragon, and out of the mouth of the beast and out of the mouth of the false prophet. For they are the spirits of devils, working miracles, which go forth unto the kings of the earth and of the whole world, to gather them to the battle of that great day of God Almighty." In verse 16, he gathers them together into a place called Armageddon. This must be symbolic since the plains of Megiddo in Palestine cannot possibly hold the armies of the world that take part in this great battle. Like Joel's "valley of decision", Armageddon connotes a world-wide situation rather than a restricted geographical location.

The books of the Apocrypha are not generally regarded as canonical scripture. However, there is a scene depicted in II Esdras 13 which nearly parallels the Biblical description. It certainly represents Jewish thought in the period in which it was written. Beginning in verse 29, we read, "Behold, the days come when the Most High will begin to deliver them that are upon the earth. And there shall come astonishment of mind upon them that dwell on the earth. And one shall think to war against another, city against city, place against place, people against people, and kingdom against kingdom. And it shall be that when these things shall come to pass, and the signs shall happen which I showed thee before, then shall my Son be revealed, whom thou sawest as a man ascending. And it shall be, when all the nations hear his voice, every man shall leave his own land and the battle they have one against another. And an innumerable multitude shall be gathered together, as thou sawest, desiring to come, and to fight against him. But he shall stand upon the top of Mount Sion. And Sion shall come, and shall be shewed to all men, being prepared and builded, like as thou sawest the mountain graven without hands. And this my Son shall rebuke the nations which are come for their wickedness, with plagues that are like unto a tempest; and shall taunt them to their face with their evil thoughts, and the torments wherewith they shall be tormented, which are likened unto a flame; and he shall destroy them without labor by the law, which is likened unto fire. And whereas thou sawest that he gathered unto him another multitude that was peaceable; these are the ten tribes, which were led away out of their own land in the time of Osea the King, whom Shalmanasar the king of Assyria led away captive, and he carried them beyond the River and they were carried into another land."

This passage from II Esdras, purported to be written by Ezra the scribe, reveals several points worthy of note. First, it shows the belief that there will come a time when God will deal with the heathen world. Secondly, it reveals the belief that the heathen are both mad and evil in their rebellion against God. Thirdly, it shows that in Jewish thought, the ten tribes were a separate people from the Jews, and will be revealed to the world at the time when God deals with the heathen nations.

Throughout Ezekiel 38 and 39, the weapons used in this great war are described as primitive weapons. Is this because Ezekiel could not conceive of modern weapons, and used the imagery of weapons he knew as symbolic of whatever weapons may be used in a future time? Will peace break out all over the world, and nuclear weapons and other modern arms be destroyed by mutual agreement, leaving the northern armies at great advantage because of manpower alone? Will this give meaning to I Thessalonians 5:3 which reads "For when they shall say, Peace and safety; then sudden destruction cometh upon them"?

The place of burial of the invaders in this great battle is said to be "on the east of the sea" in Ezekiel 39:11. Which sea? The Mediterranean or the Pacific Ocean? Consider the following. In verse 12 the time required for burial is seven months, and in verse 14, the search for the dead requires seven months. If one half the Israeli army were to stretch in single file from the Dead Sea to the Mediterranean, joining hands, and march northward, every square inch of the entire country all the way to Lebanon could be seen in seven days. This point alone eliminates Palestine as the scene of the great battle.

Throughout these two chapters of Ezekiel, frequent mention is made of Israel and the mountains of Israel.

So?

In Genesis 17, Abram's name was changed to Abraham, which means a father of a multitude of nations. In Genesis 48:19, this promise is specifically transferred to Ephraim, the son of Joseph, the son of Israel. Nowhere in the Bible is this promise ever given to a people called Jews. It is unscriptural and nonsensical to think that all the nations prophesied for Israel could ever squeeze into the small land of Palestine. Forgotten are the words in Jeremiah 3:14 which speak of a representative return, "one of a city, and two of a family, and I will bring you to Zion."

In prophetic language a mountain represents a government or a nation. Now if Gog attacks the mountains of Israel then there must be more than one nation under attack. Would not Gog mount an attack against all the nominally Christian nations of Europe as well as North America? Nothing less than a world-wide crisis is depicted by Ezekiel, and the nations being attacked are none other than the promised nations of Israel.

The number of the slain in this great battle is multitudinous. Therefore the burying place must accommodate a multitude. Such a place is provided, and in Ezekiel 39:1 it is called Hamonah, which means the place of a great multitude. The word connotes a noisy tumult, a great mob, hence, Mobtown.

One of the purposes of this great conflict is stated in Ezekiel 39:21, which says, "And I will set my glory among the heathen, and all the heathen shall see my judgment that I have executed, and my hand that I have laid upon them." Another purpose is stated in verse 22: "So the house of Israel shall know that I am the Lord their God from that day and forward." Yet another purpose is in verse 23, "And the heathen shall know that the house of Israel went into captivity for their iniquity; because they trespassed against me, therefore hid I my face from them". And in verse 25, "Therefore thus saith the Lord God, Now will I bring again the captivity of Jacob, and have mercy upon the whole house of Israel, and will be jealous for my holy name, after that they have borne their shame." Continuing in verse 27, "when I have brought them again from the people, and gathered them out of their enemies' lands, and am sanctified in them in the sight of many nations, then shall they know that I am the Lord their God which caused them to be led into captivity among the heathen: but I have gathered them unto their own land, and have left none of them anymore there. Neither will I hide my face anymore from them: for I have poured out my spirit upon the house of Israel, saith the Lord God."

This is surely the great unveiling of history. How can the house of Israel know that they were sent among the heathen because of their sin unless they know that they are the house of Israel? This prophecy cannot possibly apply to the Sephardim Jews who have always known who they are. Also the rest of the world has known who they are. It is the northern tribes of Israel, the House of Israel, who disappeared from history after the Assyrian captivity. It is this house of Israel who will be revealed to the heathen nations and to themselves as a consequence of this great final conflict of history.

In verse 29, the Lord God will pour out his spirit upon the house of Israel. Is this the completion of the great prophecy of Joel which was only partially fulfilled on the day of Pentecost?

In Ezekiel 38:12, it is said that Gog and Magog attack the "people that are gathered out of the nations." If ever there was a gathering place, it is North America, not Palestine. It is our national heritage that we are a people gathered from the northern European nations, particularly the Protestant nations, during the first centuries of our existence. It is America, not Palestine, which is the land of opportunity: It is America which is the Promised Land in the minds of suffering millions.

When Jews from Eastern block countries reach Vienna, half of them decide to go to America. Of the half who go to Israel, a large number decide after a short stay to go to America or Christian countries in Europe. Although there was a rush of Jewish immigration into Palestine following World War II, the net Jewish population of the state of Israel has actually declined in more recent decades. If what is happening in Palestine is the promised return of the Jews to their ancient homeland, then why are they refusing to return? There are about as many Jews in New York city as there are in the state of Israel. Why do they not want to return? Can it be that they know their lot is better in a free America than it would be in socialist Israel?

In Zechariah 10:7-10, it is said of Ephraim (not the Jews), "I will hiss for them, and gather them; for I have redeemed them: and they shall increase as they have increased. And I will sow them among the people: and they shall remember me in far countries; and they shall live with their children, and turn again. I will bring them again also out of the land of Egypt, and gather them out of Assyria; and I will bring them again into the land of Gilead and Lebanon; and place shall not be found for them." The message is to Ephraim, a prophetic name for the northern kingdom of Israel, which was taken from Gilead and southern Lebanon into Assyria as captives. The Jews are not included in this statement.

There is another gathering mentioned in the scripture. In Zephaniah 3:8, we read, "Therefore wait ye upon me, saith the Lord, until the day that I rise up to the prey, for my determination is to gather the nations, that I may assemble the kingdoms, to pour upon them my indignation, even all my fierce anger: for all the earth shall be devoured with the fire of my jealousy." And in Joel 3:2, "I will also gather all nations, and will bring them down into the valley of Jehoshaphat, and will plead with them there for my people and for my heritage Israel." Again, in Isaiah 24:21-22, we read, "And it shall come to pass in that day, that the Lord shall punish the host of the high ones that are on high, and the kings of the earth upon the earth. And they shall be gathered together, as prisoners are gathered in the pit, and shall be shut up in the prison, and after many days shall they be visited."

Two great gatherings, each the antithesis of the other, will be involved in this crisis of the ages. One is the gathering of the heathen in their vaunted strength. The other is the people of God, left powerless by their own folly. It is God himself who has the victory, and it is God Himself that the people praise.

What about China? As a Japhetic people they could well be included in the hordes of Gog and Magog; or they could remain a large heathen people over whom the people of God reign.

And what about the time of Christ's return? We are not told. In Isaiah 26:20-21, we read, "Come, my people, enter thou unto thy chambers and shut thy doors about thee; hide thyself for a little moment, until the indignation be overpast. For, behold, the Lord cometh out of his place to punish the inhabitants of the earth for their iniquity: the earth also shall disclose her blood, and shall no more cover her slain." It certainly sounds as if resurrection is not far from such a deliverance. If there is resurrection, then there is the One who has won the victory over death and the grave. We shall know when God wants us to know.

If this scenario is any where near the correct one, then we can expect no lasting solution to the problems of the tensions between atheistic communism and the Christian west. We can expect the Christian west to deteriorate further until it can be fulfilled that "The Lord shall judge his people, and repent himself for his servants, when he seeth that their power is gone."

Bibliography

1. Dunlap, Reginald Edward, Jr. *The Coming Russian Invasion of America.* Ontario, California: Published by author. 1978.
2. Foster, Thomas. *When Russia Attacks America.* Richmond, Victoria, Australia. The Crusade Center.
3. Saba, Michael. *The Armageddon Network.* Brattleboro, Vermont, Amana Books. 1984.

Chapter 19
The Bulwarks of Zion

We now return to the central thesis of this presentation. If we cannot trust the Bible concerning the promises God made to Abraham, then why should we trust the Bible concerning the promises God has made through Jesus Christ?

The answer to the second part of this proposition is simple and can be expressed in one word: Experience. The experience of millions of confessed believers who claim changes within. The experience of an inner warmth as the Holy Spirit enlivens our lives. The experience of a change in life's goals. The experience of freedom from the practices which have enslaved us. The experience of changed attitudes toward our loved ones and neighbors. The experience of a deep desire to know more of God's word and his purpose for our lives. The experience of tens of thousands of men and women who have gone to other lands, even to the frightful conditions of savage people to take to them the message of love and forgiveness. The experience of millions of martyrs who through the centuries have bowed their necks to the executioners or stood chained to a stake while flames licked their faces. Yes, experience, the verification of the gospel of salvation through Jesus Christ.

Now the first part the proposition can likewise be answered with one word: History. The history of the children of Israel in their deliverance from Egypt, and their conquest of the land promised to Abraham, Isaac and Jacob. The history of the tribes of Israel during the kingdoms of David and Solomon. The history of Israel in their disobedience of the law of God and their consequent banishment from the land for a time (until the land enjoys her sabbaths, Leviticus 26:34). The history of the Judah remnant which brought forth Jesus the Messiah. The history of all the people of Israel during the centuries of domination of the gentile world powers of Babylon, Medo-Persia, Greece, and Rome.

In Matthew 13:44 there is a short, but very significant parable "Again, the kingdom of heaven is like unto treasure hid in a field; the which when a man hath found, he hideth, and for joy thereof goeth and selleth all that he hath, and buyeth that field." In the original Scofield Reference Bible, Dr. Scofield writes in his notes on this parable, "Our Lord is the buyer at the awful cost of His blood, and Israel, especially Ephraim, the lost tribes hidden in the field, the world, is the treasure. The divine Merchantman buys the field (the world) for the sake of the treasure, beloved for the father's sake and yet to be restored and saved. The note of joy is also that of the prophets in view of Israel's restoration." The New Scofield Reference Bible makes no mention of this.

Referring to the key words in this parable in a good concordance will reveal some interesting confirmations of Dr. Scofield's thoughts.

1. Israel is the Treasure.

Exodus 19:5. "Now therefore, if ye will obey my voice indeed, and keep my covenant, then ye shall be a peculiar treasure unto me above all people: for all the earth is mine." Psalm 135:4. "For the Lord hath chosen Jacob unto himself, and Israel for his peculiar treasure."

2. Israel was Hid in the World.

Psalm 83:1-4. "Keep not thou silence O God, hold not thy peace, and be not still, O God. For, lo, thine enemies make a tumult: and they that hate thee have lifted up the head. They have taken crafty counsel against thy people, and consulted against thy hidden ones. They have said, come, and let us cut them off from being a nation; that the name of Israel may be no more in remembrance."

Isaiah 49:2. ". . . in the shadow of his hand hath he hid me, and made me a polished shaft; in his quiver hath he hid me." Isaiah 51:16. ". . . I have covered thee in the shadow of mine hand, . . . and say unto Zion, Thou art my people." Hosea 5:3. "I know Ephraim, and Israel is not hid from me."

3. Israel was Found.

Deuteronomy 32:9-10. "For the Lord's portion is his people; Jacob is the lot of his inheritance. He found him in a desert land, and in the waste howling wilderness." Hosea 9:10. "I found Israel like grapes in the wilderness."

4. The Lord has Joy.

Zephaniah 3:17. "The Lord thy God in the midst of thee is mighty; he will save, he will rejoice over thee with joy; he will rest in his love, he will joy over thee with singing."

5. The Lord Sells All He Has.

Deuteronomy 28:68. ". . . Thence shall ye bé sold unto your enemies for bond men and bond women, and no man shall buy you."

Judges 2:14. "and the angel of the Lord was hot against Israel, . . . and he sold them into the hands of their enemies."

Isaiah 50:1. ". . . Where is the bill of your mother's divorcement, whom I have put away? Or which of my creditors is it to whom I have sold you? Behold for your iniquities have ye sold yourselves, and for your transgressions is your mother put away." (Note: Only Israel, never Judah, was divorced.)

6. The Lord Buys the Field.

Psalm 74:2. "Remember thy congregation which thou hast purchased of old; the rod of thine inheritance, which thou hast redeemed." Isaiah 52:3. ". . . Ye have sold yourselves for nought; and ye shall be redeemed without money."

I Corinthians 6:20. "For ye are bought with a price: therefore glorify God in your body, and in your spirit, which are God's."

I Peter 1:18-19. "For as much as ye know that ye were not redeemed with corruptible things, as silver and gold, from your vain conversation received by tradition from your father; but with the precious blood of Christ, as a lamb without blemish and without spot."

Matthew 20:28. "Even as the Son of Man came not to be ministered unto, but to minister, and to give his life a ransom for many."

John 3:16. "For God so loved the world, that he gave his only begotten son, that whosoever believeth in him should not perish, but have everlasting life."
Matthew 13:44 could now be paraphrased, "Again, the kingdom of heaven is like unto Israel hid in the world, the which when God finds, he hides, and for joy thereof goes and sells his only son and buys the whole world for the sake of Israel."

When the kingdom of Judah was facing captivity in Babylon, Jeremiah had a vision of two kinds of figs, and received a message to the effect that only the good figs would return to Jerusalem after 70 years captivity. After the 70 years, Cyrus, King of Persia, issued a blanket invitation for any among the captives to return to Jerusalem who wished to do so; and the word whosoever is used in the invitation. In Ezra 1:5, we read, "Then rose up the chiefs of the fathers of Judah and Benjamin, and the priests and the Levites, with all them whose spirit God had raised to go up to build the house of the Lord which is in Jerusalem." Who were those whose spirit God had raised? Were they not the very ones God told Jeremiah would return after 70 years?

The cross is sufficient for the whole world. The "whosoever" of John 3:16 is an open invitation to the whole world. Now who do you suppose responds to this open invitation? Who, unless it was the people God proposed to save? Isaiah 45:17 says, "But Israel shall be saved in the Lord with an everlasting salvation." In Jeremiah 30:10, we read, "Therefore, fear thou not, O my servant Jacob, saith the Lord; neither be dismayed, O Israel: for, lo, I will save thee from afar, and thy seed from the land of their captivity."

There was an angelic messenger to Joseph in Matthew 1:21 who said, "Thou shalt call his name Jesus, for he shall save his people from their sins." In Luke 1:54-55, we read, "He hath holpen his servant Israel in rememberance of his mercy; as he spake to our fathers, to Abraham, and to his seed forever" and in verses 72-73, we find, "To perform the mercy promised to our fathers, and to remember his holy covenant; the oath which he swore to our father Abraham."

Now if God notes the fallen sparrow, if he guides the Arctic tern and golden plover across thousands of miles of trackless sea, if he warms the hearts of the Good Figs of Judah to return to Jerusalem after 70 years of captivity in Babylon, then can He not cause the wandering tribes of the House of Israel to respond to the preaching of the gospel of Jesus Christ wherever they be hidden among the gentiles? Are they not counted as gentiles since their divorcement from the laws of God in the days of Jeroboam their King? Why cannot God let down his net into the sea of humanity and bring up a catch which includes the fish of his pleasure as well as the rough fish which have to be discarded?

Also, if the punishment and banishment of Israel for sin occurred among flesh and blood people of Israel, then why not look for salvation of flesh and blood people of Israel according to the promise of the covenant and the announcement of the prophets? If the promises are to have only a spiritual fulfillment, then why not begin the Bible with John 1:1? Why any Old Testament at all? If the people who were punished were real, then why not the people who are saved, who were promised this salvation?

Is it surprising that in the few centuries preceding the return of Jesus Christ there would be a people who are actively the servants, the witnesses, and the messengers of God in the world? The Bible nowhere states that this function of the people of Israel would ever be transferred to another people. Just as there was a time of punishment, so is there a time of restoration. Just as there was a time of dying, so is there a time of coming alive again. Just as there was a time when Israel disappeared from history, so is there a time of emergence in history. Just as Israel broke the covenant of Sinai in Old Testament times, so Israel shall be brought into the bond of the new covenant in New Testament times, the times in which we now live.

According to Galatians 3:17, "And this I say, that the covenant, that was confirmed before of God in Christ, the law, which was four hundred and thirty years after, cannot disannul, that it should make the promise of none effect." The covenant to Abraham, the covenant of promise, still stands. It was confirmed by

Jesus Christ. The covenant of Law at Sinai did not abrogate one word of it. The Abrahamic covenant is totally unconditional. It is an announcement of God's intention in history.

God's promise to Abraham, in Genesis 17:4, was plain and positive that Abraham would become a father of many nations, and the very name Abraham emphatically so indicates. This promise was specifically transfered to Ephraim by Jacob in Genesis 48:19. The promise to Abraham included land. How much? Enough to sustain God's people in their earthly mission? To believe that one small nation under the leadership of antichristian non-Abrahamic Jews in a small spot of ground in Palestine can ever consummate the purposes of God through Abraham in history is the height of superficial study. Read the Word! Believe God!, Abraham did.

How much land? Romans 4:13 tells us that the promise "That he should be heir of the world was not to Abraham, or to his seed through the law, but through the righteousness of faith". Yes, heir of the world. The promises to Abraham constitute the charter for the Kingdom of God on earth. Some believe that the Church is the Kingdom. Then why pray "Thy kingdom come, thy will be done on earth as it is in heaven," if the church is already here and the kingdom is only spiritual?

The only land Abraham ever possessed was a small plot he bought from Ephron the Hittite for a burial ground for his beloved wife, Sarah. Abraham recognized that the promises of God were for a long time to come. He never lost his sense of pilgrimage. He knew he was but a sojourner in a land he did not possess. Through the eyes of faith he looked for a city that was nowhere in sight. "For he looked for a city which hath foundations, whose builder and maker is God" (Hebrews 11:10). What a faith!

There is such a city. It has a name. The prophets call it Zion. It has a foundation, for in Isaiah 28:16, we read, "Therefore thus saith the Lord God, Behold, I lay in Zion for a foundation a stone, a tried stone, a precious corner stone, a sure foundation...," Yes, Jesus Christ, the head stone of the corner, is the foundation of Zion.

THE BULWARKS OF ZION

Zion is the name of the hill which David took from the Jebusites. It is the hill in the southwest corner of the old city of Jerusalem. David lies buried there. Later, Zion was the name given to the whole of Jerusalem as the place of the temple. In the writings of the prophets, Zion is still future and is associated with the purpose of God in establishing his kingdom over all the earth. Just as Armageddon and Babylon have worldwide connotations, so does Zion!

Zion is the city whose builder is God. Psalm 102:16 states, "When the Lord shall build up Zion, he shall appear in his glory." In Psalm 87:5, we read, "And of Zion it shall be said this and that man was born in her: and the Highest himself shall establish her."

Because of the historical and topological connection between the hill of Zion and the city of Jerusalem, Zion and Jerusalem are used somewhat interchangeably. However, in the literature of the prophets, Zion is used in a stronger sense for the restored center of God's domain. It is the place of God's throne. In Psalm 146:10, we read, "The Lord shall reign forever, even thy God, O Zion, unto all generations." Also, in Psalm 48:2, we find, "Beautiful for situation, the joy of the whole earth is Mount Zion, on the sides of the north, the city of the great King."

In II Samuel 7, God promised David a perpetual throne, so the great King is none other than the son of David, Jesus Christ. Speaking of the Prince of Peace, in Isaiah 9:7, we read, "of the increase of his government and peace, there shall be no end, upon the throne of David, and upon his kingdom, to order it, and to establish it with judgment and with justice from henceforth even forever. The zeal of the Lord of hosts will perform this." Again, in Jeremiah 23:5, we read, "Behold the days come, saith the Lord, that I will raise unto David a righteous Branch, and a king shall reign and prosper, and shall execute judgment and justice in the earth." Amos speaks of this renewal of the throne of David. In Amos 9:11, we read, "In that day will I raise up the tabernacle of David that is fallen, and close up the breaches thereof; and I will raise up his ruins, and I will build it as in the days of old."

The throne of David in Mount Zion will have particular meaning to the people of Israel, who are to be restored in the latter days, a designation for our present age. In Jeremiah 30:9, we are told, "But they shall serve the Lord their God, and David their king, whom I will raise up unto them." In Jeremiah 33:25-26, we read, "thus saith the Lord; if my covenant be not with day and night, and if I have not appointed the ordinances of heaven and earth, then will I cast away the seed of Jacob, and David my servant, so that I will not take any of his seed to be rulers over the seed of Abraham, Isaac, and Jacob: for I will cause their captivity to return, and have mercy on them." In Hosea 3:5 we find, "Afterward shall the children of Israel return, and seek the Lord their God, and David their king; and shall fear the Lord and his goodness in the latter days." In Psalm 149:2, we read, "Let Israel rejoice in him that made him: let the children of Zion be joyful in their King."

Ephraim-Israel and Judah-Israel are each to participate in this promised restoration. In Jeremiah 31:16, we read, "For there shall be a day, that the watchmen upon the mount Ephraim shall cry, Arise ye, and let us go up to Zion unto the Lord our God." In Ezekiel 37:22 and 24, we read, "And I will make them one nation in the land upon the mountains of Israel; and one king shall be king to them all: and they shall be no more two nations, neither shall they be divided into two kingdoms any more at all: and David my servant shall be king over them; and they all shall have one shepherd."

With regard to Judah, we find in Psalm 69:35, "For God will save Zion, and will build the cities of Judah: that they may dwell there, and have it in possession." In Isaiah 65:9, we read, "And I will bring forth a seed out of Jacob, and out of Judah an inheritor of my mountains:and mine elect shall inherit it, and my servants shall dwell there." Finally, in Joel 3:20-21, we see, "But Judah shall dwell for ever, and Jerusalem from generation to generation. For I will cleanse their blood that I have not cleansed: for the Lord dwelleth in Zion."

Yes, Zion will be the dwelling place of God. Psalm 132:13 states that "The Lord hath chosen Zion: he hath desired it for his habitation. In Isaiah 12:6, we read, "Cry out and shout, thou inhabitant of Zion: for great is the holy one of Israel in the midst of thee." Zechariah tells us to "Sing and rejoice, O daughter of Zion: for, lo, I come, and I will dwell in the midst of thee, saith the Lord."

Is all this a picture of some disembodied spirit world with no physical properties? Consider Isaiah 2:2-4, which says, "And it shall come to pass in the last days, that the mountain of the Lord's house shall be established in the top of the mountains, and shall be exalted above the hills; and all nations shall flow unto it. And many people shall go and say, Come ye, and let us go up to the mountain of the Lord, to the house of the God of Jacob; and he will teach us of his ways, and we will walk in his paths: for out of Zion shall go forth the Law, and the word of the Lord from Jerusalem. And he shall judge among the nations, and shall rebuke many people: and they shall beat their swords into plow shares, and their spears into pruninghooks: nation shall not lift up sword against nation, neither shall they learn war any more."

If we are to reign with him, over whom shall we reign? Does not this passage in Isaiah give us a picture of nations being subject to Christ who rules in Zion with his saints? Is not this great city of Zion the city which Abraham sought? Can we not look forward to a time when the seed of Abraham serve God in proclaiming full salvation to all nations of the earth? Has God's promises to Abraham failed? Have Bible commentators, in their rapturous rush to glory, passed over some fundamental facts of prophetic fulfillment? Is Abraham's kingdom to be forgotten? When God promised Abraham "kings shall be of thee," does that not include David and Christ, the Son of David? Do we utter vain words when we pray "Thy kingdom come"?

Just as the prophets of old failed to separate the first and second advents of Christ, do not men today fail to separate the accomplishment of the promises of Abraham and the final state of the creation in eternity? Is there not a difference between Abraham and Eden?

Just before the ascension of Christ, the disciples asked Him, "Lord, wilt thou at this time restore again the kingdom to Israel?" He did not reprimand them, nor tell them they did not understand what the kingdom would be like. He only told them they would not know the time of the restoration of the kingdom, but rather they would be empowered to be witnesses to him to the uttermost part of the earth. Jesus tells us in Matthew 24 that after this witness is made, then shall the end come. The end of what? This present world order to be followed by the Kingdom. Then He who went into a far country to receive for himself a kingdom shall return and put his kingdom into operation (Luke 19:12-27). There have now been many generations of witnesses who followed the disciples in this task of witnessing, and we are nearing the culmination of this phase of the program of God.

We have made our witness to both men and nations. We are still making it. We have made our witness to men through the evangel of the churches. We have made our witness to nations through the posture and policy of our government in behalf of a world order of peace and public righteousness and by promoting liberty for the oppressed people of the world. No other people in all the world's history have done more to alleviate suffering, encourage freedom, promote health and advance prosperity than have the nations of the Christian West.

We are not commissioned to change the world, but to witness to the world. God takes care of the changes.

Now there is something amiss in the camp of the saints. We have not given God the praise and thanksgiving for his manifold blessings upon us. We take credit for the measure of prosperity we enjoy. The foreigners in our midst do not see that the better life is due to a loving heavenly Father who has poured out his blessings upon us, and we do not tell them. Due to a gross misinterpretation of our laws and our heritage, God, as author of our liberties is no longer honored in our venture.

We are being sabotaged through drugs, sex, disobedience,

lawlessness, and pride. We no longer recognize sin, because as mere animals, anything we do is without moral value. That is what we and our children are being taught. Assuredly, we shall be chastised for our apostasies. We may even suffer persecution if we are truly faithful to His commandments.

Our entrance into the Kingdom will not be easy and comfortable, just because we place much value on ease and comfort. Our entrance into the kingdom will be through purgation, not pride. It will be through chastisement, not indulgence. In Hebrews 12:6, we read "For whom the Lord loveth he chastiseth, and scourgeth every son whom he receiveth." Proverbs 3:11 tells us "Despise not the chastening of the Lord."

Through trials and labors, through commitment and service, we are coming to Zion. We sing, "We're marching upward to Zion, the beautiful city of God." In Psalm 48:2, we read, "Beautiful for situation, the joy of the whole earth is Mount Zion, on the sides of the north, the city of the great King." In verse 12 and 13, we read, "walk about Zion, and go round about her:count the towers thereof. Mark ye well her bulwarks, consider her palaces; that ye may tell it to the generations following." In Isaiah 52:7, we find, "How beautiful upon the mountains are the feet of him that bringeth good tidings, that publisheth peace; that bringeth good tidings of good, that publisheth salvation; that saith unto Zion, Thy God reigneth!" Hallelujah!

Amen!

A Personal Epilogue

Any system of interpretation of prophecy is developed upon the basis of facts, in this case, the text of the Bible and the record of history, and certain basic assumptions of the interpreter's own choice. The system is then organized into deductions, inferences, analyses, hypotheses, and theories which are presented to others. This has been attempted in Part III of this book as a Theory of History. In doing so, the principle of interpretation developed by the leaders of the Reformation has been followed. The principle is simple: read the Book and look out the window. If what you think you see is not to be found in the Book, then either we have poor eyesight or God is not in control of what is going on.

This presentation is an attempt to show the correlation between prophecy and history. Will the events of the centuries fit into the mold of prophecy? Did God really tell his servants the prophets what he intended to do? How far along in the purposes of God has history brought us? What part do we play? There are many more questions, and many answers have been proposed.

I was born while Theodore Roosevelt was President of the United States and before the Scofield Reference Bible was ever published. Among my prized possessions is a wrapped-up copy of the Scofield Bible presented to me when I graduated from high school. I have had and still have other copies. I grew up with it. I knew nothing else until I heard a remark made by Dr. G. Campbell Morgan in a sermon he preached in Knoxville in his later years. He disagreed with Dr. Scofield, whom he knew personally, regarding some point of interpretation and I was surprised. For the first time I realized that Dr. Scofield's notes were but one man's understanding and teaching of the scriptures, and were not at all to be accepted as being on the same level as the Bible itself.

My defection from Scofield began in earnest more than fifty years ago when another preacher said some things that were new and strange to me. My first reaction was, "That's not in the

Bible!" When I went home and looked, the preacher was right. The things he said were in the Bible. It was then that I decided that I had better read the Bible to see for myself what was really in it. It took me six months and I have never been the same.

One of the features of Dr. Scofield's commentary which I have retained is his clear distinction between Israel, Judah, and the Jews. The failure of others to do this has led to questionable exegesis on the part of a number of men.

It was not until after World War II that I became convinced of the validity of the thesis developed in this book. It has become a viable and rational system of correlating history and prophecy. The proposition is simply that the promises to the people of Israel, particularly to the people of Joseph, are being fulfilled today and in recent centuries in the history of the Christian nations of northern Europe, and in their national offspring, the United States of America. If this claim is distasteful, then one must fault God for ever choosing Abraham in the first place. We possess the material blessings promised to Israel, especially Joseph. We are the people of the New Covenant, a Christian people. We are performing the task given to Israel to do: witnessing to the world in behalf of Jesus Christ.

After reading this book, some will attempt to dismiss it by tagging it, or by putting a label on it, or by discarding it into a category of unimportant or distasteful or heretical teachings. This is no answer at all to the ideas presented in this work. Any answer must be in terms of a better and more realistic interpretation of God's prophetic word. If we cannot correlate history and prophecy, then where in the world has God been in all these centuries?

The future has been dealt with only as the scriptures reveal the plan of God. It is impossible to make specific predictions. All who have tried have failed. The Bible nowhere tells us that we can predict future events by our knowledge of his plans. However, because he has revealed his plans, we can be assured of God's ultimate victory. The plan is there for all to read. The schedule is beyond our discernment.

A PERSONAL EPILOGUE

The last three chapters of this book could be dubbed "The Tale of Three Cities." The first is Babylon, or Mammon, which must be destroyed. The second is Gog and Magog with the assembly of the heathen which must be conquered and buried in Hamona, or Mobtown. The third is Zion which must be restored if the Promises to Abraham are ever to be consummated. God did not promise Eden to Abraham, but rather promised a progeny which would be instrumental in bringing the earth back to Eden, under the leadership of Jesus Christ.

Sometimes I feel as if I were but an observer as I watch the things that are going on. I know that this old body of mine has to participate in the ordinary struggle for food, clothing, shelter, and the rest of it. But when you look at the world scene, do you have an overview of it from the standoint of the Scriptures, so that you can sit on your little hill, with the Bible in one hand, and a newspaper in the other, and say, "This is the greatest show ever, this is the main event, this is what the Book is all about, this is surely God's doing." We are commanded to watch, not sleep as others do. We are commanded to occupy, not wait in idleness. We are commanded to pray, not to worry or fret ourselves.

"So beloved, let us love one another, for love is of God. And now little children, abide in Him, that when He shall appear, we may have confidence,and not be ashamed before Him at His coming."

Even so, come, Lord Jesus.

PART IV
PLOWED GROUND:
APPENDICES

Appendix A
The Abrahamic Covenant

The Promises	Given to Abraham	Given to Isaac	Given to Jacob	Inherited by
1. I will make of thee a great nation and many nations.	Genesis 12:2	Genesis 26:3-5	Genesis 35:11	Joseph, Gen 48:15-20
2. The seed shall be as numerous as the stars of heaven, the dust of the earth and the sand of the seashore. The many seed	13:3 15:5 22:17	26:4 26:24	28:3 28:14	Joseph, Gen 48:16, 49:22
3. Kings shall come to thee	17:6		35:11	Judah, Gen 49:8-10
4. Material prosperity	12:2		27:28	Joseph, Gen 49:25-26
5. A great and strong people	12:2		27:29	Joseph, Gen 49:24
6. To thy seed will I give this land, from the river of Egypt to the river Euphrates.	12:7 13:15 15:18 17:18	26:3-4	28:4 28:13 35:12	All tribes of Israel, Num. 26:51-56 Josh. 11:23 Josh. 14:1-5 Ez. 11:15
7. I will bless them that bless thee and curse him that curseth thee.	12:3		27:29	All tribes, Numbers 24:9
8. In thy seed shall all the families (nations) of the earth be blessed. The one seed.	22:18	26:4	28:14	Christians, Gal 3:7-29

Appendix B
The Chosen Seed

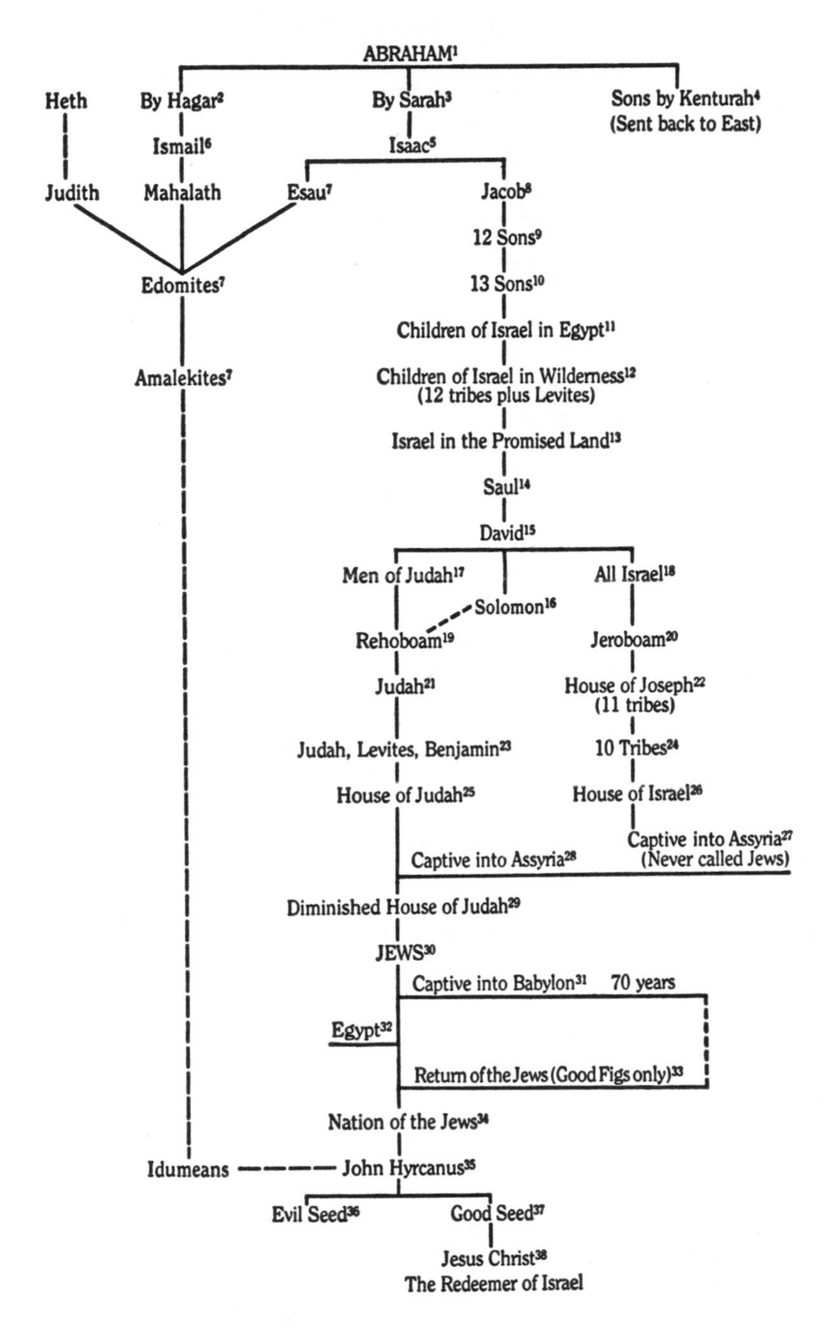

Appendix B
The Chosen Seed
References

1. Abraham - Genesis 12:1-4, 15:1-6, 17:1-14
2. Hagar - Genesis 16:1-16, 17:20-27, 21:9-21
3. Sarah - Genesis 17:15-19, 18:9-18
4. Keturah - Genesis 25:1-6
5. Isaac - Genesis 17:15-19, 21:1-8, 22:1-14, 26:1-5
6. Ishmael - Genesis 17:20-27, 24:12-18
7. Esau - Genesis 25:19-34, 26:34,35, 27:ALL, 28:9, 36:1-12, Exodus 17:8-16
8. Jacob - Genesis 25:19-34, Chapters 27-32, 35:1-7
9. 12 Sons - Genesis 35:22-26
10. 13 Sons - Genesis 48:1-7
11. Israel in Egypt - Exodus:All
12. Israel in the Wilderness - Numbers 2
13. Israel in the Promised Land - Judges:All
14. Saul - I Samuel:All
15. David - I Samuel, II Samuel
16. Solomon- I Kings 1-11
17. Men of Judah - II Samuel 2:4, 5:5, 19:40-43, 24:9, I Kings 1:9, 4:25
18. All Israel - II Samuel 2:4-9, 5:1-5, 14:25, 15:6, 18:17, 19:11,42,43
19. Rehoboam - I Kings 12:1-15, 11:43
20. Jeroboam - I Kings 11:26-40, 12:All, 13:33,34
21. Judah Alone - I Kings 12:20
22. House of Joseph - II Samuel 19:20, I Kings 11:28-31, I Chr. 5:2
23. 3 Tribes - I Kings 12:21, II Chr. 11:1,13
24. 10 Tribes - I Kings 11:31, II Samuel 19:43
25. House of Judah - I Kings 12:21-23
26. House of Israel I Kings 12:25-33
27. Israel into Assyria - II Kings 17:6, 18:9-12, 15:29
28. Judah into Assyria - II Kings 17:19, 18:13-16, II Chr. 32:1
29. Diminished House of Judah - II Kings 21:14-16, 23:1,26,27
30. Jews - II Kings 16:6, 25:25, II Chr. 32:18, Jer. 38:19, 40:11-16, 52:28,30
31. Jews into Babylon - II Kings 24:8-17, 25:1-7,21, Jer. 24:All, 40:11-16, 52:28,30
32. Jews into Egypt - II Kings 25:22-26, Jer. 43:1-7
33. Return of Jews - Jer. 24:5, 29:1-14, Ezra 1:5, 4:1, 10:9, Neh. 11:1-4
34. Nation of the Jews - Ezra 6:7,8,14, Josephus, Ant., Book XI, Chap V, Sec. 2
35. Idumeans become Jews - Josephus, Ant., Book XIII, Chap. IX, Sec 1
36. Evil Seed - Matt. 13:24-30, 36-43, John 8:37,39,44, 10:26, Matt. 23:29-36
37. Good Seed - Isaiah 41:8, 44:3, 45:25, Jer. 31:27, Matt. 13:24-43, Rom. 9:7
38. The Redeemer of Israel - Matt. 1:1, Luke 2:34,38, 24:31, Gal 3:16-19

Appendix C
The Divided Kingdom

		NORTHERN	SOUTHERN
1.	Common Name	Israel (I Ki 4:25)	Judah
2.	Corporate Name	House of Israel (Jer 3:18)	House of Judah
3.	Covenant Name	House of Joseph (I Ki 11:28)	House of David
4.	Poetic Name	Ehpraim (Jer 31:9)	Zion
5.	Number of Tribes	Ten (I Ki 11:31)	Two + Levites (I Ki 12:21)
6.	Capital City	Samaria (I Ki 16:24)	Jerusalem (II Sam 5:6-9
7.	Dynasties	Nine	One (David)
8.	Duration	250 Years	390 Years
9.	First King	Jeroboam	Rehoboam (I Ki 12)
10.	Last King	Hoshea (2 Ki 17:6)	Zedekiah (2 Ki 25:7)
11.	Primary Worship	Calves, Baal (I Ki 12:28 - I Ki 16:31,32)	Jehovah, Baal (Hos 11:12 - II Ch 24:7)
12.	Place of Worship	Dan and Bethel (I Ki 12:29)	Jerusalem (I Ki 12:27)
13.	Captivity	Assyria, 722BC (2 Ki 17)	Babylon, 586BC (II Chr 36)
14.	Prophet of Judgment	Hosea, Amos (Hos 1:1 - Am 1:1)	Jeremiah (Jer 1:1-3)
15.	Prophet of Hope	Isaiah (Is 40:1)	Isaiah (Is 40:1)
16.	Raw Material	Potter's Clay (Jer 18:6)	Broken Bottle (Jer 19:10)
17.	Metaphor	Vine (Hos 10:1)	Figs (Jer 24 - Joel 1:7, 12)
18.	Final OT State	Divorced (Jer 3 - Hos 1:9)	Unfaithful (Jer 3)
19.	History	II Kings 17	II Chron. 36
20.	Promise	Many Seed (Gen 15:5 - Gen. 48:14-28 - Gen 22:17)	One Seed (Gen 49:10 - Gen 22:18)
21.	Inheritance	Birthright (I Ch 5: 1-3)	Scepter (Gen 49:10)
22.	Appointment	Kingdom (I Ki 12:21)	Throne (II Sam 7:17 - I Chr)
23.	Function	Dominion (Ps 114:2)	Sanctuary (Ps 114:2)
24.	World Identity	Gentiles (Amos 9:9,-Hos 1:9)	Jews (Ezra, Neh)

Appendix D
Calendars and Time Cycles

The construction of a calendar is tricky business. Nature does not cooperate very well with our number system. We cannot count months or years with whole numbers. The time it takes for the earth to go around the sun is 365 days 5 hours 48 minutes and 46 seconds, or 365.2422 ... days. It is the fractional part of a day which gives us trouble.

The average time it takes for the moon to go around the earth with respect to the sun, that is, from full moon to full moon, is 29 days 12 hours 44 minutes and 35 seconds, or 29.53059.... days. Now these two numbers are irrational numbers, which means that they would never come out even nor repeat themselves, no matter if you carried them to millions of decimal places. Moreover, the quotient of one divided by the other is also an irrational number. We are left with the necessity of making approximations.

The problem can be illustrated with a bicycle ride along a marked pavement. Assume that the marks are painted every 1297.56 inches and that the circumference of the front wheel of the bicycle is 81.6816 inches. Start with the valve stem of the front tire just above a mark on the pavement. How far must the bicycle travel until the valve stem is again just above a mark on the pavement? Will it ever happen again exactly? In 16 rotations of the front wheel, the bicycle travels 16 X 81.6818 inches or 1296.9056 inches which is 0.5544 inches short of being over a mark on the pavement. This number 16 becomes an approximation for the relationship between the circumference of the wheel and the marks on the pavement.

To see how this idea applies to the measure of time, start at the time of a full moon at midnight on December 31 of any year, which would be the beginning of a new year. Now let the moon roll around the earth in months (29.53059 days) and the earth roll around the sun in years (365.2422 days). How long would it be until there is a full moon at exactly midnight on December 31 again? The answer? Never!

So we have to resort to approximations.

The Babylonians kept a sacred calendar of 360 days to the year with the arbitrary addition of 5 or 6 extra days, called intercalary days, to keep this calendar in step with the seasons. The Hebrews kept a lunar calendar of 12 lunar months, lasting 354 days. In order to keep the calendar in step with the seasons, in 7 of 19 years there was a year of 13 months. The Mohammedans keep a strict lunar calendar of 12 months to the year and let their New Year begin at any season of the year. Today, we keep a calendar of 365 days with one intercalary day added to February every 4 years, called leap years. This overcompensates, since the fractional part of a day above 365 is not quite one fourth, so every 100 years we leave out a leap year. This overcompensates in the other direction, so every 400 years we keep the leap year. This rule would keep us going for more than 10,000 years.

The first approximation we find to reconcile the month with the year is 315 years, with a difference of only 1 hour 48 minutes. Now eight times this period is 2520 years, a number which is the lowest common multiple of all the digits, 1 through 9. Dividing by 7, the quotient is 360, which suggests the 7 times of Nebuchadnezzar's debasement on a year for a day time scale. One half this amount is 1260, a number we find in both Daniel and Revelation. It is also expressed as time, times, and the dividing of time, 1260 days, and 42 months. It is significant to note that there are absolutely no natural phenomena which corresponds to these time cycles if they are interpreted as literal days, but represent very accurate natural time cycles if interpreted as years. Remember that in Genesis 1:14-16, God said that the two great lights that he made to rule night and day were to be for signs, and for seasons, and for days and years. Therefore, the motion of the celestial bodies were to be the basis of calendar making and the measure of time.

The seventy weeks of time in the ninth chapter of Daniel is

conceded by the vast majority of Bible commentators to mean seventy weeks of years, since seventy literal weeks is only about one year and four months. This is certainly not enough time for anything of prophetic significance to happen. Therefore, the seventy weeks interval is understood to mean 490 years.

Likewise, the seven times of the course of history as it pertains to God's people is understood to mean 2520 years. One half of this period is mentioned as 1260 days, 3½ times, on 42 months and used symbolically in prophetic scripture. As mentioned elsewhere, the most accurate application of this longer time interval to history is the duration of the desolations of Jerusalem. The city was captured by Nebucadnezzar in 604 B.C. In exactly 2520 years, the city was set free by General Allenby in 1917 A.D. The calculations are simple, involving one quirk of calendar arithmetic. There was no year zero. December 31, 11:55 P.M., in the year 1 B.C. was only 10 minutes away from 12:05 A.M., January 1, 1 A.D. This means we cannot apply the ordinary rules for adding and subtracting positive and negative numbers in going from B.C. to A.D. dates. Look at the arithmetic.

2520	year interval
604	B.C. capture fo Jerusalem
1916	
+ 1	for no year Zero
1917	A.D. Recapture of Jerusalem by a Christian Power

Because the exact date of Old Testament events are not accurately known, it is not possible to make calculations for other intervals as well as for the capture and release of Jerusalem. Therefore, close approximations should suffice to show the application of the 2520 years to the pairs of correlative events.

It was 2520 years from the division of Israel into two kingdoms following the death of Solomon to the execution of Mary Queen of Scots and the establishment of a unified throne under Elizabeth I.

It was 2520 years from the defection from temple worship and the introduction of worship of the golden calves under Jeroboam until the intense years of the English Reformation which brought us a pure religion.

It was 2520 years from the first Assyrian captivity of the kingdom of Israel in 745 B.C. until the establishment of a new nation born in Freedom during the American Revolution in 1776 A.D.

There is another time scale given in the Bible which confirms these considerations. In 2 Peter 3:8 we read that "one day is with the Lord as a thousand years, and a thousand years as one day." This would be based upon Psalm 90:4, which reads, "For a thousand years in thy sight are but as yesterday when it is past, and as a watch in the night." Is this time scale applicable to the people of the House of Israel to whom Hosea refers in Hosea 6:2, "After two days will he revive us: in the third day he will raise us up, and we shall live in his sight?" The midst of the third day on this time scale could well be the 2520 years.

In both Daniel and Revelation we find references to one half this grand cycle of history made in the form of 1260 days; time, times and the dividing of time; and 42 months. In general, these references are made concerning persecuting powers which afflict the people of God before the coming of the Lord. Therefore, these references must concern the latter half of the 2520 years, or 1260 years.

It was 1260 years from the establishment of the code of Justinian in 538 A.D. in which the Bishop of Rome was granted supreme authority, until the removal of the Pope from the city of Rome by the armed forces of Napoleon in 1798 and the institution of a civil code which replaced the Justinian.

By another calculation, it was 1260 years from the death of Phocas, the Eastern emperor, who in 606 A.D. conceded that the Bishop of Rome was the supreme head of all the churches, until 1870, when the pope was stripped of all secular power and the Papal city transferred to the government of Italy. Since 1870, the Popes have exercised ecclesiastical power only.

Regardless of exact calculations, it is an established historical fact that the Papacy ruled over the secular kingdoms of Europe for about thirteen centuries.

Likewise, in the East, it was Mohammedan powers that ruled

for about thirteen centuries, including both the Saracen and the Turkish phases of this rule. As noted elsewhere, this rule ended in 1917 A.D. with the surrender of Jerusalem to the British. It is interesting to note that the Turkish coins of that year bore the Mohammedan date 1335, based upon a lunar calendar beginning in 622 A.D., the year of the Hegira of Mohammed. Is this related to Daniel 12:12? The submergence of Israel among the Gentiles in Old Testament times was a process, not a single event. Then may we not expect the emergence of Israel out from among the Gentiles to be a process also, extending over a period of years? In Luke 2:34, Simeon said to Mary, "Behold, this child is set for the fall and rising again of many in Israel." If Israel fell, then will not Israel rise again? When they rise again, will they not be Christian, since the new covenant was made with them according to Jeremiah 31:31-33?

It is virtually impossible to find any dated events late enough in the Old Testament from which the 2520 years have any future fulfillment as of now. All such intervals have expired. Yet there is a deep-seated and widespread feeling among God's people that tremendous events lie just ahead of us. Is this the Time of the End spoken of in Daniel 12:4? All attempts to use these time cycles to make predictions for future events have ended in failure. They attest to God's control over history, but do not allow us to become prognosticators.

Appendix E
Three Little Words

Much is being taught and written today concerning the Second Coming of Jesus Christ. As the woes of the world increase and the complexities of government seem to exhaust the wisdom of rulers, it is only natural that Christians who place a great deal of confidence in the Bible should look into it for some clear understanding of the meaning of our lives in the world today, as well as for comforting hope for whatever lies ahead.

Is this meaning and this hope to be found in the ideas most frequently presented to our people through the countless radio programs and the prolific literature concerning the prophetic Scriptures? What is most popularly taught and received should be examined from time to time in the light of ever more exacting study of the Word of God. History itself has a way of correcting theories and hypotheses based upon a study of the Bible by Godly men.

It was not until well into the nineteenth century that Christ's second coming was considered to be in two different phases separated by a seven year period of intense tribulation. Although the general scheme of which this particular teaching later became a part was introduced by the Jesuit Ribera in 1690, the division of the second coming into two parts was an innovation initiated and developed by Irving, Maitland, Burg, Darby, and their followers in the Plymouth Brethren movement and the Powerscourt conferences of the midnineteenth century in England. Without going into a detailed discussion of the entire framework of the Futurist system of interpretation, let us look at just this one point of the separation of Christ's coming into two phases; the one concerning Christ coming FOR the Church, and the other, after the great tribulation, when Christ comes WITH his Church to reign on the earth.

The idea that Christ comes FOR the church is nowhere expressly stated in Scripture. It is an inference based upon certain presuppositions that some scholars deem implied in Scripture. The passage which many agree described Christ's coming FOR the church is in 1 Thessalonians 4:13-18. We should expect the word FOR to be in this passage, but it is not there. Instead, in verse 14, we find the word WITH, as well as in 1 Thessalonians 3:13, used in conjunction with His coming. This point is usually omitted in discussions on this subject. In fact, many discussions begin with verse 15 of chapter 4, thus avoiding the issue. Much emphasis is placed upon the word COMING in verse 15, and it is this word and its use we should examine.

The English word "coming" is translated from the Greek word PAROUSIA. In Thayer's Greek-English Lexicon, we find the word PAROUSIA defined first as "presence" and secondly as "the presence of one coming; hence, the coming, arrival, advent." It is used frequently in reference to the second coming of Jesus Christ. This is the word used in 1 Thessalonians 3:13, where the word PAROUSIA is linked to the word WITH.

There are two other words that pertain to the second coming that are usually assigned to Christ's coming in glory at the end of the period of tribulation some seven years after His coming FOR the Church. The first is the Greek word APOKALYPSIS which means "revelation", and the other is the Greek word EPIPHANEIA which means "appearing". The first of these is recognized in the title to the last book of the New Testament, which is ordinarily called the "Apocalypse" or Revelation. The second is used in liturgical churches in the form of EPIPHANY. Throughout the remainder of this study, the forms PAROUSIA, APOCALYPSE, and EPIPHANY will be used in reference to these three words regardless of the particualr spelling in the Greek. The APOCALYPSE and the EPIPHANY are considered to be appropriate descriptions of Christ's coming in glory WITH His saints after the great tribulation, while the word PAROUSIA is applied to the coming FOR the Church before the tribulation begins.

Now let us look in the New Testament and see how these words are used in the various passages pertaining to the second coming.

The first use of the word PAROUSIA is in Matthew 24:3, when the disciples ask the Lord some questions. In answer to these questions, Jesus used this word PAROUSIA in verses 27, 37, and 39. He uses it in connection with the brightness of His PAROUSIA in verse 27, and with respect to the evil days as in the time of Noah in the other verses. Another word for "come" or "coming" is used frequently throughout this passage, but it is the word ERCHOMAI which is the ordinary word meaning "coming on the way."

Now it is interesting to note that in Luke's account of this very same discourse (Luke 17:22-37), there is a difference. Instead of PAROUSIA, verse 30 reads, "Even thus shall it be in the day when the son of man is revealed." The word used is a verb form of the noun APOCALYPSE. Is Luke talking about a set of events entirely different from those in Matthew? Did Luke forget that Jesus used the word PAROUSIA as told by Matthew and jump seven years beyond to refer to some other event? Or advent? Is it possible that these two words are so equivalent that they are interchangeable, and Luke's passage is identical to Matthew's passage, allowing for the personal differences in recording the Divine Message that are permissible in any doctrine of verbal inspiration short of a dictation theory?

The next use of PAROUSIA is by Paul in 1 Corinthians 15:23. Here the subject being discussed is the resurrection. Paul says, "Christ the first fruits, afterward they that are Christ's at his PAROUSIA."

There should be no difficulty regarding this passage. In reading 1 Thessalonians 4:17, which states that believers shall be caught up (raptured) to meet the Lord in the air, many people assume that Christ does not complete his journey to the earth on that occasion, but takes his church away for a time before returning WITH it in glory. If PAROUSIA means "coming to be present with," then this interpretation would indicate that this meeting with Christ in the air is our PAROUSIA to Him, and not His PAROUSIA to us. Verse 17 does not discuss the events following this meeting because the purpose of the passage is to explain the fate of dead believers with respect to the resurrection, stated in verse 13.

An illustration might be helpful. When a home-town football team has won a game played in some other city, and flies back home, it is not unusual for a crowd of supporters to go the airport to welcome the team back home. These fans do not board the plane and fly away into the wild blue yonder with their heroes. They join the team in completing its journey into the home town. This would be a PAROUSIA of the team, remembering the meaning, "coming to be present with".

Why this bit of foolishness? In I Corinthians 16:17, Paul, writing from Ephesus, says, "I am glad of the PAROUSIA of Stephanus and Fortunatus and Achaicus, for that which was lacking on your part they have supplied." Well, did these men get there, or not? Did they turn around at the city limits of Ephesus and go back to an undisclosed destination? They brought something which supplied Paul's needs, and therefore must have completed their PAROUSIA to Paul in Ephesus. In II Corinthians 7:6,Paul says "--comforted us by the PAROUSIA of Titus." Did Titus reach Paul, or not? Even if Paul met him, did Titus not complete his journey? The plain meaning of words would indicate that Titus went all the way into Ephesus to see Paul, and provided him with consolation and comfort as related in verse 7. When we are caught up to meet Christ in the air, is this not a joyous welcome to Him, a happy joining with Him as He completes His glorious return to the earth in majesty? In Phillipians 1:26, Paul writes, "That your rejoicing may be more abundant in Jesus Christ for me by my PAROUSIA to you again." Did Paul intend to go only to Neapolis on the coast and not complete his journey inland to Philippi? Would it have made any difference if some of the Philippians would have met Paul at Neapolis and accompanied him during the rest of the journey? Or did Paul expect some of the Philippians to meet him at the port and sail away with him without ever going to Philippi?

In I Thessalonians 2:19, Paul writes, "--Are not even ye in the presence of our Lord Jesus Christ at his PAROUSIA?" The phrase "in the presence of" does not contain the word PAROUSIA, but can properly be translated "before", having a positional meaning. When Christ comes to be present with us at His PAROUSIA, then we are "before" Him.

The word PAROUSIA is used again in I Thessalonians 5:23 where Paul says, "--and I pray God your whole spirit and soul and body be preserved blameless unto the PAROUSIA of our Lord Jesus Christ." No comment is needed here nor in II Thessalonians 2:1. In II Thessalonians 2:8,9, we find, with regard to the Wicked (One), "-and shall destroy with the brightness of his coming," or "with the EPIPHANY of his PAROUSIA." Now this is interesting, since many teach that the EPIPHANY is a word applied to Christ's coming in glory at the end of the reign of Antichrist, and here it is used in conjunction with PAROUSIA. How could this be if the events described by the two words are separated by seven years? Is it not more acceptable to believe that the PAROUSIA will be characterized by great brightness as indicated in Matthew 24:27? Is not the EPIPHANY of Christ's PAROUSIA in sharp contrast to the PAROUSIA of the Wicked One?

James used the word PAROUSIA twice, in verses 7 and 8 of chapter 5, urging believers to be patient until the PAROUSIA of the Lord. This passage presents no difficulty.

In II Peter 1:16,17, Peter uses PAROUSIA in a way that obviously refers to Christ's first coming, since Peter refers to the transfiguration which he witnessed. In II Peter 3:4, doubters are to express contempt for the idea of another Parousia of Christ in view of the long time which transpires. However, in verse 12 of chapter 3, believers regard the PAROUSIA with eager expectation. In connection with the PAROUSIA, a judgment by fire and intense heat is involved as indicated by the word "wherein". This is usually not considered an event that goes with the rapture of the church, but here it is described as a feature of the PAROUSIA.

In I John 2:28, believers are enjoined to have confidence and not be ashamed at His PAROUSIA. This raises no question with regard to the timing or nature of the second coming.

So far, we have considered every use of the word PAROUSIA in the New Testament. All 22 of them. In seven of these passages no doctrinal or timing problem is presented. There are questions which have been raised regarding the other verses in which PAROUSIA occurs. Some of these questions cast serious doubt on the application of the word PAROUSIA to an early phase of Christ's second coming in advance of his coming in glory.

Now let us look at the word APOCALYPSE and its usages in the New Testament. There are several passages where the word is translated revelation without any reference to the second coming, but there are several passages in which a relation is stated or implied.

In Romans 2:5, the revelation (APOCALYPSE) is related to the day of wrath and judgement.

In Romans 8:19, the word APOCALYPSE is translated"manifestation". "For the earnest expectation of the creature waiteth for the manifestation of the sons of God." Later, in verse 21, this waiting on the part of the creature or creation is for the "adoption, to wit, the redemption of our body." If the redemption of our body is our resurrection, then this must occur at the APOCALYPSE of us who are the sons of God. This passage relates the resurrection, usually associated with the PAROUSIA, with the APOCALYPSE. Therefore, these must be synonymous or simultaneous. This is also borne out by Paul's use of APOCALYPSE in I Corinthians 1:7, which reads, "So that ye come behind in no gift, waiting for the coming (APOCALYPSE) of our Lord Jesus Christ." Are we waiting for the PAROUSIA or the APOCALYPSE of Christ? The word "wait" is hardly appropriate for the attitude of believers that have already experienced the rapture. Again, are not these two words used with regard to one and the same event?

In the last part of I Peter 1:7, we read, "-at the appearing of Jesus Christ." The word is APOCALYPSE, not EPIPHANY, indicating that both the writer and the translator may have exercised a choice of words.

In I Peter 1:13, we read, "-and hope to the end for the grace that is to be brought unto you at the APOCALYPSE of Jesus Christ." Notice that our hope is with respect to the APOCALYPSE of Christ. Could Peter not have used PAROUSIA?

Now let us look at the third word we are studying. In I Timothy 6:14, Paul admonishes believers to "keep this commandment without spot, unrebukable, until the appearing (EPIPHANY) of our Lord Jesus Christ." Keeping a commandment is hardly an admonition applicable to believers already having their glorified, resurrected bodies during a seven year absence from the earth, which would be the case if the EPIPHANY is delayed seven years beyond the PAROUSIA.

In I Timothy 4:8, mention is made of a crown of righteousness appearing (EPIPHANY) of the great God and our Saviour Jesus verse reads, "Awaiting and looking for - the blessed hope, even more than one viewpoint.

A very interesting use of EPIPHANY is found in Titus 2:13, which reads, "Looking for that blessed hope, and the glorious appearing (EPIPHANY) of the great God and our Savior Jesus Christ." Now some insist that the reference is to the two separate phases of Christ's second coming, the first alluded to by the words "blessed hope," and the second by the word EPIPHANY. It is claimed that the wording sets forth a distinction, not a parallelism. The transliteration from the Greek reads as follows: "Awaiting the blessed hope and appearing of the glory of the great God and Saviour of our Jesus Christ." There is no comma in the Greek, and there is no definite article "the" before the word "appearing." Thus the "and" joins the hope and the appearing rather than separates them. In the Amplified New Testment the verse reads, "Awaiting and looking for the blessed hope, even the glorious appearing of our great God and Saviour Jesus Christ." Why this difference? Is there a real difference? The Greek word for "and" is KAI. The Greek word for "even" is this very same word KAI. The English chosen by the translators is more or less up to the judgment of the translator. The New American Standard Version agrees with the King James. However, the RSV, the NEB, Weymouth, Williams, Verkuyl, Beck, Young, Phillips, and the Today's English version all make no distinction between the blessed hope and the appearing, linking them together in a variety of ways. It may not be an exact translation, but could we not read, "the blessed hope which is the glorious appearing, etc.?" All these versions mentioned, and perhaps more, would allow this interpretation. The idea that two separate events are in view in this verse is only an inference based upon the presupposition that there will be two events, and is not a necessary or justifiable interpretation or induction from this verse at all.

In summary, these three words, the PAROUSIA, the APOCALYPSE, and the EPIPHANY, all apply to the second coming of Christ and are used interchangeably and in juxtaposition in the New Testment in the several passages dealing with the second coming. They describe the different facets of the same great event; the one and only glorious PAROUSIA, APOCALYPSE, EPIPHANY of our Lord Jesus Christ. Jesus is coming to earth again.

Even so, come, Lord Jesus.

Appendix F
The Great Seal

What symbolizes America? Our flag? Our national anthem? Our material wealth? Our armaments? The need to agree upon a proper symbol representing our nation was a real problem in the early days of our country. The problem was recognized immediately after the signing of the Declaration of Independence. The men who pledged their lives, their fortunes, and their sacred honor were concerned that the young nation would be duly recognized by the other nations of the world.

On July 4, 1776, before the ink had scarcely dried on the signatures of the Declaration of Independence, the Continental Congress resolved that Dr. Franklin, Mr. John Adams, and Mr. Jefferson be a committee to prepare a device for a Seal of the United States of America. The Congress desired to complete the evidences of the independence of the United States by formally adopting an official sign of sovereignty and a national coat of arms; and, in the resolution, one design was to serve both purposes. The committee had no precedent to follow.

When a nation signs an agreement with another nation, what signatures are written on the papers? In Europe, the signet ring of the reigning monarch was impressed in the wax which sealed a document, and that signet ring had on it the coat of arms of the king's own family. He personally stood for the commitments of his kingdom. We could not use anything like that in a republic. Of what value is the President's ring? The committee conceived the idea that an allegorical design significant of the fortunes and destiny of the United States would be more appropriate.

In a letter written by John Adams to his wife we have an account of the first proposal. "Jefferson's idea was that we use some kind of a picture of Israel in the wilderness, under a cloud of fire. Franklin's idea was a picture of Moses and the Children of Israel standing on the bank of the Red Sea, watching Pharoah's army being drowned in the waters with an inscription around it saying "Rebellion to tyrants is obedience to God."

The final report of the committee described a very complicated design having a variety of figures on it, including a picture of the goddesses of liberty and justice, the coats of arms of all the thirteen colonies, a glory cloud, and the motto "E Pluribus Unum." The report of the comitttee was tabled. It is noteworthy that Franklin's idea, "Rebellion to tyrants is obedience to God," was used by Jefferson as his own personal motto the rest of his life.

There were several elements in this first design which were used later. The Latin phrase "E Pluribus Unum," a triangle with an eye in it, and rays of glory emanating from some central design were kept.

In the summer of 1777 our minister to France tried to borrow some money to help finance our revolution, but the French moneylenders wanted to know who would sign the notes. The minister complained to Congress that he had no written device to use in contracting loans. Someone found the original charge to the first committee, and a second committee was appointed. Its report to Congress was sent back to the committee and became lost. The shield, the olive branch, the thirteen stars, and the date 1776 were items proposed by this committee.

In May, 1782, a third committee was appointed which consisted of Arthur Middleton of South Carolina, Elias Boutennet of New Jersey who knew something about coins and medals, and Edward Rutledge of South Carolina, who was educated in Europe. All these gentlemen were presumed to have some knowledge of heraldry and symbolism. They were smart. They hired an expert. They employed the services of William Barton, the son of an Episcopal minister in Philadelphia. William Barton was a profound student of heraldry, and he was an artist. He created a very complicated design about 4 x 6 inches in size, consisting of a complex assortment of symbols, retaining the eye in the triangle, and introducing an eagle. Elaborate as it was, this design was adopted by the committee and reported to Congress. The Congress referred it to the Secretary.

Who was the Secretary? Charles Thomson, the only Secretary ever to serve the Continental Congress. Charles Thomson was not only a patriot, but an accomplished Bible scholar. He published an English translation of the Septuagint, which was the Greek version of the Old Testament dating from about the third century B.C. He published a Harmony of the Gospels, and commentaries on the Epistles. This man was very knowledgeable about the Scriptures.

Charles Thomson suggested some changes in the design of William Barton. He placed the eagle in the center with a bundle of arrows in his left claw and an olive branch in his right claw. Above the head of the eagle he placed a constellation of thirteen stars surrounded by a cloud of glory. There were red and white diagonal chevrons across the shield held by the eagle. He retained the phrase "E Pluribus Unum." For the reverse side of the design a pyramid was made large and central with the triangle containing the eye suspended above it. Rays of glory emanated from this capstone. A motto, "Annuit Coeptis," meaning "He (God) has prospered our undertaking," the date 1776, and another motto on a scroll, "Novus Ordo Seclorum," meaning "A New Order of the Ages," were placed around the pyramid. These suggestions were accepted by Barton who made some additional minor changes. He changed the diagonal chevrons to vertical pales and the rising eagle to a dislayed eagle. All these ideas were radical departures in the use of symbols. The final design became the work of these two men, who then resubmitted it to the Congress.

Now is the time for everyone reading this to examine the design of our Great Seal. It is on the back of a one dollar bill. People see these two circular designs many times as they handle dollar bills, but few know of their historical background. Look at them carefully as you read the following quotation.

This is the action of the Continental Congress on June 20, 1782. "On the report of a Great Seal, to take order. The device for an armorial achievement and reverse of a Great Seal of the United States in Congress Assembled is as follows: Arms, the paleways of thirteen pieces, white and red, the chief, blue. The escutcheon on the breast of the Americn eagle displayed proper, holding in his dexter talon an olive branch and in his sinister a bundle of thirteen arrows all proper, and in his beak a scroll inscribed with the motto, 'E Pluribus Unum.' For the crest over the head of the eagle which appears above the escutcheon, the glory, or breaking through, a cloud proper, surrounding thirteen stars forming a constellation, silver on an azure field. For the reverse, a pyramid unfinished, in the zenith an eye in a triangle surrounded with a glory proper. Over the eye these words, 'Annuit Coeptis.' On the base of the pyramid the numerical letters 1776 and underneath the following motto, "Novus Ordo Seclorum." Then followed a number of remarks and explanations, explaining the meaning of the various parts of the entire design and their colors. One excerpt reads, "The eye over it (the pyramid) and the motto allude to the many signal interpositions of Providence in favor of the American cause."

The entire report is in Charles Thomson's handwriting and is endorsed by him, "Device for a Great Seal of the United States in Congress Assembled, passed June 20, 1782." By this action this design became the official symbol and signature of our nation. This Seal identifies us as a nation among the other nations of the world.

The front of the Seal bearing the eagle is very familiar. It is displayed in many places. Adaptations of it are used for the President's seal, and for several cabinet members and departments of our government. The reverse of the seal was placed on the one dollar bill in 1935 but has never had any other public use in the history of our nation, until very recently. The Seal preceded the Constitution by seven years, since the Constitution was not ratified until 1789. When the first Congress elected under the Constitution met, it reaffirmed this Seal as our sovereign signature and national symbol. There has never been any change in this.

The Seal is used as follows: On all civil deputations, commissions of high ranking officers, treaties and international agreement of all kinds, the President signs the papers and the Secretary of State affixes the Seal which is the official signature, since presidents come and go. The actual seal is a brass casting in two parts, one with the design raised, and the other with the design depressed so that when they are forced together the design is embossed on the paper between them. The castings are very durable, and only a few have been used since 1782.

In a biography of Charles Thomson there are many revealing insights into the thinking of the men who founded our country. What did these men know and believe that made this symbolism acceptable to them without debate? For one thing, they knew the Scriptures of the Holy Bible. Charles Thomson was thoroughly saturated with the Sacred Writings. It seems incredible that William Barton would be unfamiliar with them. Then what are some of the Holy Words that could be associated with these allegorical designs on our Great Seal? We are accustomed to terms such as eagle, stars, glory cloud, and shield. However, it is in the symbolism of the reverse side of the Seal that we see the more esoteric meaning of the symbols. The following quotations will illustrate this point.

"The Lord is in his holy temple, the Lord's throne is in heaven, his eyelids try the children of men."

"The stone which the builders refused is become the headstone of the corner."

"Now ye therefore are no more strangers and foreigners but fellow citizens with the saints and of the household of God, and are built upon the foundation of the apostles and prophets, Jesus Christ himself being the chief cornerstone in whom all the building fitly framed together groweth unto a holy temple of the Lord, in whom ye also are builded together for a habitation of God through the Spirit."

Notice that by design the pyramid is unfinished with a suspended apex stone. No stone can go into the building of the pyramid unless it conforms to the pattern of the headstone. The angle must be just right. The foundation stone is above, not below. The Scriptures are very clear concerning this chief cornerstone or headstone of the corner, and the geometric design of our Seal reflects this wonderful idea.

Now none of this was put into words by Charles Thomson or William Barton, or even by members of the Congress. Then why did they adopt this symbolism so readily? They knew its meaning. It symbolized their whole system of knowledge and faith. It was their public philosophy. It was their heritage from the English Christian philosophers who inspired them to do the impossible.

Yes, we have a heritage of a Christian nation. Our written institutions were created by men who imbibed the principles of liberty and freedom from the great Christian leaders of the seventeenth and eighteenth centuries. The fountainhead of our ideals was in English Protestantism, not French rationalism as some would have us believe. Our rules of conduct, both public and private, are based upon a Christian doctrine of man and society. Such rules will not work successfully when this philosophical base of our society is changed. We cannot play football with baseball rules. Our society cannot endure if pagans dominate it.

We have a mission. Not imperialism, whether it be political or economic, but a mission of enjoining the peoples of the world to live together in love, forebearance, and cooperation under the sovereign leadership of God. Never before in history has a nation been called upon to give so much of its substance and its talents to help other nations in need. When has a people been so magnanimous in its treatment of its former enemies? We have fed them and set them upon their feet to the point of making economic competitors of them. This is unique in history. Some of us do not like the way we have gone about it in our foreign aid programs, but demands are upon us, and we respond to these human needs because we are that kind of people. Who else is there who can or will do it?

We have a King. This Seal, this signature of the United States of America, identifies us as the people whose King is God. Is there any other ultimate interpretation of this symbol? Because we recognize that we operate under God's sovereignty, then we are stewards of a system of government intended to bring about the righteous ordering of society.

In recent years we have had several court decisions regarding religion in our public life. The doctrine of separation of Church and State was never intended to separate this nation from Almighty God, but only that as a national government we were not to be concerned with the ecclesiastical divisions within the Church. For a few, just a handful of godless people, to tell Americans that we cannot pray corporately in public gathering is a gross misrepresentation of our national heritage and our national character. Our Constitution is the governmental instrument of a people who know God as their ultimate ruler.

One way of clearing the air would be for Congress, by a joint resolution, to reaffirm our acceptance of this Seal as our national symbol, with full knowledge of its inner meanings, and call to the attention of the American people that we were founded by men of faith; that our national well-being depends upon a continuation of the acceptance of God as our Sovereign, and that our continuing prosperity depends upon His continuing providence. It is both timely and appropriate to do this. Such a reaffirmation is for Congress alone to do, because only Congress as direct representatives of our people can give expression to the character of our nation. It is interesting to note that in the stained glass window of the Prayer Room of the House of Representatives in the Capitol in Washington, the Great Seal is the main design, and the pyramid side of the Seal is at the top of the window. This places our national Headstone above all else when the time comes for our national leaders to pray.

One of the Commandments reads "Thou shalt not take the name of the Lord thy God in vain". This word "take" means to take up, to lift up, to bear aloft as on a banner, to use as a label. The people of America have been known and recognized throughout the world as a Christian nation. We have borne the name of God in the midst of our neighbors. Many of us feel that something has gone wrong in recent years. Have we forgotten? God can still deal with nations, and a nation can yet honor God and His Holy Name.

"If my people, which are called by my name, shall humble themselves, and pray, and seek my face, and turn from their wicked ways; then will I hear from heaven, and will forgive their sin, and will heal their land."

Truly it was said by the Psalmist, "Blessed is the nation whose God is the Lord."